Metaphor-phosis: Transform Your Stories from Pain to Power

Lesley Tierra

BALBOA PRESS

A DIVISION OF HAY HOUSE

ISBN: 978-1-4525-5601-7 (sc)
ISBN: 978-1-4525-5600-0 (e)

Library of Congress Control Number: 2012913748

Balboa Press books may be ordered through booksellers or by contacting:

Balboa Press
A Division of Hay House
1663 Liberty Drive
Bloomington, IN 47403
www.balboapress.com
1-(877) 407-4847

Because of the dynamic nature of the Internet, any web addresses or links contained in this book may have changed since publication and may no longer be valid. The views expressed in this work are solely those of the author and do not necessarily reflect the views of the publisher, and the publisher hereby disclaims any responsibility for them.

The author of this book does not dispense medical advice or prescribe the use of any technique as a form of treatment for physical, emotional, or medical problems without the advice of a physician, either directly or indirectly. The intent of the author is only to offer information of a general nature to help you in your quest for emotional and spiritual well-being. In the event you use any of the information in this book for yourself, which is your constitutional right, the author and the publisher assume no responsibility for your actions.

Any people depicted in stock imagery provided by Thinkstock are models, and such images are being used for illustrative purposes only.
Certain stock imagery © Thinkstock.

Printed in the United States of America

Library of Congress Control Number: 2012913748

Balboa Press rev. date: 9/13/2012

Contents

Thanks-Giving

When I hear from students and patients about how much their lives have changed, and that even their friends, family, and partners see this and positively comment on it, I have even more gratitude to my teachers for their many gifts. Each one has taught me invaluable lessons and has shared incredible knowledge, tools, and techniques.

To all of my teachers, I give great thanks and love. Know that your wisdom and guidance has not only helped transform my life but also, through me, that of many others as well. And so it is to you who have shown me the way, whether you are consciously aware of it or not, that I dedicate this book: my parents; Granny; husband, Michael, and son, Chetan; brother, Rick, and sister, Jane; and the rest of my family, Mary Jane, Lee, Lesley, Noel, Brannan, Nancy, Megan, Colleen, Mark, Michael, Shasta, Senta, Beau, Justin, Tyler, Kai, and Natalie; Karen, Lee, Jon, Dave, Wendy, Polly, Ken, Jimmy, Lynn, Annette, Arlene, Carl, Jack, Mel and the R.E.M. Institute, Sam, Mariah, Lissa, Earlyne, Robert and Sita Chaney and Astara, Baba Hari Dass, Sai Baba, Darlena, Savarna, Grandmother Evelyn Eaton, Jill, Beth, Marjorie, Elsa, Suzanne, Sarah, Lauren, Margaret, Rasa, Karen, Sue, Maia, Korie, Heidi, Lisa, Aviva, Tom, Jen, Dov, Alberto Villoldo, Linda Fitch and The Four Winds Society, Peggy, Barbara, Jerry, Drunvalo, and the patient and supportive Inkslinger's Maia, Wendy, Andrea, and Bonnie. And an especially big thanks to Barbara Brundage for shifting me into gear to write this book, Anne de Courteney for her insightful editing and Darlena LaOrange for her astute editing and front cover design.

Introduction

I once sat in the middle of a butterfly migration. I lived outside of Cleveland at the time and was eating breakfast on my apartment deck high above the ground. Something caught my eye, and I glanced up. Shock stilled me. Thousands of monarch butterflies colorfully crowded the air while winging southward. Never since have I experienced this wonder except to see ribbon strands of monarchs drape the eucalyptus trees in Santa Cruz.

Monarchs summer in Canada and then fly to Mexico or to mid and southern California to winter. Driven by their internal urgings for self-preservation, these North American butterflies have a wingspan of three and a half to four inches and are the only ones that make a massive journey of up to three thousand miles (4,828 kilometers).

We also have strong internal urges—the urge to migrate to our true selves, to be seen and loved for who we really are, to be fed and nourished by our soul's food, and to freely explore, grow, and shape our dreams and visions. We may start as caterpillars, uncertain about our lives, just wanting to do or be something different from what we are now. Yet we, too, have the capability to shift into something even greater: our butterfly selves.

For most of my life, I have acted as a "midwife for the soul" by helping people "birth" their authentic butterfly selves. In doing so, I've learned that many people's illnesses stem from deeper sources of emotional, mental, or spiritual issues. I have addressed physical healing through herbs, diet, and lifestyle habits in my prior books, particularly *Healing With the Herbs of Life*. Here in *Metaphor-phosis*, I focus on healing through the powerful forces on the emotional, mental, and spiritual levels.

Stories as Our Guides

Butterflies have long amazed me. They undergo an incredible transmutation, starting out as one thing and ending up as something entirely different. You too can transform your life so that it looks and feels completely reformed. And this deep internal shift is possible when you change your stories.

Stories rule your life. They define who you are, how you see others, and what happens to you. All your joy or despair, fulfillment or bereavement, freedom or imprisonment is due to your stories. Some stories are supportive and enlivening while others are limiting or even detrimental. Many stories are about how others see you and how you interact with the world. Still more are about your deep wounds and limiting beliefs.

In turn, stories create cyclical patterns so you experience the same things over and over whether you want to or not. The secret of your stories is that you generate experiences and circumstances in alignment with them. If you believe you are unworthy, you will find evidence to support this. Like a laser light seeking its target, you filter all nonsupporting proof so it can't be seen or doesn't seem to exist. We find what we are looking for, and our stories and beliefs determine what that is.

Whether you yearn to claim your power, be more creative, discover your destiny, heal your body, repair a relationship, clear anxiety, resolve depression, fix one small area of your life, make a major life change, or generally up your game, breaking cyclical patterns is necessary to transform your stories.

We are Meant to Transform

We are all meant to transcend our caterpillar selves and become beautiful, free butterflies. But many of us get caught in our chrysalises, the pupa stage when the caterpillar's body is digested to form the butterfly. This is staying in meltdown, never changing into the potential new form. Reliving past wounds keeps us in the chrysalis of such goop.

Must you do years of therapy or meditation or leave your job or relationship to break free? Or are you doomed to a life of repeated abandonment or continual struggle to achieve your goals? And can you really change anyway since wherever you go and whatever you do, you always take yourself along? How do you fly from the winter of your life into a summery land?

By unleashing your subconscious hold on your stories and beliefs, you can sail along life's updrafts rather than struggle in eddies. Then you don't repeatedly circle the same spots and miss opportunities to explore new land. When you digest and reshape your wounds into a new form, it is possible to transform your life. And when you truly transmute old stories, you can spread your wings to soar from the past and feed on the sweet nectar of your desired life instead.

Yet the help available to support this process usually only suggests where to go and who to be; it doesn't give complete tools to fully get there. Further, it may also tell you to just wake up and choose something different or else simply affirm what you want instead. But these don't always work.

To truly eliminate cyclical issues, it's necessary to clear their roots from deep within. This is because 95 percent of who you are is memorized as habit in your subconscious mind. That means the hidden part of you automatically pursues repetitive actions and reactions based on decisions you made from your upbringing, past experiences, and cultural, racial, and gender influences.

So how do you actually diffuse old stories so new ones stick? How do you change repetitive experiences, heal wounds, and, even more, create a life in which you thrive? Is it truly possible to fully transform your life?

True Change Is Within

Yes! *Metaphor-phosis* teaches how to find and neutralize limiting patterns and guides you through choosing a new story in alignment with your greater life's purpose. It offers a simple and effective method for shifting forms within the chrysalis of your being so you can fly free with the stories you crave.

To change your stories, therefore, it's necessary to reprogram your subconscious and to do that, you have to access this hidden part of yourself. Typical methods don't usually work here, however, such as changing your mind, trying to figure things out, affirming something else, or emotionally expressing how you feel. Rather, other keys are needed, ones that can unravel the subconscious grip on your stories, for only then can a new life manifest and stay.

This means the true change you seek is not in the outer world. The caterpillar doesn't expect to be costumed as a butterfly and presented with nectar to sip. As well, the blame game doesn't work. Reciting old scripts such as, "My mom did this to me," "My dad was never around," or "I can't do such and so because my partner or boss will get angry" will prevent the change you desire. Rather, the caterpillar must dissolve for the butterfly to form. It is the inner world that needs to transform.

The keys that unlock your subconscious inner world are found within the innate wisdom of your heart and body. They are unique to you and are immediately and easily accessible. In *Metaphor-phosis*, both are combined with the power of universal stories—metaphors, myths, and images—because these are loaded with archetypes that teach deeper truths and hold universal meanings. Additionally, they bypass mental and emotional loops to connect you with your authentic self and Source energies, the place of deep wisdom where true, lasting transformation occurs. And such a shift not only positively affects you but others too.

The Butterfly Effect

The Butterfly Effect states that small changes can have big effects. That is, a small change in one part of the world can trigger a huge change in another. This is true for your inner and outer worlds as well. Just making a small shift inside, such as clearing a limiting belief, can alter your outer world greatly.

For example, I knew a woman who always had difficult conversations with her parents. She felt as if she were going into battle and would prepare herself as such. When she processed this belief, she realized that she loved the drama; getting ready for battle was like acting in a play. Once she understood why the battles happened, she wondered, "How stupid is that decision?" As a result, she neutralized this belief and the meetings with her parents became harmonious.

This realization not only affected my friend but her parents' lives also. When she shifted internally, it impacted other people. This is the power of clearing our limiting patterns and core beliefs: through transforming ourselves, we can transmute the world. Change starts at home; it truly is an inside job.

My Story

I spent years enslaved by my stories. They controlled my life along with my happiness. Although I craved joy, contentment, and ease, I felt empty, alone, and unable to find my place. When I learned how to identify my stories and release their grip, I found new freedom— freedom to be who I yearned to be, to express my gifts and passions, and to experience true contentment and joy.

But this did not occur all at once. My life journey led me on a determined path to this point. Like all of us, I am still in process, still growing, learning, and evolving. Yet I have discharged enough energy from my stories that many no longer control me; instead, like compost, they nurture my growth.

My personal soul's journey has led me to study many different spiritual, psychotherapeutic, and healing traditions for over forty years. Each has helped tremendously, yet all have also been a piece in a much larger puzzle. In the last decade, that puzzle has come together to form a definitive structure and outline. What I offer in *Metaphor-phosis* is the synthesis of my studies and explorations that have not only helped me but many others as well.

What This Book Includes

Like migrating animals have hidden ways of determining their flight patterns, so too do we have methods to help us along life's journey. While some signposts are hidden, they can be detected with specific techniques. There is much available to guide us through the migration of life.

Metaphor-phosis does just that. Through four sections, it details the power of your stories; how to identify your stories, patterns, and beliefs; how to diffuse the subconscious grip on your stories; and how to create and live the stories you desire instead.

Within each section, I first share my personal stories and experiences to demonstrate how I identified, shifted, and recreated them. Then I provide explanatory material with specific steps and instructions for undergoing your own metamorphosis. Lastly, I include tools and techniques to achieve these steps and live your desired life.

What Is *Not* Included in This Book

There are two subjects I have purposely excluded from this work: ego and karma. Here's why.

Ego means the psyche, or identification with individual existence. Yet to most it means egotism, conceit, and self-importance. It is the "what about me" part of us. Working with the ego usually defines it in an antagonistic position as something to overcome, conquer, sneak around, detach from, or otherwise diminish. This creates not only a latent adversarial position with your self but also sets up a type of "enemy" that is so powerful it seems impossible to change. Most of us view the ego as a sort of super-monster we must overcome but from which we can never really be free. This puts us in a victim role where the ego acts upon us, takes our power, or causes us to feel or behave as we do.

And yet we have egos for a reason. The ego provides self-identification, which is very useful and even necessary to survive in a corporeal body living in the physical world. As well, it motivates and develops who you are. The key is to not make your ego an all-powerful monster but to shift from the "little me" to your soul and its language of universal stories. Instead of identifying with your ego, connect with your authentic self and your soul's journey.

Karma is the law of cause and effect, like Newton's Third Law of Motion that states for every action there's an equal and opposite reaction. This means that the type of energy you put out is matched by an equal and like energy that comes back. However, most view karma as a punishment. I did such and so, and thus, this is what happened to me in return. This is also a victim role that keeps you trapped as being powerless about what happens to you. Worse yet, many people use it as an excuse to avoid change.

Put this law of cause and effect, or motion, to work for you instead. Face forward with what you yearn to experience and give to others what you desire to receive back. Then the law of equal energy will return to you in like. The Metaphor-phosis process frees up limiting energy so you can do just this.

Answer the Call!

We each get "telephone calls" from the universe, advising us it's time to change. It can occur any time, but such calls are obvious at turning points in life, such as graduation, marriage, and midlife. As well, they can arise through accidents, death, trauma, shock, and illness. These calls are opportunities to listen and grow. They are the times to assess what needs releasing, changing, or fostering so you can develop your full potential instead.

These calls are usually soft at first with a gentle intuitive nudge that says, "Pay attention! Heads up!" If you ignore it, the ring can get louder and more insistent until it eventually screams. By that time, we are already in deep trouble, such as bankruptcy, degenerative health, finalized divorce, or irretrievable job loss. Such crises arise when we don't heed the earlier calls.

Be alert for the universe's first gentle hints; pick up the phone and listen. It's an opportunity to awaken and transform so you align with your authentic self. Saying yes to your call initiates the rebalancing of your life and energizes helpers, such as angels, to come to your aid. So say yes to your call; say yes to the message. Say yes to your self! When you do so, you embark on a healing path and your soul's journey.

This book is the user's manual I wish I had been given when I was born. Now it's the legacy I pass on. May this book empower your life transmutation as this work has helped to metaphor-phosize mine.

Lesley Tierra
April 10, 2012

Prologue

As I was writing this book, I developed a horrible bout of eczema on my arms and chest. While I had some eczema as a child and a small patch as an adult, neither episode was like this. I ceremonially processed the eczema through the techniques in this book and clearly heard that I'm growing new skin but need to shed my old skin first for that to happen. To do this, I must tell my story, for that is how to honor it. In other words, I needed to fully acknowledge my experiences for the eczema to go.

And so I listened. I went through dozens of journals to re-examine my past and began to tell my story. As I did so, I gained enormous insight into particular events that I had already known about but now saw in a different way. As I wrote, my eczema started to clear. For almost a year, I had been dreading telling my story, fearing it and pushing it away until the last moment. This journey gave me the courage and impetus to write it.

Our inner guidance speaks loud and clear; we have but to tune in and listen. I thought I had listened to mine, and sometimes I did. Yet many times, I didn't act on what I had received. This led to a long journey, one that took me through metaphorical death and back. Through that arduous descent and return, I learned how to closely listen to and trust my self.

We all live from our stories. They determine our core beliefs, how we see the world and the experiences we have. What happens and doesn't happen to us all ultimately stems from our stories. When you discover and clear them, however, true lasting life transformation occurs. This happens not through stuffing, ignoring, or endlessly processing them or hoping they'll disappear. Rather, for our wounds to heal, we must go through them. We need to embrace our wounds to finally release them.

Your life is actually in your hands right now. You have but to listen to your heart and act on what you receive. I learned my life was in my hands only after I reached a breaking point. This occurred years after I had been studying and using many self-help techniques. The key piece came after I learned the power of my stories and how to diffuse their grip. But first came the breakdown ...

My shaking hand held the phone close to my ear as I waited for Mariah to answer. She was the only one who could help me now. I sat at my dining table, gazing out the window, but unable to take in the broad vista of winter gardens, cottonwoods, and redwoods that blanketed the ridge before me.

"Hello?" Mariah thankfully answered.

"Mariah, I don't know what to do!" I blurted out and then burst into tears.

"What's wrong?" Immediately alert, Maria probed for my needs.

"Everything!" I cried. "Nothing works anymore. I don't know who I am. I can't stop crying. I don't know what to change or how to fix things. Nothing makes sense in my life."

I had hit rock bottom. Years of sleeplessness and stress combined with my midwestern talent for presenting a put-together persona had taken its toll. I had to face it—I could no longer keep it together but was rapidly falling apart. Yet another sleepless month left me in emotional turmoil. I tried to hold it inside, but it leaked out the edges like the tears now escaping my eyes.

"This is hell. Absolute, silent-killer hell," I gushed. "And it does kill. It kills health. It kills joy. It kills my ability to have friends or do what I want. It's a prison of intense limits, limits of what I can eat, do, or be. It limits my mind, desires, and abilities. My only desire right now is for sleep, and that's exactly what eludes me. It has stripped away years of my life. Chink by chink, it has taken my youth. My face is lined from lack of sleep."

As Mariah listened compassionately, I angrily flicked off the tears rolling down my cheeks. *If I'm not careful, I'll melt into nothingness,* I thought to myself. The heat in my head was unbearable, and my heart pounded erratically. I tried to distract myself but could only think about how lack of sleep was a thief. It slipped into my nights and stole away my life, piece by piece. I lived around this thief, afraid of what it would take from me next.

I'd already given up reading, friends, sweets, eyesight, my dancer's muscles, evenings out, teaching engagements, and oh, so much more. I lived around exercise and bland food just to keep it all together. I stopped all work at five, as I could only focus on one thing at a time. I couldn't go places much any more. I was a prisoner of tiredness. *Got to get a nap, be in bed by ten, get up in the morning and go to clinic, take care of matters, try to be present for my loved ones,* reverberated through my head.

I didn't have the energy to do what I wanted. Even talking exhausted me. I couldn't help people as I used to. My strength waned and memory faded. Lack of sleep had made me overly sensitive. Loud noises and voices grated my ears. Even electromagnetic fields bothered me. One day, I felt the erratic field of our power lines ten feet away, which hit me like a wall of angry bees.

Some experience the pain of a lost relationship, unfulfilled career, or financial ruin. For me, my body failed me nightly while daily I paid the price. I wanted to play cello as before, but it took too much effort now. I wanted to garden again, but I had no energy. I missed dance, but my muscles were too weak. I couldn't socialize, read, or travel anymore. Everything had been stripped away from me, bit by bit.

Most people don't get it. They think sleep is a birthright we all enjoy or an obtainable commodity. But you can't go to the store or restaurant, order ten hours of sleep, and expect it to be served up. Most people get crabby from losing a single night's sleep. Try twenty years!

I used to have it all together. I had a wonderful husband, special son, terrific children and grandchildren, beautiful home in an ideal place, right-livelihood work I loved, and books and teaching opportunities. And yet it was as if I had an invisible handicap that no one could see. I was pinned down, a reluctant hermit, and I hated it.

Worse yet, I didn't know who I was. What I used to hold dear, I no longer wanted and didn't know how to replace. I was unsure of everything and had energy for nothing. What I missed the most was being joyful. I used to be filled with spirit and the joy of life. Now my internal landscape was barren, just like the garden I could no longer tend. I was truly falling apart.

"So why don't you just let yourself fall apart?" Mariah finally asked. That thought stopped me. Why not indeed? After all, that's what my body was obviously doing. And yet I didn't want to freak out my partner or son, and I wanted to be present for them, not a heavy weight around their necks. Being a heavy weight around my own was enough.

But even more, I admitted to myself, I was afraid to fall apart. I, who had always had it together, who always kept a dozen balls in the air, who always had been mentally sharp, and who always achieved, accomplished, and did what I wanted, couldn't even imagine allowing myself to fall apart. And yet intuitively I realized that was exactly what I needed to do.

In those long, dark hours of January, Mariah convinced me to come visit her and attend a weekend bodywork seminar together. It would release my stress, she urged, and give me breathing room. So I went. And thus began my long ascent back to the land of the living and eventually to the thriving as well.

My life had not always been so dramatic or in breakdown, however; in fact, far from it.

I

Born to a typical, midwestern family outside Detroit, Michigan, I was the middle of three children, each spaced two years apart. My parents loved and cared for us well, of that there's no doubt. I grew up in a wonderful neighborhood in two different houses, both of which I loved. There was a local community swimming pool, neighborhood games, and lots of trees, gardens, and yards to explore.

We lived so close to the Detroit Zoo that I could hear the lions roar at night along with the elephants trumpeting and the monkeys chattering. Rather than scaring me, these sounds made me feel right at home. We'd set up lemonade stands for the visitors who parked on our street. The neighborhood kids later gathered to play ball games or hide-and-seek. Every winter, my mom made an ice rink in our backyard or we'd go sledding when my dad was home.

It was an idyllic childhood in many ways. I didn't suffer any of the major traumas or abuses many people endure. And yet I still managed to get wounded as do we all. Later, I considered these wounds as part of my path for growth in this life, but now I could only sustain their pain.

When I turned two and my brother was born, my mom came down with pneumonia and was taken to the hospital. All I remember is screaming with fear as two burly men strapped mom down and carted her outside. My granny came to care for us, and her gentle hand and expansive love soothed me. I had found a second mother who I adored to the day she died at nearly ninety-eight.

Next, I have a very clear memory around age four or five when my best friend's dad arrived home one day. He immediately swept her into his arms, held her on his lap, and asked about how she was. I was shocked. Although I was a daddy's girl and idolized my father, he never hugged or held me. He gave me horsey rides and carried me piggyback, even played tickling games. But he never held or hugged me. All I knew then was that it was something I wanted too but didn't know how to get.

A couple of years later, that childhood playmate found another friend and I saw less and less of her. To compound everything, my sister endlessly occupied my parent's time, or so it seemed to me. My dad—so full of fun and adventure when he was around—traveled a good fifty percent of the time and just wasn't there. I not only felt alone but left out, and that there wasn't enough love, space, or attention for me. My childhood wounds deepened.

At the same time, my baby brother was the little lamb of the family and so could do no wrong. When he turned five, he found a best friend and became all boy. After being my live baby doll for five years, this was a blow indeed. I didn't understand his masculine energy; it was too rough and unpredictable. When my brother suddenly sprouted legs and testosterone, it was a shock.

I saw little of him the next twelve years and, in truth, cut him out of my awareness. To this day, I have little recollection of his life during those years. It wasn't until I was seventeen and he taught me yoga that we connected again. Since then, he's remained one of my most precious friends. However, when I see pictures of his life then, it's still a surprise. I truly had blanked him out.

My sister and I had more interaction but not pleasant. She was either very upset or very happy; either way, it seemed she'd do whatever possible to torment me. Her behavior attracted punishment or other negative attention, so I learned to distance myself from her actions and be very good. I didn't want the kind of attention she received.

Over time, my sister and I fought more and more. Because we shared a room, it was hard to get away, plus we couldn't have been more opposite. As my mother often said, you could draw a line down the middle of our room and clearly see the difference. She was messy; I was neat. She wanted to stay up late and get up late; I wanted to sleep early and get up early. She loved loud music; I preferred softer fare, and so on and so on.

Because my sister was older, she took that to mean she was the boss and so did everything her way. All I could do was keep my belongings as I wanted, but all else went as she chose— music, lights, and noise at night with darkness and quiet in the mornings. As I grew older, I complained more and more until one night, I had had it.

My dad was out of town and my mom was at a PTA meeting while my sister babysat my brother and me. Our homework done, the three of us laid watching TV on my parent's bed, but that was not enough for my sister. She kept tossing about, bouncing up and down, pushing me away and other such things so I couldn't watch the show or relax.

Finally fed up from years of such treatment, I fled the house and stumbled in the dark all the way to our grade school to find my mother and complain. This was a good half mile away, and although I knew the path well, it was scary. Plus I knew I was on thin ice by leaving home alone at night. However, anger fueled my steps until I finally arrived and realized that I'd have to walk into the school to find my mom or else wait outside. Even more scared of facing all those people, I decided to wait in the bushes by our car until she came out.

It seemed ages until she did, but it was probably only a half hour or so. When mom finally emerged, I began to run out and greet her until I discovered she was talking with a friend. So I hid again. Even though I yearned for my mother's safety and support, I just couldn't embarrass her in front of her friend, and so with sinking heart, I watched her say good-bye, get into her car, and drive away.

It was a long walk home. My anger gone now, the path seemed more fearful than before, probably fed by my anticipation of what would happen after I got home.

Mom was mad all right. She threatened me with her worst, Dad's punishment when he returned from his business trip, but somehow this seemed muted. Indeed, when Dad did come back, he did nothing. Not long after, my parents announced we were moving across the street into a slightly bigger house, where I got my own bedroom. A miracle had occurred!

In that new house, my life unfolded and blossomed. I hung out with my three best friends as we explored the mysterious and mystical, such as lateral thinking puzzles and playing with the Ouija board along with baking lots of cookies, of course.

Around age thirteen, after yet another session of listening to a friend's problems and giving support, I had an epiphany: My purpose in life was to help people. I had no idea how or what form this would take, I just knew that's why I was here and what I would do. It was in this manner that I survived junior high and began high school.

My high school was huge, with over four thousand students. I loved many of my teachers and classes and began writing poetry, even placing second in our school contest. I joined the synchronized swimming team, had a duet with the club president, and was slated to be the next vice president. I tried out for cheerleading and, at five nine, amazingly missed joining the shorter group by one person. I even had a respectable relationship with my sister when, alphabetically arranged, we sat together in French class and competed for the highest grades. My friends were many and varied, and life was great. I had found my place. I belonged.

Then one night when I turned fifteen, my mom announced that we were moving again. This time it wasn't across the street or even across town but to a different state entirely. I was stunned. Ripped away from my friends, I felt like a flower that was nearly blossomed, stripped petal by petal, and thrust into a desert. I no longer had my place and had to start over again. Thus began what I thought of as my dark years that lasted until I was nearly twenty-seven years old.

The new high school was much smaller and more provincial; the kids thought they knew it all but had no idea of what they were missing. There was no pool, so I had to drive to a local YWCA to swim synchronized. It took a long while to develop new friends, but eventually I found my way and made the best of it. I even ended my senior year as class treasurer. Still, I felt displaced, uncertain, and alone.

I did manage to play my teenage role, however. I thought my boyfriend, Ken, was more deprived and felt compelled to help him. That included borrowing my parents' car one summer day to supposedly visit a friend. Instead, I actually drove across the state line to Pennsylvania, where I visited Ken at an evangelical church camp, where he nearly convinced me to jettison my college and career dreams to move out of state. Instead, I'd settle down, marry him, and we'd live near home.

As we sat in a church service, I prayed and prayed for an answer. The minister urged us to follow the Spirit within and come declare ourselves at the altar. For the first time, I felt an alien urge inside that overpowered me. I just had to go up front. At first, I held back, too embarrassed to follow it, but the force grew too strong. I found myself walking up front and kneeling. I prayed even harder, unaware of what the minister said or did, and then heard a very clear voice in my head. It was simple but direct: "Tell your parents." And then the force stopped.

I returned to my seat and later told Ken my experience. He trusted it too, so I drove home to confess everything I had originally intended to hide, including dropping college and getting married. Now what underage teenager would steal across state lines for a forbidden visit with her boyfriend and then go home to spill the beans? Only one with such a strong directive from an otherworldly source! And that's exactly how I felt.

As soon as I told my parents, everything moved into high gear. Our minister was called over to counsel me. My granny was arranged to hostess me. My dad stood guard over me. Within two days, I was flown to New Orleans to spend the rest of the summer with my granny but not before a dramatic finale with Ken standing in the driveway yelling up at my window for me to come down and leave with him, me upstairs shouting down my undying love and devotion to him, and my dad in between holding a shotgun at the front door. I guess my "good girl" role had lapsed and transformed into "holy terror" instead.

My parents' protection saved me. With my beloved granny, I gained distance and perspective. She never said a word about the matter but gave me the space I needed to grieve, release guilt, and eventually emerge quite glad I had escaped a bad relationship that would have derailed my life. Instead, we rode out Hurricane Camille together, never leaving her house on Saint Charles Avenue or losing power despite the cyclone winds pushing trees parallel to the ground and blowing all the store windows out less than a mile away. In another month, I returned home and finished my senior year, boyfriend-less and glad.

What followed was typical for those times—college trailed by marriage and work for a big corporation. College started out tough until the spring of my freshman year when I found friends and activities I loved. I began to think I had found my new place and community again when the Kent State shootings occurred.

Snipers immediately moved to our Ohio University campus only three hours away. Overnight, the entire sixteen thousand-student body school closed and all were sent home regardless of several remaining weeks and finals to take. We didn't get to say good-bye to friends, sweethearts, or teachers; we just packed and left. It felt like eating the most delicious dessert imaginable and the waiter whisking it away beneath your fork. Once again, I was taken from my place and people.

My sophomore year started out well enough until near the end of the first semester when I discovered that I hated my major. I'd sit in study hall fighting back tears, unable to focus from my despair. This bloomed into a full existential crisis. What did it all matter? Who was I? What was I going to do with my life?

No specific answers came, so I eventually settled on another major. However, it never felt right, just something to do to complete college and begin earning a living. Increasingly, I felt like I didn't belong. Then I found a new boyfriend, Jim. Exciting and intellectual, he joined me the following summer for a vacation from my job at a resort in New Hampshire. We traveled and camped through many of the New England states and developed a close bond.

Not only did we share nature's beauty but also similar thoughts around my favorite author then, Hermann Hesse, especially his books, *Siddhartha* and *Magister Lodi*. Further, Jim had been raised on an apple farm, which fertilized my own ancestral farming genes. I felt right at home again in this budding romance. When I arrived back at college, however, Jim announced he wanted to see other girls, and my bubble burst.

Somehow, I made it through my junior year. My only consolation was studying Abraham Maslow's work. I loved his concept of self-actualization and instinctively knew achieving that was the inner direction of my life. The following summer, I worked as a temp at a company near home and there met my husband-to-be, Carl. I immediately ended college a quarter early and got married.

Carl was charming and romantic but very controlling. He managed to orchestrate every detail of our lives, from buying a new car every year with our joint earnings while I took the daily bus to downtown Cleveland until I finally had my own car (a VW bug with 95,000 miles) to developing few friendships outside the marriage, rarely entertaining, seeing my parents only twice a year even though they lived fifteen minutes away, and never using the china or silver we received as wedding gifts because we didn't have the crystal yet (and never did).

Something was very wrong with this picture; I felt like a hostage in my own life. It took me four years to realize I was trapped in a life I neither liked nor wanted. And so I began a PhD program in psychology and Organizational Development at a local institute. It was through my own counseling sessions there that I realized how truly unhappy I was.

I didn't seem right working for a big corporation at their whim and will. I hated being promoted because of the impending Equal Rights Amendment (ERA) rather than for deserving it, as I knew I did. Not only did I feel imprisoned in my marriage, I was also sick of living in the cloud belt of Cleveland where we defined the sun as something that shone two days a year.

What hatched from this discontent was a plan to drive west, explore our beautiful country, and enter a period of self-exploration. I had friends, or friends of friends, in several states with whom I could stay, and at one point, my husband and another couple would join me to backpack

Glacier and Waterton National Parks in northern Montana/Southern Canada. I took the leap and a five-month sabbatical from work to head on what I called my "Journey West." When I began the trip, I felt ecstatic to finally be on my own.

Started as a PhD project, my Journey West ended as a life transformation. All went as expected until the day I left Ames, Iowa, in sweltering 113 degrees and over 100 percent humidity. Since I wanted to make it to my next destination by the end of that day, I drove unceasingly across the southern border of South Dakota with little food or water. I almost made it. Entering the Rose Bud Sioux Indian Reservation near the Badlands, I fell asleep at the wheel and crashed my car into a steep ditch.

Dazed, I got out and stared at my gear strewn across the road and shoulder. I didn't know what to do or think, only stare at what I had done. Here I was in the middle of nowhere, stranded, car-less, friendless, and still an hour or so from where I was to stay with people I barely knew. I was in shock.

Literally within a minute, a big blue Chevy pulled up, and seven or eight Indians piled out. They immediately began to stuff my belongings into large plastic garbage bags and called the local police. At the same time, the elderly grandmother wrapped me in her big, soft arms and told me she'd pray for me in her "special nightly way" as she said (which later I assumed to be a pipe ceremony).

The Indian policeman arrived, and everyone loaded my stuff and me inside his pickup truck. I was taken to the local Indian hospital where I was x-rayed and patched up. Thankfully, I walked away with only my little finger cut despite the car being totaled. From there, the Indians called my sister's friends, with whom I was to stay, and these kind folks came to retrieve me.

What special people found me! They had no questions or concerns with what I had done, just offered help and friendship. I called my husband, and he made arrangements to fly out and pick me up in a few days when we would resume my journey with our backpacking plans. In the meantime, my life had changed.

As I was now "grounded," I sat outside for hours in the stark beauty of that land and thought how the cathedral of nature was best of all. I learned a few Native American traditions from my host family, who had a young child along with an adopted Indian teen. I felt a part of this friendly, loving, supportive community, even though I was only there for less than a week.

During this week, my host family took me to a rendezvous in northern Nebraska, a gathering where people dressed and lived in the traditional Wild West fur trapper and trader ways. There, a rough-looking man in buckskins and a beard halfway down his chest stepped into the group where I stood, pointed at me, and said, "Meet my wife." And so began my friendship with Sam and the next chapter of my life.

When I told Sam about my Journey West, he invited me to visit the ranch he managed outside West Yellowstone. We parted with this intriguing possibility, and shortly after, my husband arrived. Instead of being happy to see him, however, I was upset and aloof. Within the last three weeks, I had found family and community, flexed my wings, expanded my horizons, and opened my mind. Out from under his romantic and controlling sway, I had started to become a free woman, but I didn't yet know how far I really had to go for this to be true.

Backpacking together was miserable. Except for our friends and the glorious scenery, the trip was a disaster. After our friends left, we spent another ten days backpacking the Olympic Mountain range, exploring the rainforests of western Washington, and visiting the gorgeous Japanese gardens of Seattle. Increasingly, we became more and more distant. One did not fight with Carl; instead, we had cold wars, and the air between us was frigid indeed. I could not and would not step back into our past relationship. Things had changed too much. I was out from under his thumb and was finding myself.

When Carl flew home, I happily resumed my Journey West. In a rental car now, I visited the stunning Oregon coast, the misty redwoods of northern California and the mysterious Crater Lake. I loved camping by myself, meeting new friends, and following my instincts. Ultimately, I did stop at Sam's ranch. There I soaked up Montana's expansive sky, explored its magnificent land, and learned about Sam's unusual lifestyle. I was hooked on the West; it was in my blood.

Before I left the ranch, Sam made another fascinating offer: I could live in his empty trailer rent-free in Jackson Hole, Wyoming. As I made my way home, I imagined this new life and made plans to save money so I could move west. I stopped in Milwaukee, visited my best friend from college, spilled my guts, and gained the support I needed to make this big shift. I was ready to step into the unknown and claim my dreams.

And so I did just that. Back home, I thankfully found that Carl had already moved out. I happily returned to my parents and set about my new plans. It was time for a complete life change—divorce, quit big business, and move from Cleveland to a new land where I could explore my path in life. And thus began the "magic" years, as I called them, years of blossoming, exploration, and spiritual awakening, years that nourished me like my early teens—until insomnia claimed me, that is.

In Jackson, I taught photography to children as part of the Artists-in-Residence program, sold my photographs to painters and sculptors and at fairs, and danced with a local school. This is also when I first met Mariah. High in the Montana mountains at another rendezvous Sam and I attended, Mariah had parked her big white van so she could camp and take a much-needed break from her own family woes.

We immediately bonded. During one of our many long hikes accompanied by captivating talks, I had another awakening. On top of one of those mountains, the hole that I had increasingly felt inside became clear: What I had so deeply missed the last five years and the hollow I needed to fill was spirituality.

I realized this as Mariah told me about Astara, an organization that taught Eastern and Western mysticism, which spoke deeply to my heart. After years of searching and eventually discovering that I'd be "damned" no matter which religion I followed—and I had explored many of them—I finally found what rang true within me.

During the following Wyoming winters where I now lived with Sam fifty miles south of Jackson and a five-mile snowmobile ride to our neighbor-less cabin that I had helped build, I studied the lessons from Astara and devoured Earlyne Chaney's teachings like a starved animal. Sam worked long hours making muzzle-loading rifles in a tiny nearby shed, so I sat alone reading or snowshoeing the mountain slopes to follow moose, elk, deer, rabbit, or coyote tracks.

Even though my spiritual needs were now being fulfilled and Sam was full of fascinating stories about his years as an adopted child of Pearl S. Buck, one of the characters on *Mr. Roger's Neighborhood* and a frequent movie consultant on Civil War weapons, I felt more and more isolated in all other ways. Although it was a beautiful and even majestic existence with no running water or toilet facilities and the Wind River Mountains outside our front door, it was extremely lonely, as well.

I increasingly felt disappointment from Sam, who wanted me to be someone other than I was. He wanted me to wear long skirts and dresses, be skilled at home crafts, embrace his remote lifestyle, and want all of that too. But I still needed people. I had to find myself. I wanted to discover and express who I was, not fulfill his desires, and that was difficult to do in such a remote place. It became clear again that I still felt alone, left out, and isolated. I was neither in my place nor with my people. I was an impostor.

And so I moved away from Sam and Wyoming and moved in with Mariah in Montana as she, too, was divorcing. We spent several nourishing months together until she left for her new life and I headed to Astara on a work-trade position for the summer. Sam and I had visited their campus twice before, and I wanted to support their work, so I moved to southern California, another strange land to midwestern eyes, so filled with sunshine, palm trees, and stimulating people.

I spent four months at Astara, and magical they were. I met people from around the world, received a tarot reading from which everything came true, and had amazing spiritual and "cosmic" experiences, such as being spontaneously gifted exactly the amount of money I needed to pay off my credit card bill!

Having spent all my savings by now, I taught one yoga class a week to put gas in my car and launder my clothes. All the rest I earned through work-trade. I knew I couldn't stay there past summer, and I wondered what to do next. As my life had beautifully unfolded so far, I trusted that would happen again, and indeed it did.

During a workshop at Astara, I met someone who told me about polarity therapy in Santa Cruz. I decided to attend a weekend class there and fell in love with the place—ocean *and* mountains along with many diverse people. I was hooked! There I learned about Heartwood Institute's Holistic Health Practitioner Program and knew I needed to pursue this as my next career. I had begun to explore herbs and natural medicine at Mariah's, and here was my chance to study more.

Back at Astara, I planned my move to Santa Cruz. I'd obtain my needed credentials and move to Jackson to set up a healing practice. My work-trade ended, and I headed to Wyoming to stuff my belongings into a U-Haul. After one last drama with Sam, I drove to Santa Cruz for a two-year stay.

The first day of my new class on herbal healing, I walked into the building, saw my teacher, and instantly "knew" him. Two days later, when I learned of possible work-trade to help pay for my schooling, this teacher, Michael, gave me the job of typing up some lessons for his herbal correspondence program, The East West Herb Course, that he had begun to write for his newly formed East West School of Planetary Herbology.

Everything felt magical around Michael, even the very air itself. An herbal master, he had directly learned the power of plants while living on the Blackbear commune in Northern California and by sitting at the feet of early herbal pioneers, Dr. Christopher and Norma Meyers. Also an incredibly generous man, Michael helped many of his students launch their diverse careers. I was one of them although not without some tough times. It's hard to marry your teacher and establish an equal relationship. This didn't happen immediately, but rather through years of friction as two very independent people bumped up against each other like rough diamonds in a tumbler.

And that was it. I never left California to live elsewhere. After a rocky start, I formed a relationship with Michael, helped him develop the new course and school, completed my holistic health practitioner requirements, and began studying acupuncture. I helped raise two of his four children, birthed our son, became licensed in acupuncture, set up a practice, and began to teach and write books. I had found my new home and path. Or so I thought.

Over the next twenty years, I began to get sick. It didn't help that I had become vegetarian through the influence of my spiritual beliefs. Frequent bladder infections or sore throats plagued me. After our son was born, I began to have light sleeping problems. The more I extended myself outwardly, the more health issues I seemed to have. I took on more and more responsibilities and slept less and less.

Regardless of sleep, or lack of it, my spiritual studies expanded. I explored Native American traditions with Grandmother Evelyn Eaton, shamanic journeying with Elsa Etcheverry, and yoga/meditation with Baba Hari Dass. I did two vision quests and later helped co-lead women on vision quests with my teacher and friend, Beth Beurkins. My clinic thrived as I worked from 8:30 a.m. until 7:30 p.m. daily with barely a break. I still oversaw our herb course, taught throughout the United States and England, and wrote several books.

At the same time, motherhood was an all-encompassing role for me, and I threw myself into all my son's activities. I cooked all our food, read nightly stories to him, shuttled him to and from Waldorf School a half hour away, and attended all his ball games and piano performances. I also went to all his piano competitions up through the 2009 Van Cliburn. I loved every moment.

As I did so and accomplished my outer activities and studies as well, my inner world became a very different place—a descent into eventual meltdown. I'd go nights with little sleep, sometimes two hours before teaching a day-long class or just three hours a night for three nights in a row before clinic. I consumed every herb possible along with homeopathy and both helped a great deal, yet during the bad times, I had to take medications, hormones, or other support. You name it, I tried it. Still, sleeplessness plagued me for over twenty years.

Exhausted and perimenopausal, I not only felt uncomfortable in my skin, I also no longer knew who I was or what I was doing. All I could do was put one foot in front of the other. Finally after yet another bad month of impossible sleep, I could no longer hold it together. I was falling apart. And that's when I picked up the phone and called Mariah. Soon after, I embarked on a path that taught me the power of my stories, which delivered me from my pain.

The Stories of Your Life

Do you feel like the same thing happens to you over and over?

Do people treat you in similar ways?

Do you feel stuck in repeating negative patterns?

Or do the voices in your head continuously tell you that you aren't successful, attractive, or appreciated, or that you are clumsy, inartistic, invisible, or a failure?

Such repeating thoughts or events arise form the stories you hold, which, in turn, determine how you interpret, respond to, and inadvertently create what happens in your life. Limiting stories hold you back from experiencing the life you desire. So can you change your stories and beliefs? Can you experience the life of your dreams?

Yes, you can! And the power to do so lies in discovering and changing your life stories.

Your Stories

We love stories. Most of us heard stories as children and then began to read them ourselves. We saw stories in movies and on TV. While young, we developed stories about the world and ourselves to help us feel safe and to make sense of what happened around us and to us. As we grew older, we told stories to others—stories of what happened, stories of what we wanted to happen, and eventually, stories of what we expected or thought would happen. All the while, we absorbed family, cultural, racial, gender, and religious stories as well.

In fact, stories define us. When we meet people, we generally first share a personal story, such as our names, where we live, what work we do, if we have children, even our health issues. Like coordinates on a map, these stories pinpoint us. While some stories benefit us by telling us that we are worthy, loved, successful, and have many opportunities or much abundance, other stories limit us.

For example, you might desire wellness, but if you hold a hidden core belief that you have to work really hard to get what you want, the result is adrenal exhaustion instead. In another case, you might desire an intimate relationship, but your subconscious[1] cyclical pattern of abandonment causes you to be defensive and protective, pushing away potential partners instead of attracting them.

Stories Form Patterns and Core Beliefs

As you repeatedly think about and tell others your stories, they strengthen and intensify. Soon you'll find that the same things happen to you again and again. Repetitive stories create patterns, where the theme of the story repeats regardless of time, place, or people involved.

Stories also create core beliefs. A belief is a thought that you continue to think. A core belief is a thought that you think over and over with strong conviction. Eventually, you no longer consciously think about it because it is now an unshakable knowing and certainty. You are so sure about this belief, that you don't even question it.

> ### Jim's Core Belief
> Jim hated his job because his boss was condescending and overbearing. Jim quit this job and found a new one in another city. It was even in a different field. His new boss was great and everything went well until a special project began.
>
> The manager of the new project arrived and at the first meeting treated Jim in a condescending and bossy way. The people, place, and even career had switched, but Jim experienced the same haughty treatment by a superior. This is because he held a core belief that authority figures were arrogant and derisive. Because of this, he lived his story again and again regardless of where he lived or what he did.

We hold our beliefs near and dear not because they're true but because we either want them to be true or we want to be right. We even attract experiences to prove that they are true and that we are right. Have you ever heard the old saying, "You can move away, but you take yourself with you"? That happens because *your inner world attracts what happens to you in your outer world*. Your stories filter your experiences no matter where you live or the people who surround you.

Patterns and Core Beliefs Form Life Themes

Many of our stories form patterns so huge that they create life themes. Life themes are the main patterns that repeat throughout one's entire life. They hold your greatest power, as they are the patterns you experience over and over until you learn their lessons, understand their teachings, and receive their gifts.

---

1   Medically, it's called the "unconscious," but the term Jung coined, *subconscious*, is commonly used now.

There are a number of life themes unique to each of us, but five main ones seem common to most people:

- unworthiness
- helplessness
- hopelessness
- abandonment
- distrust

Life themes can arise in any realm—love, work, career, creativity, finance, and so forth—or occur in multiple areas of your life. Even though so many of us share the same life theme, how it manifests in your life is unique because the mix of your stories is exclusive to you.

Life Themes Help Form Your Soul's Journey

When you look back over your life and see it as a whole, patterns or themes emerge. It's as if your life has been purposefully composed, like a painting, book, or symphony. Far from being a series of arbitrary surprises, your life has a consistent plot. And not only have specific people been agents in your life, you've been an agent in theirs.

The composite of your life themes, beliefs, set of behaviors, and life purpose creates your unique soul's journey. It is the overall pattern of your life, like a grand symphony or play. It's also one of the main reasons you're here, what you've come to develop or shift about yourself so you can fully blossom. As you identify and change your stories, your full potential and power grow and you soar along and even guide your soul's journey.

Where Do Stories Come From?

Stories come from three sources: conscious, subconscious, and inherited.

Conscious sources include your upbringing, life experiences, childhood issues, wounds, roles, identities, and other

---

Soul Versus Spirit

There's often confusion between the terms *spirit* and *soul*, for many view them as the same. Here, spirit is the spark of Source energy that is the consciousness in all life, while the soul is your eternal perfect Self that dwells in infinity. Sometimes called the Higher Self, your soul is your authentic self that lives in a body on the physical plane. It is the source of life, energy, and wisdom that comes from Source energy. As your individual expression of the Divine, it collects experiences throughout all times and places where it undertakes lessons to grow and develop. The soul envelops and protects the spirit.

environmental influences, such as culture, race, and religion. Any experiences with strong emotional impact produce a story. In other words, your history and environment create your stories.

Subconscious sources include what becomes so deeply embedded or rote that we're not even aware or conscious of it anymore. Actually, most of the brain's activity goes on beyond our conscious awareness. This includes our core beliefs, cyclical patterns, life themes, wounds, roles, and identities.

You can even live out a story that's not your own but has been inherited or passed down to you from an ancestor. I knew a man whose grandfather and father both died at the age of thirty. As this man approached that age, he developed many health problems. When he came to me, he just knew he was going to die when he turned thirty. We uncovered and cleared the ancestral pattern and his health returned. Now he's well beyond that age.

Stories Inform and Shape Your Life

Once a story is born, it begins to inform and shape your life. It becomes a tape or track that continuously runs in your head. You repeatedly think about it and then tell yourself and others about it. Soon you begin to expect the same experiences, for this is now "truth" in your life. And so it is, for the universe proves you are right, that what you think and believe is true. Even more so, you believe it is Truth with a capital T and Reality with a capital R.

For example, when Zack's partner left him, the pain was so great that he decided to never let that happen again. In his next relationship, when he felt it turn sour, he left the relationship first. As that felt better, he left first again in the relationship after that. Eventually, Zack developed a problem with commitment so that even though he deeply desired to have a long-lasting intimate relationship, it never happened. Zach was too afraid the woman would leave and that he would experience terrible pain again, so he would never commit to a relationship but would always leave the woman first.

Susie had the same core story and issue—a partner left that caused her severe emotional pain—but she chose a different reaction. Instead, she only entered into superficial relationships from then on. She appeared carefree, like a flitting moth, but actually her behavior arose from a subconscious pattern to protect herself from further pain.

A third person, Karen, also shared Zack's and Susie's story, but her response was to gain weight. She didn't even want to attract a partner so she wouldn't suffer the horrible pain of a broken relationship. Weight protected her from risking another partner who might leave and hurt her again.

Your Imagination and Emotions Fuel Your Stories

Repeatedly thinking and talking about your stories give them power. They are fueled by the images you hold and the emotions they invoke. How you see the story in your mind's eye and imagine it takes place keeps it alive. How you consider or react to a story gives it power.

> **You Are Right Either Way**
> Henry Ford knew what he was talking about when he purportedly said, "Whether you think you can or think you can't, you're right."

Images of past experiences, present ideas, and future expectations guide every aspect of your being. These images are imbued with strong emotions of how you felt or will feel, and both inform your future. When your thoughts dwell on what someone did or said, you also empower the story and keep it alive. As a result, when a similar circumstance arises, you are easily triggered. This reaction occurs because of the stories you hold. In other words, your story has now entranced you.

Exercise

Learn to Identify Stories

The first step to shifting your stories is to identify them. It's hardest to see our own stories, so start with others'. However, keep what you see to yourself!

To start seeing stories, take the eagle-eye view and observe other people. Family gatherings are great times, especially during holidays when everyone's stories are especially "up." But you can observe stories anywhere and anytime—a movie, radio or TV show, or something you overhear in a store, during a meal, or at work.

As you listen to other people's stories, avoid judgment. Just observe so you can identify the stories when they arise and learn when people are speaking from their patterns. See how stories hook people and how in turn this creates their behavior and others' responses too.

Next, start to identify your own stories. The best way to do this is to observe your life as a mirror. Shift your perspective so you see yourself within the context of your whole life. Look at what happens to you, watch how you respond, and see what you experience. These mirror your beliefs and stories.

As well, observe the stories you tell to others. Do you often tell this particular story? Where do you feel the most energy in the story? Where do you feel its energy in your body? Listen to the words you use and statements you make. Most of them are automatic and so reflect your subconscious beliefs. What are you really telling others about yourself?

Observe, and do not judge. Remember that stories aren't good or bad. Rather, just become aware of the stories, the patterns they form, and how you and the world respond in turn.

The Power of Your Stories

Stories are powerful indeed. They hook you, keep you in pathological relationships, shape your perceptions, inform your future, and determine your health. However, you can change your stories, for you are the source and power of the transformation you desire.

Stories Hypnotize You

Stories work by hypnotizing you. When you tell yourself the same stories over and over, you eventually believe them. You think that's how life is, and that nothing else is possible. This is what happened to me before, this is how people treated me in the past, and so this is what will happen to me in the future. Now a story is born. It has become a creed, your ultimate Truth and Reality. This is the process of how you hypnotize yourself.

We allow into our worlds the suggestions we accept or already believe, and we generally don't allow the suggestions we don't accept or believe. As children, we accept suggestions from our parents, siblings, friends, teachers, race, culture, and religion. We believe what they say and do as Truth about the world and ourselves.

With maturity, we begin to not accept some of these stories and choose our own. However, most of us stay hypnotized with the original suggestions and believe there is no other possible way. Even more, when we encounter beliefs foreign to our own, we think they are wrong and we are right. Wars are fought on this basis alone.

The suggestions you don't accept or allow are just as important and powerful as the ones you do. You might exclude the suggestions that you are successful, partnered, wealthy, lovable, smart, or respected. Such limiting suggestions don't allow you to experience what you do desire.

For example, most of us have entranced ourselves into believing that we are victims to our genes, that we inherit certain genes but not others and there's nothing that can be done about it. However, science is now determining that your environment is what influences your genes and determines if genes are read or not. This new science, called epigenetics, has far-reaching implications on our lives.[2] But to work with these fascinating possibilities, it's first necessary to awake from the hypnotic belief that you can't influence your genes.

Stories Hook You

This is important: *Stories are neither good nor bad.* Good things happen. Bad things happen. Indifferent things happen. Life dishes out tragedies, invasions, and holocausts. It brings birth, survival, pain, love, and death. We all experience events that cause joy or suffering. But do you have to suffer to grow? Do you have to suffer your whole life? And should you expect to keep suffering in your future?

> **Source of Your Experience**
>
> **We are not responsible for everything. People perpetuate crimes. Acts of nature occur. Others can be jerks. Tragic things happen. You can only be responsible for yourself; you can't change other people.**
>
> **In the example of a book hitting your toe, the story behind your response of anger or irritation could be: "I always get hurt," "I'm clumsy," "The world is out to get me," or "Bad stuff always happen to me." It doesn't matter what the story is; what matters is that you reacted and so are hooked by it.**
>
> **See yourself as the source of your experience and how to respond. This is the only area where you are responsible and can make a difference.**

Your beliefs determine whether or not you suffer. *How you respond to what happens is what matters, not what happens itself.* And how you respond is due to the story, pattern, or limiting core belief you hold, consciously or subconsciously.

When you react to something, you are "hooked" by it. When you blame others for your feelings, you are hooked. When you react negatively, you are hooked. When you react violently, you are hooked.

It is the emotional charge you hold behind a limiting story or belief that hooks you. Hooks are anything with a charge that evoke strong emotion or grab and hold your attention and energy. The stronger you feel or react to an experience, the more energy it has and the more it has hooked you.

For example, if you drop a book on your toe, you could pick it up and realize it opened to the passage you were looking for or else read something inspiring and helpful. You could also shrug, rub your toe, and walk away. Or you could get angry and throw the book at something, yell at your kid, or get increasingly irritable

---

2   Epigenetics includes anything other than DNA sequence that influences the development of an organism. Epigenetics literally means "outside conventional genetics."

throughout the day. The story is the same—the book hit your toe—but how you respond to it reveals if you're hooked or not.

Stories Keep You in Pathological Relationships

We love to play starring roles in our stories. Even if we tell a story about someone else, we insert ourselves in it through implication. Most stories have three main roles: hero, victim, and villain. Each of us tends to play one of these roles more than the other two, but in actuality, we play all three of the roles at different times and in different areas of our lives. We can even switch between them in a moment or play all three in rapid succession.

The hero rescues, helps, or saves someone or a situation. The victim blames everyone else for his problems and says, "They did this to me," "Poor me," "I'm left out," or "Everything bad always happens to me." The villain perpetuates a situation or acts on other people and situations and so is often called a perpetrator (a term more easily adopted by many, for who likes to admit they are a villain?).

Playing any one of these roles means you also need the other two roles to occur in order to act yours out. For instance, what would stories be without a hero or heroine? We idolize them along with the obstacles they overcome and goals they achieve. Yet how can you be a heroine without a villain or something to overcome? And a hero needs someone or something to rescue, so this creates the role of the victim as well.

The hero looks out for, or tries to overcome, the perpetrator and seeks to help or rescue the

Our Different Hooks

When Julie asked Ken what he thought about her new outfit, he said, "That's interesting." Julie could have responded in any number of ways, but because she held a core belief that she was unattractive, she immediately wanted to crawl into a hole. As a result, she remained withdrawn and sullen throughout the rest of the evening.

If only Julie had considered that Ken really meant her outfit looked different than what she normally wore and so appeared interesting to him, she might never have reacted and could have enjoyed her evening. Instead, her core belief of being unattractive filtered what she heard so she didn't allow for other possibilities. When Julie didn't hear Ken say she looked good, her old belief that she was unattractive hooked her. This triggered the bad feelings from her story so they colored the rest of her night.

Two other people were in the room when Ken made his comment, but because they held different core beliefs, they responded differently. When Pattie heard Ken say Julie looked interesting, she just shrugged, whereas Sally playfully tapped Ken on the arm and told him he looked interesting too. Neither woman was hooked in the same way as Julie.

victim. The hero could be an activist group, a politician, or even your aunt who brings over desserts to cheer you up. The victim blames the perpetrator and seeks to be rescued or saved. The victim could be a culture, a racial group, or your coworker who feels his boss repeatedly berates him.

The perpetrator seeks a victim to act on and avoids or sabotages the hero. The perpetrator could be a corporation polluting the air, a different political group than yours, or even the neighbor's dog that messes your lawn. It could also be someone who instigates new laws, establishes a group effort to clean up the neighborhood, or continually names the elephant in the room so no one ignores it.

These three roles—victim, hero, and perpetrator—form what is called a "pathological triangle" in which all three parts are codependent. Interestingly, none of these roles see themselves clearly. Often a villain believes he's a hero or a victim, and the victim might see herself as a hero. Behaviors can play any of the three roles, too, such as an addiction.

Stories Shape Your Perceptions

Perception is not the event or circumstance in itself, but the meaning you give to it. This meaning is shaped by your stories and beliefs regardless of whether you share a twin, family, bloodline, culture, race, religion, spiritual approach, or career. *It's not what happens to you that matters. It's how you perceive what happens that does.*

Beliefs and stories are filters, like wearing glasses. Your perception is a unique perspective, like your own colored lens that tints how you see life. Your personal lens filters other ways of seeing life, sometimes to the point that you don't even know or accept that other possibilities exist. Your lenses only allow you to see what matches your stories and beliefs. They keep you stuck in a slanted perspective.

Blind Men and The Elephant

There's a parable from India about blind men and an elephant. A group of blind men touched an elephant, but each felt a different part. One man at the trunk said the elephant was shaped like a curve. Another by its ear said the elephant flapped back and forth. A third by its hide said the elephant was rough and hairy. All the men were right, but each only had part of the picture.

The men defined the elephant according to their perception from where they stood and from what they could experience from that place. When they compared notes, each story differed and conflict ensued. In reality, a much bigger picture (the entire elephant) with more possibilities existed (the elephant in a larger landscape) than any of the three men knew.

Stories and Your Health

Like all the other stories in our lives, we love to play the blame game with our health issues too. But health is actually an "inside job." This means that most health problems are due to emotional or spiritual issues that are derived from your cyclical patterns and limiting beliefs. When you uncover and clear the hidden emotional or spiritual issues that underlie your health condition, the issue "miraculously" clears up.

Some people have health issues a very long time with great impact on their lives. If this occurs, the underlying issue is a part of their soul's journey. Healing such health issues usually takes time and repeated work since there is more to clear and much to learn from them.

No matter what health issue you have, you can alter how you respond to it even if you can't fully heal. There are always people who in the most dire, horrific, or difficult circumstances are still cheerful and loving while others whine with a mere cold or skin outbreak. It is not the health issue itself that creates suffering or triggers reactions but how you respond to it that does. When you unhook from your stories, your reactions and responses vary as well.

The power of placebo demonstrates the power you have over your health. A placebo is an inactive substance given in trials as a control treatment. It is a purposeful deception of which the imbiber is not aware. People believe they are taking a medicine that will correct their condition while actually they may be taking an inert tablet. Regardless of which is taken, a high percentage of people experience a perceived or actual improvement with the placebo, as do those taking the real medication. In this case, people are essentially tricked into replacing one story with another. The power of placebo is the power of our stories not only on health but on all areas of life as well.

Heath Issues

A friend of mine had chronic shoulder pain. She tried everything on the physical level to clear it but nothing worked permanently; the pain always returned. At the same time, she juggled two households for two years. It was not until three days after she sold one of the houses that her shoulder pain disappeared.

Years ago, I had a patient with multiple sclerosis. Acupuncture and herbs helped tremendously but only slowed the progression of her disease. One day, she told me about being sexually abused as a child and described that she dealt with it by lying stiff as a board, pretending she couldn't move, in hope the abuser would stop. The multiple sclerosis had literally manifested the feeling of that image in her life.

I knew a man whose kidney stone pain was managed through acupuncture, diet, and herbs for over a year. The day he passed his dreaded CPA exam, he also passed the stone, pain free.

Stories Inform Your Future

Stories not only inform who you were and are now, they also predict who you will become. *Chronic thoughts invite matching experiences to happen.* Sometimes this creates an internal tug of war. When one part of you wants something to happen but another part doesn't believe it's possible or holds hidden subconscious programming that doesn't allow it, you stay in limbo, wanting something but never really experiencing it.

Moving through life while focusing on the past is, simply put, like driving while looking through the rearview mirror. The old stories, dramas, and patterns that dominate your life determine how you feel, what you can or cannot have or do, and how you behave. We tend to play the blame game, blaming what doesn't work in our lives or what we don't experience on what "he said" or what "she did" or on how our parents treated us. This is focusing on the past and living through the rearview mirror.

Changing Your Stories

Can you truly shift your stories and reshape your life and future? How do you "turn around" to drive your life while looking through the front windshield? And can you create what you desire instead?

Yes, you can change. Even in the most difficult of circumstances, you can evolve beyond your present state of being, limiting stories, and core beliefs. Indeed, you are meant to shift your stories and reshape your life, just like the caterpillar is encoded to become the butterfly. There's an intrinsic, authentic self to let out. However, it can't emerge from its chrysalis until it goes through a metamorphosis. And your metamorphosis occurs when you neutralize and shift your stories. This is the key to changing your life.

You Are the Source of Change

To transform your life, you must first diffuse the energy behind your stories so you can clear their hooks. Positive thinking and affirmations can help, but because stories are dominated by subconscious patterns and beliefs, they ultimately control your life regardless. It is like trying to get rid of a weed: If you just pluck off the leaves and stems, the weed will grow back. Rather, you must dig out the root of the story in your subconscious to be rid of the weed. Only then can the beautiful garden you desire bloom and grow.

To dig out the weed and unhook from your stories, some of us must *first stop expecting a better past*. Reliving the past only reinforces it and keeps pain alive. This is driving while looking through the rearview mirror. Instead, acknowledge your past for its teachings and gifts, for only then can it fully let go. Doing so shifts your stories' grip so you can align with and manifest your authentic self. That means you don't have to wait for someone or something to correct the situation for you; rather, you can transform your life now. The power to change is internal, not external.

Eventually, you'll come to see and understand that everything you say and do is a story, and that everything you hear and see is a story too. The question is, are you bound, limited, hooked, or held back by your stories, or do your stories serve you so that you live your highest potential and greatest dreams?

It's an Inside Job!

Perhaps one of the greatest held secrets is that your outer life shifts around your inner life. **To truly change your outer life, it's necessary to first shift your inner life.** Everything else mirrors and follows that. In fact, you have always been creating your life although you haven't necessarily been aware of it.

Look at the life you are living, and that is the life you have been creating. This is actually the secret of secrets—that you are already dreaming your world into being. *You* are the one. So why not dream in what you desire instead? Once you've neutralized your old patterns and beliefs, this is exactly what is possible.

You Have a Choice

By now a part of you might believe you can transform your life but another part might say, "Yes, but life isn't like that. Life is hard. I grew up in the ghettos (or on a farm or in a country) where every day was a life-and-death struggle. So all of this is very nice to think about, but it's just not realistic." Or, "Everything doesn't happen because of what I think. The universe is vast and complex. Lots goes on that doesn't have anything to do with me. I don't have control over my neighbors, country, or other people."

The universe *is* vast and complex. Life *can* be a daily struggle. Uncontrollable events *do* occur, such as natural disasters, crimes, or societal changes. Incidents happen that are undeserved or even horrible, such as losing a loved one, being in a tragic accident, suffering childhood abuse, or living through civil war. Further, we can't alter other people or take responsibility for them. Some people *are* abusive, dishonest, selfish, self-absorbed, or irrational. So how do we deal with such circumstances and people? How do we still create lives of peace and contentment? Is it really possible?

While many factors are beyond our influence, how you respond to what happens is within your control. If you are hooked by a story or pattern, you will react from the belief you hold. This is what you can adjust. You can discharge the energy from the pattern, release the story's hook, and choose to respond in another way. You can then create what you desire to experience instead.

Move from Victim to Director

Nancy came from a dysfunctional and neglectful family. For years, her parents wouldn't listen to or believe her. Even as an adult, her parents treated her disrespectfully. Whenever her mom came to her house, she would spread all of her stuff across Nancy's dining room table even though Nancy asked her not to. She requested that her table stay clear to eat on, yet her mom ignored this request.

Nancy spent years crying, lost in self-pity and feelings of not being smart enough and that no one believed in her. Finally, she had had enough and began to work on herself. She learned to love and respect herself and, through this inner shift, adjusted how she responded to her outside world, even in the seemingly small things.

Without making a big fuss, she cleared off her dining room table, and when next her mom appeared, Nancy pointed to a place on a side table and said to put her items there. Amazingly, her mom did so without questioning or ignoring her.

No blaming, anger, or arguments occurred to facilitate this transformation. Rather, Nancy found that her own newly developed self-love and self-respect enabled her to act differently in the outer world, and her mom responded accordingly. Her mom didn't change; Nancy did. Through this, Nancy was able to experience what she desired instead.

Say Yes to Your Journey

So say yes to yourself! Say yes even though there's not enough time, money, space, or energy; say yes even though you have small children to care for; say yes even though you think your partner or family won't understand; say yes even though your job won't "allow" it; say yes even though your friends don't support you; say yes even though you have health issues; say yes even though you have a million other reasons why you can't. Choose to say yes to your Self, and step into your future. Choose to say yes every step of the way, every minute of your day. Answer the call, and watch your life transform.

My Experience With Metaphor-phosis

When you change yourself, your outer world shifts too. I've seen this happen over and over in my life and with clients and students. It always seems amazing and miraculous, but it happens. Here's an example of how I transmuted my stories and, as a result, my future. It's a simple one and yet has had a deep influence on my life.

I am part of some professional groups, and at one of the group's annual meetings, I always felt left out, unseen, and unappreciated due to a life theme of unworthiness. I didn't really seem a part of the group although I knew or was friends with most of the key members.

When I learned how to clear my stories, I identified and recognized the unworthiness theme and all its implications in my life. Over time, I focused and worked on shifting that story. At the next annual meeting after this inner work, my experience was the total opposite from any previous ones. I felt seen, respected, included, and involved with everyone there. In fact, I called it a "love fest" to myself because of all the love and respect I felt from its members. I was even invited to teach on a cruise through one of those people, fulfilling a dream of mine.

Ever since then, I have felt included and seen by the members of that group. The people themselves didn't shift, and I didn't alter my perceptions of them. Rather, I cleared my old core belief of feeling unworthy and left out. This relinquished my rearview mirror approach and enabled me to look out the front windshield so I could see and experience what I desired instead.

Exercises

Exercise One: Identify Your Role

Observe the stories you tell to others. Reflect on the roles you hold. Now identify yourself on the pathological triangle. Who do you think you are in the story—heroine, victim, or perpetrator?

Exercise Two: Recognize Positive Core Beliefs and Patterns

It is always best to begin seeing what *is* working in your life rather than what isn't. You know very well what isn't working, so tally what does work for you. Positive core beliefs and patterns are the ones that enhance positive emotions, support your life vision and goals, and bring you love and joy. Make a list of these along with answers to the following:

- What beliefs support you now?
- What cyclical patterns occur in your life that you like?
- Which stories make you feel good?
- What positive things do you believe about yourself?
- What positive things do you know to be true about yourself?

The Biology of Your Stories

Your stories not only affect your perception, but they also live in and affect your body. Did you know that

- there's no difference between what you imagine and what you actually see because the same areas of the brain light up either way?
- the brain can't tell the difference between a real danger or threat and a perceived or imagined danger or threat?
- a repeated emotional response actually rewires your brain?
- belief and perception control your biology and not the other way around?
- if you can't control your emotional state, you are addicted to it?
- signals from your environment (thoughts, images, emotions, and invisible energies) change how your DNA expresses itself in your body?
- the subconscious mind is running you on autopilot most of the time because 95 percent of your brain's activity occurs beyond conscious awareness?
- people with multiple personalities have different illnesses with each personality, such as allergies, and diabetes?
- your stories and feelings create a resonance that attunes to similar resonances in other people and events?
- belief and perception control the expression of your cells, and your stories control your beliefs and perceptions?

The body never lies. It holds tremendous wisdom and all of our information. Any memories, emotions, stories, trauma, core beliefs, and ancestral patterns live in your genes, cells, blood, tissues, muscles, organs, and brain. Your stories live in every part of your body and manifest through it as well.

Have you ever had someone touch a certain place on your body and suddenly had a memory bloom forth, complete with smells, sounds, and emotions? It's as if a movie played back with all its sensory experiences from another time. This is because that touch unleashed the story that's stored there. This means you can go to your body to learn your stories.

Usually we're not aware of the multiple physical functions occurring on a cellular level that act together to store stories. Our bodies do a remarkable job in memorizing them so they are put on automatic pilot and the mind is freed to process cognitive functions instead.

Remember, stories shape your perception. In turn, perception controls your behavior and your genetics. In fact, you can even alter the read-out of your genes! This might seem amazing or even impossible, but this is what you are already doing all the time, though you may not know it. Belief, perception, and emotion control your biology as much or more than the other way around; it's the way you respond to your environment that controls how your cells respond in turn. To understand this, it's helpful to look at how your brain and cells work and how environmental signals affect you too.

The Brain and Your Stories

Your brain is actually comprised of four sections, each sitting on top of the other. First, you have a reptilian part in the brain stem that's associated with all of your autonomic functions, such as heartbeat, breathing, and body temperature. This "lizard" brain is all you really need to survive in the world. It also activates your subconscious programming to store the experiences you repeat over and over so your body memorizes them and they become second nature.

The subconscious includes your habits, skills, core beliefs, cyclical patterns, and stories. If you were repeatedly told as a child that you were clumsy, this is where it's stored, and because the subconscious doesn't analyze anything, it was stored as truth.

According to cognitive neuroscientists, we are conscious of only about 5 percent of our cognitive activity, and ***"… our behavior depends on the 95 percent of brain activity that goes beyond our conscious awareness."***[3] The reptilian area of your brain is the most active part because it's the microprocessor that fuels and drives the rest of the brain. The subconscious beliefs you hold about life drive your actions and reactions. This is where you mostly create and perceive your world. This means your subconscious programming has a tremendous influence on how you behave and who you are.

The mammalian part of your brain includes the limbic system and sits on top of the reptilian brain. It is considered the chemical brain because it secretes a chemical with your every thought and feeling. Additionally, it's the brain of primitive instincts that operate from the four Fs: fear, fighting, feeding, and fornication. This is where your fight-or-flight response occurs,

---

3   "Mysteries of the Mind, Your unconscious is making your everyday decisions," Marianne Szegedy-Maszak, *U.S. News and World Report*, posted Feb 20, 2005; February 28, 2005 issue. Accessed May 30, 2012. http://health.usnews.com/usnews/health/articles/050228/28think_2.htm.

which causes the gut to squeeze shut and the blood vessels and forebrain (conscious reasoning and logic) to shut down so blood flows to the arms, legs, and hindbrain to control reflex and reactive behavior.

Amazingly, ***the mammalian part of your brain can't tell the difference between a real danger or threat and a perceived or imagined danger or threat.***[4] It also can't tell the difference between a threat that occurred two years ago or twenty years ago. Instead, the memories are bundled in neuro-pathways within the brain, which, when activated by a threat (real or imaginary), cause you to relive that traumatic event all over again. The fight-or-flight response can be triggered through stress or an emotional reaction just as easily as through a real danger. This brain is a part of the subconscious too.

The neocortex is the third part of the brain. Also known as the frontal cortex, it sits right above the limbic brain in the frontal lobe and forms the walnut shape on the outside of the entire brain. This frontal cortex comprises 40 percent of the entire brain. It's the executive or the thinking brain, which determines what you pay attention to so you can single-mindedly focus for an extended time and make decisions. This is the brain of conscious awareness.

The fourth area of the brain, which appeared most recently (about one hundred thousand years ago), is the "spiritual" brain. Located in the prefrontal cortex at the forehead, Neanderthals didn't have this brain (and so were known as "low-brows" because of their backward sloping foreheads. Our foreheads slope forward because we have this newer brain structure).

The spiritual brain allows us to step into communion with Source[5] energy. It is the transcendental brain, the brain linked to our soul, or Higher Self. This is the brain that's awakened through meditation, prayer, stillness, journeying, and similar activities. This brain is activated when you are in higher consciousness.

In terms of your stories, the reptilian and mammalian parts of the brain have the greatest impact on your biology. Together, they include your automatic and subconscious programming and the chemicals surging through your body. This is key because of how these store and activate your stories through thoughts, images, and emotions.

Associative Memory and Your Stories

The brain builds its stories through associative memory. This is important because an associative memory includes not only the many details of one story but connects with other stories as well. For example, your concept of love is built from many different ideas. If you associate love with disappointment because of past events, when you think about love, you

---

4   Joe Dispenza, D.C., *Evolve Your Brain* (Health Communications, Inc., Deerfield Beach, Florida), 2007, p. 272.

5   I use the term *Source energy* to encompass the many names people give to the conscious life force energy that infuses all life, such as God, Goddess, Divinity, Great Spirit, Allah, Yahweh, and the void.

experience the memory of pain, sorrow, or even anger. In turn, the story may be linked to hurt, which may be partnered with specific people, which then connects back to love. A memory triggers an entire story with relationships to several emotions and past experiences.

Your "Neuro-Net" and Stories

Your brain is constructed of a "neuro-net" made of tiny nerve cells called neurons. These link with other neurons that wire and fire together and send messages between each other, sort of like your own personal Internet. If you practice the same thing over and over, those nerve cells develop a long-term relationship to store the associated memories in your subconscious. *A repeated emotional response rewires the brain.* If you get angry, sad, frustrated, or suffer on a daily basis, you develop a superhighway between nerve cells that quickly activate.

For example, as a child, I had teachers who told me that I wasn't artistic. One particular event was so firmly programmed in my subconscious that even to this day I can vividly recall the situation, complete with sounds, colors, words, emotions, and action, just like a mini-movie.

As an adult, I learned photography and was eventually invited to give my own show. However, I couldn't believe this was possible because I believed I wasn't an "artist." Every time I heard that word, I cringed inside and withdrew, as it triggered fear and self-doubt. It took me years to release those emotional reactions, but eventually I acknowledged myself as an artist and my neuro-net rewired to support this new belief.

The good news is that your neurons do respond to new environmental signals and can break long-term wiring relationships and create new ones. When you respond differently to your environmental signals, another chemical of emotion is sent to bind with receptors and shift the cells anew so a different part of your DNA is read, setting an entirely separate cascade of instructions into motion.

Imagery and Your Stories

The link between images and the subconscious mind is key because *there's no difference between what you imagine and what you actually see*. Imagining an object lights up the same areas of the brain as when you actually see that object. The brain doesn't know the difference between what it sees and what it remembers because the same specific neuro-networks fire.

While the brain and body don't distinguish between an imagined event and a real one, it responds in the same way. We've all experienced how a movie or dream can have the same effect on our bodies as if it were really happening. This is the power of images.

Actual seeing occurs through the visual cortex in the brain, not with the eyes. The images that play in your brain are what you see. And yet you only see what you think is real and believe is possible. *You create images in your mind of what you think is true, and this is what you then*

believe is real. You actually create your reality this way, for it's what you perceive (or what you think or believe you see) that matters, and what you perceive arises from your stories. Your subconscious mind controls your body and habits, not your intellect or eyes.

Chemical Signals and Your Stories

Emotions are chemical signals to your cells. When you respond to your environment, the hypothalamus in your brain manufactures chemicals to match your emotions. These in turn create neuropeptide molecules (small-chain amino acid sequences, or bits of protein), which the hypothalamus then assembles into neurohormones to match your emotional state.

You have chemicals for all emotions, such as joy, love, appreciation, anger, and fear. This is the mammalian part of your brain in action; it constantly produces neuropeptide molecules from how you feel, and the resulting peptide is sent through the pituitary into your bloodstream where it finds its way to different parts of the body.

Emotions are designed to chemically reinforce something into long-term memory. This creates an addiction to that emotion because it provides a chemical "rush." Over time, you'll create situations to fulfill the biochemical craving of your cells so your chemical needs are met. You are used to the feeling, so it's familiar even if it's uncomfortable and undesired. How do you know if you're addicted to an emotion? If you can't control your emotional state, you're addicted to it; you are hooked.

But here's the big news about your emotional chemicals: According to Candace Pert, they don't just occur in the brain but exist everywhere in the body.[6] Your emotions are not just responses from your brain but are produced directly at a cellular level when the neuropeptides bind with receptors. That means emotional issues are stored everywhere, such as in your nervous system, blood, organs, bones, glands, muscles, and skin.

Even your heart holds every single neuropeptide receptor, which is why people who receive heart transplants have a personality change for several months after, as the neuropeptides and receptors there imitate the personality and emotions of the donor. Your memories are not just stored in your brain but in a psychosomatic network extending into your cells at the receptor level.[7]

---

6   Pert, Candace PhD. *Molecules of Emotion: The Science Behind Mind-Body Medicine.* Simon and Schuster, New York, NY, 1999.

7   ———. *Your Body is Your Subconscious Mind.* Sounds True, Boulder, CO, 2004, compact disc, written and performed by Candace Pert. 3 CD's (2 hours, 30 minutes), 1 study guide (20 pages). ISBN-10: 1-59179-223-1; ISBN-13: 978-1-59179-223-9; Product Codes: 0451d, w451d, aw00451d.

Cells and Your Stories

Neuropeptides are informational substances that create states of consciousness with associated physical responses. For example, excitement and anger increase gut motility while contentment decreases it. Between two and three thousand different neuropeptides integrate to act as a coordinated whole. Candace Pert calls them "molecules of emotion" because they are found in the parts of the brain related to emotions.

Once the neuropeptide molecule is sent throughout the body, it locates its particular cell receptor site, similar to finding the right house address to deliver its mail. The peptides find the receptors where they fit, bind, and open the cell, just as a key opens a lock. Then they transmit very specific instructions to the cell. This causes the cell to alter and shift, setting off a whole cascade of biochemical events. Some of these create changes in the nucleus of the cell, and others determine what part of the DNA is read.

Receptor sites receive information. They communicate received information to the cell, which tells the body how to respond. Any number of emotional reactions can cause a pounding heart, dry mouth, clenched gut, tensed muscles, or flushed face. If a particular emotion is repeatedly experienced, that chemical bombards its receptor at a high intensity. This causes the receptor to either literally shrink so there are less of them or to desensitize so the same amount of chemical elicits a smaller response. When the cell divides to create a new one, the new cell has more receptor sites for that emotion and fewer ones for vitamins, minerals, food exchange, and the release of wastes and toxins.

DNA and Your Stories

Your DNA does not act upon or control cells in any way but is a blueprint for making proteins that comprise the cells in your body. Through gene regulation, a gene "switches on or off," meaning it is either read or not read, like a blueprint to build a house. To read your DNA blueprint, the chemicals of emotion bind with their special receptors on the cells and change them. When the cells are changed, they shift so certain parts of the DNA can be read and other parts can't.

The read parts form the pattern for developing proteins; the unread parts have no effect. This means you can't change your DNA, but you can alter what is read or not read. ***In other words, your stories influence which part of your DNA is read (or not read)*** to influence the reactions and formation of your body.

Environmental Signals Control Your DNA

So what triggers this cascade of events? What are the original stimuli that set off the neurons to create molecules of emotion that in turn change cells and the read-out of your DNA?

Signals from your environment.[8]

Signals come from everywhere. They can be chemical, hormonal, drug, growth factor, and energy field, as well as your thoughts, images, and emotions. And what triggers your thoughts, images, and emotions? The stories stored in your subconscious mind. Yet it is not what really happens that matters, but your perception of these signals that does.

Back to Perception and Your Stories

Your response to environmental signals occurs from what you perceive is happening and not necessarily from what is actually occurring. And how does your perception develop? From three places—instinct, the conscious mind, and the subconscious mind. Together these form what we call consciousness.

For example, you are born with genetic instincts to heal yourself, but life can alter or cancel them because of the perceptions you acquire. As a child, you might have been told only a doctor can heal you, that you are sickly and will never be well, or that your parents had a certain illness and so you will too. It doesn't matter what is real; what matters is that your subconscious believes it as true, and so this belief continues to influence your perceptions.

Health and Your Stories

Every signal from the environment stimulates a habitual response and emotion, which in turn causes the release of the chemicals of emotion into your bloodstream to go to your cells and change them. In other words, your environment stimulates your subconscious to activate memories, which in turn causes chemicals of emotion to be released that create muscular and hormonal responses and choices of behavior (action), which in turn create new thoughts, images, and feelings, and so the cycle repeats.

All of this information on your biology and how you respond to environmental signals has far-reaching implications on health and disease. If your emotional chemistry influences what part of your DNA is read, think of how this affects your body. This entire cascade starts with your perception, which in turn is determined by your core beliefs and stories.

Signals create disease when they are inappropriate or sent at the wrong time, such as through toxins (distorts the signal); trauma (interferes with the transmission of the signal); and thought (autosuggestion infects the signal).[9] We think all the time, and thoughts produce emotions that send chemicals to bind with receptors to change the cells, so our thoughts are most powerful indeed.

---

8   The way DNA code is translated into function depends not only on its sequence but also on its interaction with environmental factors. Studies have shown that experiences in life are potentially able to induce epigenetic modifications.

9   Bruce Lipton, PhD. From a lecture on *The Biology of Belief* in Felton, Ca.

Health issues are the branch, or the shoot, of the real issue. Like weeding a garden, you must dig out the root (emotional cause) or the weed (health issue) will return. To fully heal, it's necessary to eliminate the limiting core beliefs and cyclical patterns that keep the old beliefs in place and diffuse the emotional charge that feeds the pattern.

To do this, it's helpful to stop seeing illness as something separate from you. Instead, view it as part of a larger pattern of your life. Metaphors work brilliantly for this. For example, you could see vision problems as not seeing something clearly, ear problems as not listening to yourself, digestive problems as not being able to stomach something, constipation as a hard time letting go, and bladder infections as being pissed off. The possibilities are endless.

The bottom line for health is that it's very important to not stuff or repress emotions in any way. Emotion is e-motion, or energy *in* motion. If an emotion is stopped, repressed, or suppressed, it stagnates energy and causes disease. In fact, it's been discovered that release of repressed anger even causes tumors to disappear two months later![11]

How Stories Affect Health

An interesting demonstration of the effect of our stories on health is people with multiple personalities. Some personalities have illnesses while others don't; some have allergies to cats, but others don't; some have diabetes and yet this disappears when another personality emerges! What each of these personalities perceives about their worlds is completely different, and so each one reacts and manifests something different even though they all coexist in the same body and their outer environment is the same.[10]

I'll never forget the time I had such a severely swollen sore throat that I could barely swallow, let alone talk. It lingered for days with no relief regardless of what I tried to heal it. At the same time, my partner wanted me to travel with him on a seven-hour road trip to see his mother for a few days. I certainly didn't feel well enough to do this, so I said no. He left in a huff, which made me so angry that I spent the next hour venting my emotions over this and other issues with him that I hadn't yet expressed. Within two hours, my swollen sore throat completely vanished, and I was entirely well. My not "voicing" my inner truth had been the true cause of my sore throat.

Each of us has different personalities, but they don't manifest to the extent or extreme as those diagnosed with multiple personality disorders. However, our power to manifest or vanish a disease

---

10   "The Chemical Communicators," Interview with Candace Pert by Bill Moyers, *The Truth Seeker Journal*, Volume 123 (1997). Accessed May 30, 2012. http://www.banned-books.com/truth-seeker/1997archive/124_1/15_chemical.html.

11   Pert, Candace PhD. *Your Body is Your Subconscious Mind.* Sounds True, Boulder, CO, 2004, compact disc, written and performed by Candace Pert. 3 CD's (2 hours, 30 minutes), 1 study guide (20 pages). ISBN-10: 1-59179-223-1; ISBN-13: 978-1-59179-223-9; Product Codes: 0451d, w451d, aw00451d.

is just as powerful. This is because **health issues don't start in the body but with beliefs and feelings**. In fact, viruses use the same receptors as peptides to enter cells, and if those particular receptors are filled, the virus can't enter the cell. Our emotions affect whether or not we succumb to a viral infection. For example, a cold virus uses the same receptor for norepinephrine, which flows during happy moods and blocks the receptors so the cold virus can't enter the cells. If you are frequently unhappy, the receptors are more available for a virus to bind there.

Resonance, Coherence, and Your Stories

Your stories not only affect your chemistry, they also attract similar people, events, and experiences of the same frequencies. This attraction of like energies is similar to resonance and coherence. Resonance is comparable to a vibrating tuning fork that resonates with another vibrating tuning fork if the second one is similar in size, structure, and shape. Coherence is separate parts fitting together to form a harmonious whole to establish communication, like a subatomic telephone network or a huge orchestra.

In quantum physics, non-locality means that a quantum entity influences another quantum particle instantaneously over any distance. This is called quantum coherence. Two subatomic particles once in close proximity can still communicate over any distance after they are separated. The Institute of HeartMath tested this and found that loving feelings and specific intentions altered samples of DNA in solution and produced biological effects in and out of the body even a half mile away!

The Institute of HeartMath also discovered that there's a torus around the heart, and that the heart's energy field has measurable effects on other processes in your body—on your physiology, DNA, and on those around you. Creating resonance and coherence with other people is very powerful.

Emotion is the guide to what you create and experience. As you think, you feel, and this creates a specific resonance that attunes to similar resonances in other people and events. You will then actually see and experience more of your stories because you are attuned with them. For example, before I was pregnant, I rarely saw children, but after I got pregnant, I saw children everywhere. The same happens when you're interested in something new, like a car, computer, or item of clothing, and then you see that brand everywhere when few seemed to exist before.

You make unconscious decisions and beliefs about other people through coherence and resonance. This is great if your body tuning fork is vibrating with love and bliss, but if you vibrate with anger or fear, you may not want the further experiences of angry or fearful people that you're then attracting through resonance and coherence.

Just as we don't perceive a difference between what we think is happening and what really is, so too does the macrocosm not know the difference between what you imagine and what you think or observe. Through resonance and coherence, the same experiences occur regardless of whether it is true or you perceive it as true. You attract outwardly what you emotionally feel inwardly. What you think, emote, and imagine is what you create through resonance, and your outer world matches this.

You give to others what you give to yourself. This is a very profound statement. When you criticize others, you criticize yourself; when you love others, you love yourself; when you are angry with others, you are angry with yourself. It's a continuous loop, for usually if you are angry with yourself, you'll then be angry with others. Whether or not you express your love, anger, or criticism, it's still present within you, setting up a vibration for resonance and coherence. And so your stories repeat.

Can You Change?

Can you rewire your brain and alter your biology? And can you transform your stories? Yes! Indeed, you are meant to shift your life so you align with and express your authentic self. Learn how to do so by using the Essential Tools for Change in the next section and then the three Metaphor-phosis steps.

Exercise

Self-Observation

Observe your interactions with others. What reactions do you have? What do you tend to think about most? What emotions do you experience over and over? What emotions do you express the most often? Make note of all these repeating issues, reactions, and emotions. Then ponder these questions:

- Do you want to continue reacting this way?
- Do you want to keep feeling this way over and over?
- Are you ready to change?
- Do you desire to change, or do you *want* to want to change?

Essential Tools for Change

As you begin to discover and process your stories, there are specific tools and techniques to help you quickly shift. They are so invaluable that I will bring you back to them over and over again.

Gratitude

Gratitude is one of the most powerful emotions. Feeling grateful affects every aspect of our lives and beings. It is deeper and more encompassing than acceptance, surrender, or letting go. And it not only influences the heart and mind but the body as well.

When you focus on what you are grateful for, through resonance and coherence you will draw more of those experiences to you.[12] You could be in the worst of moods and gratitude will lift you up like an express elevator. If you are emotional, give thanks for something you truly appreciate, as it's the best way to quickly change your energy. Give thanks for what you love, such as your relationships, work, home, family, or finances. This not only brings joy but also shifts your perspective about everything else.

Even at your darkest hours, there's always something you can thank—the beauty of a flower, the joy of a pet, the air that you breathe. Even just appreciating laughter, a baby's smile, or the shape of a tree can vary how you feel. Appreciate the small things, and your perspective will quickly alter.

Recently, I witnessed someone living in joy and gratitude. A paralyzed man who couldn't even hold his head up very well literally danced in his wheelchair with anything he could move—fingers, arms, eyes, head—to the inspiring New Age gospel music. His joy and gratitude spread to those around him and inspired many of us.

I learned a wonderful thanksgiving ritual from one of my teachers.[13] A traditional Peruvian offering called *apuchuta* uses two natural materials, such as pebbles, leaves, flowers, or shells. The

---

12   The Heartmath Institute discovered that feelings of love, joy, and appreciation entrain blood pressure and respiratory rhythm to the heart's rhythm. That means the heart's energy field has measurable effects on our physiology, DNA, and those around us.

13   Linda Fitch of the Four Winds Society.

first item is set down with thanks to the earth, while the second is set on top with thanks to the sky. Making ten of these little "cairn" offerings throughout the day for two to three weeks is a great way to swing one's perspective to enduring gratitude.

I also suggest you keep a gratitude journal. Every day, write ten to fifteen items for which you are grateful. Include any blessings you've experienced, no matter how small. Make a list of all you love and appreciate. The best time to do this is at night before bed. You could first write down your burdens in another journal, and then record what you appreciate. First thing in the morning, read your gratitude journal, and read it whenever you're emotionally upset as well. This can evoke a grateful state as you remember what's truly important.

Alternatively, you can use beaded necklaces or bracelets, such as a mala or rosary, to count your blessings. A dear friend and colleague[14] has her patients assign a positive major life event or memory to each bead and (after saying the rosary or mala, if desired) use the beads to remember each of the events for which they felt grateful.

Ho'Oponopono

One of the best ways I know to release the past for others and yourself is through *Ho'Oponopono*, an ancient Kahuna forgiveness technique. The meaning of *Ho'Oponopono*, "to make things right," refers to its ability to bring you into harmony with any relationship, whether you know the person or not. It even works with those who aren't alive, such as your ancestors. Ultimately, *Ho'Oponopono* recognizes our oneness with all of life and the impact we have on each other. It is a process of taking full responsibility for our actions and thoughts and the actions of others toward us.

There's a story about *Ho'Oponopono* that's circulated on the Internet, which is a fantastic example of the power of this technique. Whether true or not, it's a great story. As it goes, a Kahuna healer was called into a mental hospital in Hawaii because everything was out of control. Instead of visiting with and treating each patient, however, the doctor only went through their files for three full days. During this time, all the patients got better, some even to the point of being discharged.

When asked what he did, the doctor responded, "I was simply healing that part of me that created them." He explained that total responsibility for your life means that everything in your life, simply because it is in your life, is your responsibility.

The Inca and Navajo have a similar belief that if one individual is sick or nature is disruptive, it is due to the entire community being out of balance. Doing *Ho'Oponopono* restores balance and harmony to you and those around you.

---

14 Darlena LaOrange

Ho'Oponopono Technique:

When you find you are thinking, emoting, or reacting from a painful memory or future worry or fear, do *Ho'Oponopono*. Speak its four phrases as if to your inner six-year-old child. Say them in this order:

I love you.
I'm sorry (I apologize).
Please forgive me.
Thank you.

Repeatedly say these four phrases until your thoughts and emotions are clear. Traditionally, this process is done as an ongoing practice. It is used to clear memories from ancestors, individuals, childhood, and, eventually, all of life. It cleans memories from known issues but also those whose origins are unknown.

Face Forward

Facing forward means ***focusing on how you desire to feel*** rather than on what you actually feel. It means fully dwelling on what you desire in your life—your dreams and visions—instead of what is. Facing forward may seem strange and may contradict everything you've been taught. After all, our culture emphasizes facing "reality." While this seems logical, it actually perpetuates your current state of affairs so that your future is a continuation of your past, like driving while looking through the rearview mirror.

Instead, focus on what you desire to experience and the joy it would bring. Act from a place of excitement, anticipation, pleasure, or any other uplifting emotion your realized desire would evoke. Perceive what you desire to occur and then respond as if it were real. That means, "fake it 'til you make it." If you repeatedly focus on your desire, a door can open for the results to occur. Call it forward! Get excited! Go for it! Bring passion to your dreams, and focus on them unwaveringly.

Just as seeds need water, sunlight, nutritious soil, and weeding in order to thrive, desires require excitement, joy, anticipation, and expectation. The old thoughts and beliefs that may arise are the weeds to be dug up and "composted" (acknowledged). This compost then feeds the new growth. Until your garden is fully weeded, see it as abundantly full of all the beautiful flowers you desire. Dwell on how that beautiful garden makes you *feel* while continuously "faking it 'til you make it." *Expect* it as so, and in time, your dream garden will manifest.

Journal Writing

Stuffed or hidden emotions fester within and stagnate your energy. As most illness is caused by a blockage of energy, this has far-reaching effects. Writing in a journal provides a safe outlet to express your emotions, allowing them to surface and release before they cause health issues or damaging blow-ups.

Journal writing is different than diary writing where you record the events of your day. Instead, describe your strongest feelings and deepest thoughts. Since it's only for your eyes, write anything you want. Get it all out and on paper and express it fully.

Writing down your feelings is quite different than thinking about them. The latter creates an endless mental loop, while writing opens a door to the subconscious, creating a thoroughfare for thoughts and feelings to freely travel between the subconscious and conscious minds. Journal writing not only releases trapped emotions but also reveals inner connections, new ideas, or hidden thoughts and feelings, all of which form new meanings and possibilities.

There are a few helpful tips for keeping a journal. First, purchase a blank book that's so attractive you'll enjoy writing in it. Keep it in a secure yet easily accessible place, such as near your bed, so it's available to record your dreams upon awakening (dreams directly reflect hidden thoughts and feelings). As you write, imagine you're talking with a good and trusted friend.

It's best to establish a routine of journal writing, as this ensures its frequent and regular use. Many find that nighttime is especially good since it benefits sleep to first empty your mind and heart, offering emotional issues to your Higher Self for solutions during sleep. Regardless of any set routine, journal writing is an essential tool during any time of stress, mental or emotional upset, creative blocks, and so forth. For this reason, I suggest carrying your journal with you wherever you go so it's available when needed.

Lastly, trust the process. Even if you think you're fully aware of your feelings and have no need to write, go ahead and write anyway. You'll be surprised and amazed at what comes through and seeks expression.

Movement

Physical movement is one of the great secret keys to emotional and physical health. Movement is a fabulous way to get blood going, free stuck emotions, and release trapped thoughts. When you least want to move is usually when you need it most. Studies have revealed that physically moving your body can affect your mind, particularly helping to generate creative solutions and solve problems.[15] Emotion is e-motion, or energy in motion. This means that releasing emotions not only creates movement in your life but also movement releases emotions.

You can move in any way and at any time. Choose what you like or what seems most appropriate and accessible. You could do brisk walking, dancing, pounding pillows, stretching, or running up and down stairs. Even at work, it's usually possible to take five or ten minutes to do one of these. The form doesn't matter; moving does.

What is your favorite form of movement? Working in the garden? Riding a bike? Dancing? Swimming? Hiking? Make a list, and when you are stuck, choose something off your list and then go do it. You will be amazed at how wonderful you feel even after just five minutes.

Creative Expression

Expressing yourself creatively is another way to quickly shift how you feel. It helps to clear emotions, alter thoughts, and free your energy. Creative expression does not have to be "art" as we think of it. Rather, it can be any activity that creatively engages you.

Rearranging furniture, planning a new garden, designing a photo book, building a house project, reassembling clothes in a different way—these are just some of the myriad possibilities. If you already have a creative project, give it an hour of your time daily or even just five to twenty minutes if that's all you can spare. You don't need an entire afternoon or day to give it focus. Just planning or thinking about it can quickly shift your energy.

Reversing

Reversing is a process of reviewing your day, starting with the most recent experience and ending with the earliest. This not only strengthens memory but can also reveal connections, patterns, and messages from the universe. Additionally, you may use reversal after business meetings, projects, classes, and other events.

To do reversing, review your day (or meeting, project, event) backward from the most recent experience to its beginning. When you come to any difficult experiences, assess what happened and determine what needed to be different, improved, or rectified. You can also mentally "erase" that event and see yourself reliving it with what you desired to have happened instead. This can help you make timely course corrections. As well, you may reverse your life, year by year, asking what was most important about that year and what needed to be changed, corrected, or rectified.

---

15   "Surprising Ways to Think More Creatively," Carole Jackson, Editor, *Bottom Line's Daily Health News*, April 12, 2012. Accessed May 30, 2012. http://bottomlinepublications.com/content/article/self-improvement/surprising-ways-to-think-more-creatively.

When you reverse at night, call back parts of yourself that may have left during any difficult or traumatic experiences. This prevents disassociation, or soul loss, from occurring.

Emergency List

An Emergency List is an inventory of everything that helps you feel good, all that nurtures, supports, elevates, and inspires you. It is used whenever you are down, stuck, depressed, hopeless, or any other negative state. At such times, choose something on your Emergency List and do it. You will immediately feel better.

Many people turn to food when they are down—typically chocolate, alcohol, snacks, and/or sweets. While any of these may be on your personal Emergency List, I suggest you include what is healthy so you don't beat yourself up afterward, which only perpetuates a negative cycle.

Instead, put on your list what is easily accessible and simple, such as reading a favorite poem or an inspiring passage from a book, going outside for a walk or to sit in nature, stroking a beloved pet, writing in your journal, moving or exercising, focusing on a creative project, cooking a special meal, or other activities that elevate your emotional state. Surrounding yourself with what inspires and nurtures you will quickly shift how you feel. Make it a practice to do at least one item on your Emergency List every day.

Cleansing Bath

A cleansing bath is very useful after expressing and releasing emotions, patterns, and old stories. Simple and comforting, it cleanses toxins and releases stress. Here are a few possibilities.

Salt and Soda Cleansing Bath
Pour one cup each of salt and baking soda into warm bath water. Soak twenty minutes.

Epsom Salt Cleansing Bath
Pour one cup of Epsom salts into warm bath water. Soak twenty minutes.

Herbal Bath
Mix ½ cup each rose petals, calendula flowers, lavender flowers, raspberry leaves, and red clover blossoms. Boil twelve cups water, turn off heat, add one handful of herbal mix, and steep covered twenty minutes. Strain, and pour into bath water. Soak for twenty minutes. This may be used as a hand and/or footbath too.

Stillness

Stillness means stopping. It means just sitting or lying down without any external stimulation. It could be as simple as sitting outside in nature, or lying on the couch, bed, or the earth. Stillness could be meditating or just breathing and nothing more.

Stillness is extremely powerful. If you're driving a huge semi-truck at sixty miles per hour, it's dangerous if not impossible to quickly change directions, but if moving slowly, you can turn the instant you choose. The same is true of our lives. The more stillness we allow, the more options arise. Thoughts sort themselves out, new ideas appear, what seemed too stressful before becomes possible, anything stuffed or ignored can surface and be released—the possibilities are endless.

Slowing down actually gives you more access to time, for the more still you are, the more time expands, while the busier you are, the more time collapses (you know the old saying, "A watched pot never boils"). Stillness slows your current momentum, which in turn allows the doors to your subconscious to open so you can access its hidden knowledge. Stillness also helps you connect with your soul and Source energies.

When we sit, rest, meditate, take a siesta, or contemplate nature, we move into "being" and something interesting happens: The right brain activates so insights appear, realizations arise, and understandings click. Stillness refreshes the mind and body. It's nearly impossible to receive insights while in an active "doing" mode.

Stillness means to stop everything you are doing. Everything. Set down your cell phone, push away from your computer, put down that cigarette, stop moving, and just sit. It means completely stopping everything for the time you allow. Try stopping everything for five seconds and see what happens and how you feel. For some, it is a tremendous relief, while others may be fidgety or restless. This alone can be very revealing.

With a busy lifestyle, you may have to plan times of stillness. It doesn't matter how long you take. Stillness is so powerful that even five minutes can make an enormous difference. What matters is to be still every day at some point whenever possible.

Process Preparation

To do any of the processes in this book, it's most helpful to follow these steps: ready your space, set your intention, and go into alpha, which will be explained later. After, you are prepared to engage in your desired techniques, rituals, ceremonies, or other work. Stillness is described above. The other steps follow.

Ready Your Space

When doing any inner work, it's important to first ready your space. This can be as simple or complex as you desire. First, choose a space where you won't be interrupted for as long as you need. It doesn't have to be a special room or spot, just somewhere that supports your work. Turn off your phone and whatever else is desired to enable the quiet you need.

Now create a sacred space where you will feel safe, protected, and supported. You could light a candle, say a prayer, call in your spirit helpers and healers, and/or connect with the directions, especially the earth and sun. If you call in spirit helpers, healers, power animals, guides, guardians, or the directions, ask them to come from the highest source for the highest good for all concerned. Avoid asking "the spirits" to come because you want specific energies that will support and nourish you.

Many traditional cultures open the six directions with an offering before ceremony, calling in the powers of the east, south, west, north, earth, and sky. The earth and sun are not only archetypes but also living entities, and each direction has its own qualities as well. Additionally, you can connect with Source within as the center direction.

Many traditions use smoke or incense to prepare a space. The Native American tradition of using the smoke of burning herbs to cleanse and renew is called ***smudging***. In this case, loose, dried herbs are burned in a container, such as a bowl or shell. The smoke is then wafted over the area to be cleansed–the body, room, car, objects or whatever you choose. Herbs typically used include sage, cedar, and sweet grass.

Set Your Intention

Intention is the aim or objective you desire to achieve, the ball you set in motion for what you desire to happen. It is sending information with belief. This is like tuning the frequency of a radio station to what you desire so you can then receive it. When you purposefully set an intention, through resonance and coherence, it links with like energies to bring it about. We intend things all the time, we're just not always consciously aware of it.

Our stories and core beliefs are intentions too. Ideally, we consciously set our intentions and stay focused on them. This is what propels your desires into motion and existence. Where you focus is where energy goes. Where you set your intention is not only where your energy goes but other energies that support it as well. When you set your intention, do so with conviction, knowing that what you intend will occur. Focus on how you desire your intention to feel, and act as if it is true. In other words, face forward with your intention.

Go Into Alpha

Next, switch your brain state to alpha, and go to stillness. This slows your brain waves and gets you out of your thoughts and emotions. Additionally, it opens the door to alternative consciousness. While alpha consciousness is described in "States of Consciousness and Stories," here are a few ways to achieve an alpha state:

Slow, rhythmic breathing: Slowly inhale and exhale three to ten times, focusing only on your breath. For some, it helps to inhale to a count of seven and exhale to a count of seven, while others see numbers as they count down. You could also send love with your breath to the earth and then send love with your breath to the sky, feeling their answering love return to you in your heart.

Relax your muscles: Relaxing muscles one by one helps slow the body, ease the emotions, and still the mind. Focus on one body area at a time, and move from there. It's easiest to start at the feet, as this helps pull energy down from the head and brain, and from there move up to the calves, thighs, abdomen, torso, arms, neck, and head. Tighten each area's muscles, and then let them completely relax.

Focus on what you love: See the faces of your loved ones, friends, pets, or a special place in nature. Allow that love to expand outward to fill your body and then to surround you.

Imagery: As you count down, you can see numbers from ten to one (or five or three to one) or see yourself descend that number of stairs to the bottom step. You can also pick images to associate with each breath, such as moving from sunlight into a cool, dark cave, or walking through a forest, in a meadow, or on a beach. Stick with images that enhance your sense of relaxation and protection.

II

The bodywork weekend I attended with Mariah brought me something essential: inner stillness and peace. It relaxed my nervous system enough so that when I returned home, life was livable again. Still, I felt like I was in a washing machine on the soak cycle—hold and soak, hold and soak. And while I waited and soaked, I was cracking wide open.

Prolonged poor sleep has a powerful impact on the body. Heart palpitations; recurring sore throats; restless legs; ringing in the ears; achy teeth; bad memory; back and knee pain; headaches; body twitches; burning eyes, hands, and feet; feelings of panic or anxiety; sadness; grief; and an impression of being trapped all plagued me. The veils became so thin that I could even sense electromagnetic fields. Heightened sensitivity and lowered immunity made me controlling around my food and environment since almost anything could trigger bad sleep.

With my body failing, I felt like I was collapsing into myself. So much had been stripped away on all levels that I had nothing left to give. I held my emotions inside, not sharing how I felt. I worked a lot and did little of what I loved. With my son away at school and husband involved in music, I was alone much of the time, which intensified all my symptoms.

Things were slipping through the cracks. I felt like I was on a tightrope over a chasm, and that if I wasn't careful, I'd crash. Between fatigue, overwork, and stuffed emotions, I just couldn't hold it together anymore. A part of me wanted to quit everything and go to another land to start over.

I even felt crazy at times. It helped to learn other women in menopause often felt this way, but that didn't reduce the pain. I did the whining and complaining thing. I did the middle-of-the-night crying and railing too. I tried conventional and alternative medicines and took many herbs. All helped to a certain extent, but not enough. I was in meltdown and needed to try a different approach.

It was around this time that a friend told me about Alberto Villoldo's new book then, *Shaman, Healer, Sage.* While I read it, I had a dream about his Four Winds School and knew that was where I needed to go, which I did over the next two years. It was through the Four Winds' Healing the Light Body program that I finally learned about the power of my stories and gained shamanic techniques to clear my limiting core beliefs and patterns. It also helped me consolidate what I had already been doing most of my life through my own explorations and intuitive guidance but had not identified in such a cohesive way.

Of course, the first pattern I wanted to discover was around insomnia. As I tried to untangle my emotional turmoil and mental conflicts, themes began to emerge. I discovered them through several different techniques, such as life reviews, dreams, examining core beliefs, roles, projections and assumptions, using my body wisdom, processing emotions, journal writing, ancestral pattern and shadow work, messages from the universe, and more. Each helped distill the essence of my issues. When I noticed themes repeat, I could identify the major patterns I needed to clear. Here are some examples.

To discover my cyclical patterns and limiting core beliefs around insomnia, I tuned into my emotions. Having the typical middle-child syndrome, I never felt there was enough for me, not enough friends, community, patients, blood sugar, sweetness of life, fun, energy, abundance, immunity, love, and, eventually, not enough sleep. It didn't matter that the universe was taking care of me or that I did have friends, community, patients, love, and fun. What mattered is that I *felt* I lacked all of these.

Next, I thought about all my past relationships and how most of the major ones were with men who never seemed to love me for me but wanted to fulfill their own needs. I thought of the men I had turned away and realized they had been attentive, caring, and interested in me. What was up with that? What caused me to turn love away?

I next examined my early life. A clear memory emerged of losing my best friend at age six. We lived next door to each other and frequently played, but suddenly, she was never home or available. I felt abandoned. I decided to learn more about my childhood and see what other events might have caused the feelings of lack, loneliness, and an inability to feel loved.

I started with old photos to see what memories might arise. As I looked at shots of family trips and holidays, I remembered that although I knew my dad loved me, he never said so. I wondered why and thought about his childhood. I knew that his mother had left him when he was twelve and realized he must have rarely felt her affection. Perhaps lacking love was not just my issue but an ancestral one too.

I decided to call my mom and ask her about my childhood. I mentioned the memory of losing my best friend at age six and how lonely I had felt. As I talked, another memory materialized. I saw myself sitting on the street curb all alone one summer day, wondering where everyone was and thinking over and over, *I'm alone, I'm alone, I'm alone.*

My mom was amazed by my feelings. She told me that as a toddler I always slipped off people's laps and didn't want to be held. She also said I actually had lots of friends who wanted to play with me, but I always seemed to turn them away and isolate myself. When she said this, another image surfaced. I remembered my mom saying this girl or that asked to play with me, but I said no because they weren't the friends I wanted to play with. I craved being with my best friend and her new friends. So I *did* isolate myself! And yet the friends I *wanted* to play with didn't ask me to play, no matter how long I waited. This only compounded my feelings of loneliness back then.

It was easy to come up with other memories once the floodgates had been opened. I remembered playing on the living room floor near its curtained end around age three. I don't know what provoked this, but suddenly I realized I was alone, not just in that moment, but mostly alone in my life. My mom was occupied either with my brother the baby or my sister the problem. I had learned to be good and to stay out of the way, so it seemed the steep price I paid was loneliness.

Then I recalled a rebirthing session I had experienced in my early thirties. During the process, I flashed back to being taken from my mom after birth and left in a nursery. I felt completely alone and afraid there. All I could say to my partner in that session was, "Please don't leave me! Don't leave me!" It was as if that original strong emotional event implanted itself in the soil of my being, so when future incidents occurred to match it, that plant of feeling lonely and unloved grew taller and stronger.

Next, I pulled out the childhood autobiography I had written when preparing for my second vision quest many years earlier. As I reread it, I realized what a tremendous impact our family's move during my teen years had made on me. Before it, I had found true friends, activities, and a school I loved. The move ripped them away, so I felt disoriented and uprooted.

Again I had lost my friends. Again I was alone. This move didn't affect my brother or sister at all like it did me, but because I had experienced energetic abandonment at birth, seemed alone as a child, and then lost my best friend at age six, the move intensified these losses. It felt like a sharp knife had been driven deep inside and twisted. I recognized the move had caused soul loss, where a piece of one's self disassociates from the rest in order to handle a traumatic experience, and I wanted that part of me back.

Another memory surfaced of deciding to run away from home around age eight. I started to pack but realized I needed a suitcase. I found my mom and asked for it. When asked why, I told her what I was doing, but instead of sympathizing or asking what was wrong, she handed me paper bags. Moving forward in time, I thought about my early dates with Michael. During a class party, two of my best friends joined us in a hot tub. It really wasn't clear to me whom Michael liked best, and that fed my unloved and unwanted feelings. A pattern was emerging.

As a result of not receiving the love or nurturance I wanted as a child, I decided I had to give it to myself. Because of this, I shut down more and more to external sources until I couldn't even receive the nurturing sleep I needed. A further belief emerged that I didn't trust love would stay since it always seemed to be taken away. No wonder I didn't let love in! All of this combined together to feed a sense of worthlessness.

I had tapped into a deep hole in my heart, a very tender place that needed to be filled. I understood that it kept me working hard, trying more and yearning strongly for my people and community. My heart felt so closed that somehow I just couldn't feel love even though I knew people loved me. Instead, I'd wake up in the mornings with dreams of grief or tears of sadness.

I was amazed how the conversation with my mom had put together all these pieces. It's possible to be aware of issues in one's life and yet not identify them as cyclical patterns. We all have repeating experiences, roles, and circumstances but don't necessarily take them further. This was the case for me. I knew I had felt alone most of my life and was unable to take in love, but I never identified it as a pattern. Somehow naming it altered how I felt about it. It created distance and separation so I could claim it and no longer be its victim. All these memories now helped to identify my patterns of lack and an inability to feel loved.

A third repeating theme arose: not being able to find my place in life. I had worked on this issue for years, and it had much improved. Yet discovering my place was always at the back of my mind even with a career, clinic, and books. At this meltdown stage in my life, it appeared again, but as part of my larger soul's journey this time.

The theme of not finding my place in life first became evident through a seminal dream during my freshman year of college. It arose during a period when I felt a continuous black cloud over my head that had begun since our family's move in high school. At this point in college, I had just discovered that I hated my major and needed to choose another but had no idea what.

This confusion threw me into an existential crisis that lasted on and off for many years. This was a huge emotional switch for me, for I had come from a place of Walt Whitman's "I love life!" attitude to not knowing who I was or what I was doing. It is no accident that my dozens of journals began with this dream, and the search for my place is the common thread through them all. This is when my Rooms dream occurred.

In this dream, I entered a corridor filled with doors to many different rooms. In the first, I found people joyfully singing and playing guitars, each knowing their place in the songs. Enthralled with the rich melodies, I, too, tried to sing my song, but no sound came. No one heard me nor noticed me. I left alone.

In the next room, I found several people discussing their occupations. One man was a brilliant lawyer, another an experienced doctor, and a third a housewife with three children and a happy home. All turned to hear my achievements, but when I opened my mouth to share, I closed it without a word. There was nothing to say, nothing to contribute. I left ashamed and unfulfilled.

In a third room, I found only candlelight and people crying to their version of the Divine. Each seemed so completely happy and satisfied that I thought this must be the way. I, too, kneeled and prayed, yet I heard nothing, *felt* nothing. I tried harder until tears squeezed from my eyes. Yet still nothing came. I left unanswered.

In the fourth room, I found people sprawled all over the floor, listening and reacting to loud, thumping music. It reverberated up my spine and echoed in my head as if it were a hollow cave. I joined a group already far beyond me. They talked about peace, love, and brotherhood, about how all people were created equal and should be treated as such. Yet each time I tried to offer my comments, they were ignored. No one listened or showed they cared. I left rejected and unloved.

Back in the hallway, I paused a moment. Anger, emptiness, and frustration mounted inside. I tried to control myself, but I felt hopeless. I was about to reach my breaking point. How could all these people communicate when I couldn't even express myself? Which door is the way, *my* way? I knew there was an answer somewhere, for I could sense its presence. Yet each time I stretched out my hand, it came back empty. I had not reached far enough.

I turned to leave, and then I saw it! A door at the end of the hall beckoned to me. This was it; this was *my* room! Joy rushed through my body as I ran toward it. Yet as I did, the door grew smaller and smaller. I ran harder, faster. I reached out my hand to grasp its knob, but the door floated past me. Again I ran until I almost reached the keyhole. That's when the hall filled with swarming people.

Fighting broke out and then fire. People shouted and gasped for air. It grew even more crowded. I tried to push through but couldn't get past. I just had to reach my door before it was lost! I ran faster, pushed harder, but the people built a wall around me. My oppressed body writhed until it seemed squeezed into nothingness. All I had left was my mind. As the group moved in for the final crush, I closed my eyes, waiting for the end.

And then I woke up, sweating and sobbing uncontrollably. While I tried to calm down, I thought about the dream. The image grew hazy, but the impression it left was tremendous. I felt shaken and bereft until another realization came. I should be thankful it was only a dream, for the end never came. I'm alive and can still search for the door to my room.

Since the Rooms dream, I have searched for "my" room in life. I knew it was there, for I had seen it and felt it. However, the way was dangerous and blocked by obstacles I could not yet see, let alone move. This theme continued for decades, even after beginning my career as an herbalist, acupuncturist, teacher, and author. And now, while in meltdown, it perfectly summed up how I was feeling at the time—displaced, alone, unsure of where to go, and not knowing what to do.

After remembering the dream, I scanned my life again with this different theme in mind. I reviewed old journals along with more dreams to determine other times I had experienced not finding my place. When I stumbled across writings about my first vision quest at age thirty, I realized I had undertaken it to search for my true "room" too. It was the vision quest that definitely had assisted me in discovering my place then through a mate, family, and work.

However, during the next eight years, pent-up feelings began to plague me. I felt emotionally and verbally bound since I couldn't say how I felt or speak my truth. I felt bound by my roles, people's expectations, others' concepts of me, and the many limitations within, such as my strong inner critic who drove me to be productive, stay on top of things, do my share, and follow my "shoulds."

At that same time, my clinic still hadn't taken off, and I didn't know why. I loved my work and yet didn't seem effective yet. No longer a toddler, my son had started school, and I missed him terribly. I felt separated from my inner spontaneous and playful child and so immersed myself in work instead. Sleep issues slowly began to occur.

I felt like I could easily slip from the world with little impact on others. When I woke in the middle of the night, fears piled up and my heart pounded. I had never felt this before, and it scared me. I was so weak that I was even incapable of meditation let alone changing my negative thoughts or renewing myself. And so about eight years after the first vision quest, I did another. This one occurred with a group of women under the guidance of two leaders. It was then that the theme of not finding my place arose again.

The day before the quest, when my group went out to find our power spots for the three-day, three-night vigil, I had trouble finding mine. I searched and searched until finally I had to return. I quickly chose a place, but it didn't feel right. Later, when our leaders reviewed safety precautions, I realized that my spot was in a wash, a place where flash flood waters traveled. This was not good and I had to find a new spot.

The next morning, I felt more trepidation around finding my place than the fact I was about to spend three days and nights alone fasting on the desert floor and under the open sky. When I arrived at the spot I had chosen, it was very clear this was not my site. Not only was it not safe, it still didn't feel right either. I continued to search and finally found a perfect perch above the flood plane. I knew it was mine because it finally felt right; my gut instinct informed me as such through my body wisdom. This place protected me and brought many revelations and gifts on that quest, which still inform me today.

To me, the inability to find my spot at first was a metaphor for the larger issue of not finding my place in life. I remembered that I had worked on this theme for almost two decades now. This second vision quest helped heal this issue. After, I realized it included much more than the physical location but also encompassed people, community, work, and everything else that supported and helped me to feel at home within myself.

I knew that the family move at age fifteen had not only torn me from my friends and activities but also had taken away everything that created a sense of my people and place in life. Further, the inability to discover my place had really started when I was separated from my mom at birth. When I looked at everything together, I realized that the insomnia issue had bloomed into more deeply rooted issues than sleeplessness itself.

The themes of lack on all levels, inability to take in love, and not finding my place now formed obvious cyclical patterns that had repeated over and over throughout my entire life. I wanted to claim my deep desires instead: love, self-worth, acceptance, community, peace, and my unique place. I knew that if I didn't clear these issues, more experiences of lack, feeling unloved, and not finding my place would arise in the future, something I definitely didn't want. It was time to clear these patterns.

States of Consciousness and Stories

Consciousness is the ground of all being. It crosses all levels—physical, emotional, mental, and spiritual—and all states of awareness—conscious, subconscious, and higher consciousness. And it is expressed through the innate wisdom contained in your heart and body.

Consciousness

Conscious Awareness

Conscious awareness is our waking state and includes our daily awareness and easily accessed memories. The conscious self lives in a world of duality, a world of either/or, you or me, black or white, sun or moon, day or night, feminine or masculine, and yin or yang. The world of duality is very polarizing because it believes that we are all separate entities—you, me, us, them—and that even Source energy is removed from us.

Unconsciousness

Medically, the term *unconscious* is what encompasses all functions that occur below surface awareness. The term *subconscious* was coined by Carl Jung[16] to identify the unconscious parts of our selves. These include hidden feelings; unnoticed perceptions; unaware thoughts; automatic reactions; unknown phobias; concealed desires; forgotten memories; unacceptable ideas, wishes or desires; and traumatic memories. The subconscious also includes your automatic functions, such as your heartbeat and respiration, along with your habits and skills.

Because you are only conscious of about 5 percent of your cognitive activity (remember in "The Biology of Your Stories" we learned that 95 percent of the brain's activity goes on beyond your conscious awareness), most of your life is run by your subconscious mind. This is originally developed through two sources: as a fetus during pregnancy when you respond to stimuli and after birth when you learn through observation.

16   Carl Jung was a nineteenth century psychologist and pioneer.

The first six years of a child's life is programmable, which directly develops subconscious stories. If your parents gave you messages that you didn't deserve something, couldn't do math, weren't good enough, couldn't play sports, weren't smart enough, couldn't sing, weren't pretty, and other such thoughts, this is what you programmed as truth about yourself (and your parents were probably programmed with these messages too, so they just passed them along).

These programs became the habitual core belief tapes you learned about yourself and your life. Then your biology took over from there, sending the same chemicals for the same emotional responses and thus causing an addiction and need to experience them over and over.

This creates an entire psychosomatic mind-body network, which is activated by your perceptions and subconscious programming that are developed through your core beliefs and stories. Your body and the conditions that give rise to your health or illness are governed by your subconscious mind. In other words, your body and subconscious reflect the outer world.

Higher Consciousness

Heightened awareness that transcends the body along with any sense of time and space is termed *higher consciousness*. It includes an enhanced state of awareness all the way to transcendence reached through ecstatic prayer, deep meditation, and other numinous experiences.

We move beyond our stories when in higher consciousness. Here duality falls away and is replaced by a feeling of unity with all. Here we connect with the Source consciousness that infuses all life and know that we are all part of one collective consciousness.

Brainwaves and Consciousness

Changing your state of consciousness determines which part of your brain is active. On the other hand, changing your brain state alters your level of consciousness.

As discussed in "The Biology of Your Stories" in section I, you have four parts to your brain: the reptilian microprocessor that fuels and drives the rest of the brain and encompasses the automatic functions active 24/7; the mammalian part that secretes chemicals with every thought and feeling; the neocortex that's the executive or the thinking part; and the spiritual part that's activated when you are in a higher conscious state of awareness.

Just as each of your four brain parts have different levels of awareness, so there are four brain states of different electromagnetic frequency. Understanding these brainwaves can help you achieve alternative states of consciousness where you discover and neutralize your stories.

> ### Brain States
>
> *High Beta*: **30 Hz and above (some say 16 Hz and above): upset about something, worried, stressed, too much weighing on your heart or mind**
>
> *Beta*: **12–30 Hz: conscious mind and ordinary, active consciousness; daily activity of chores, work, studying; focused state of attention associated with normal adult waking activity; children age twelve through adulthood are most often in this state**
>
> *Alpha*: **8–12 Hz: door to subconscious; relaxation; state of calmness conducive to meditation, creativity, and assimilating new concepts; play, fun, joy, childlike, laughter, Peter Pan, "Think happy thoughts"; children ages six to twelve are primarily in this state**
>
> *Theta*: **4–8 Hz: subconscious mind; meditation, deep contemplation, dreaming, daydreaming, fantasizing, ecstatic prayer, twilight half awake/half asleep, super-learning state; reverie or trance run by the imagination; shamanic journeying; children ages two to four are primarily in the theta state**
>
> *Delta*: **.1–4 Hz: unconscious mind; deep sleep; hypnotic state; children from 0–2 are primarily in this state**

Brainwaves range from the most active to the least:[17]

Beta waves include high beta and beta. *High beta* waves are the fastest of all brain waves. This occurs when we are extremely stressed or emotionally upset.

Beta waves are relatively low in amplitude but fast. Beta is indicative of a strongly engaged mind. This is normal waking activity where we are alert, concentrating, and focused on the outer world. Here we hold active conversations, debate, argue, make decisions, teach, take exams, play sports, give presentations, analyze and organize information and work. Here we have deep attention and focus. Most people are in this state during waking hours.

Alpha waves occur when we are relaxed but still focused and aware. Alpha waves are slower but of high amplitude. We experience alpha right before we fall asleep and immediately after waking. This is where you reflect, meditate, play, and stroll through nature. This is a more internally focused and self-reflective state of mind. Here you are in touch with your intuition and psychic nature. Inner chatter quiets, and the mind stills, but you are aware and receptive.

Theta waves have even greater amplitude and slower frequency. Here is daydreaming, creativity, flashes of memories and imagery, and night dreaming. Theta is an expansive state. You might feel you are floating, and your mind

---

17   Brainwaves were first recorded by Hans Berger (1873–1941) in 1924, for which he invented the electroencephalogram. He also discovered the alpha wave rhythm known as "Berger's Wave."

flows beyond the boundaries of your body. This is also where you are in deep meditation and transcend any sense of time and space.

Delta waves have the greatest amplitude and slowest frequency. This occurs during deep sleep, profound states of meditation, or during comas.

We move in and out of these various brain states all the time. When in deep sleep, we are in delta. When we dream, we are in theta. When we first wake up and remember the dream, we are in alpha. When we get up to shut off the alarm and start the day, we are in beta. (The reason why most people can't remember their dreams is because they move directly to beta awareness and so can't access theta.)

The alpha and theta states access the subconscious mind, which is what we want to use to learn our hidden beliefs, patterns, and stories.

Alternative Consciousness

To discover and neutralize your stories, it's necessary to move out of day-to-day beta consciousness and into alternative consciousness because it moves beyond polarity of either/or to either/and and links with Source energy where all possibilities exist.

Alternative consciousness is active in two brain wave states, alpha and theta. Of these two, alpha is key because it is the transition, or "door," to reaching theta higher consciousness.

Think of beta consciousness as the room of waking consciousness. Here your brain waves move fast as you undertake and accomplish your daily tasks. On the other hand, theta is the room of both the subconscious and higher conscious states where you can access your unconscious stories. It has much slower brain waves than beta.

In the theta room, the mind is clear, receptive, and rapidly makes connections, solves problems, and has realizations. There's a sense of peace and well-being as your awareness expands and creativity flows. Theta is the best state for reprogramming your subconscious mind through such means as meditation, deep contemplation, lucid dreaming, daydreaming, fantasizing, and ecstatic prayer.

To shift from beta to theta consciousness, we need to open the door, and that door is alpha. Alpha consciousness is a state of calmness, relaxation, and play. This is when you have "light bulb" moments. Here your creative juices flow so you can recall easier, learn faster, and absorb information quickly. This level of relaxation is also essential to health and well-being and is the place of first waking up when we can remember our dreams and yet are aware we're not dreaming anymore. We can access our subconscious stories here as well.

How to Achieve Alpha Alternative Consciousness

Although one brain wave state is usually predominant, generally several brain waves are active at the same time though usually at just trace levels. We can learn to recognize when we are in which state and also how to change our brain states to achieve alternative consciousness to uncover and neutralize our stories.

When you shift your brain state, you adjust your brain and alter your consciousness, and when you adjust your brain, you shift your brain state. There are both external and internal stimuli for changing your brain state.

External Sources:
Nutrition
Supplements
Drugs
Medications
Heightened experiences
Traumatic events

Internal Sources:
Breathing
Intense thoughts or emotions
Changes in light, sound, kinetics, or other senses
Change of body position or movement
Slow, relaxing music (such as the largo movements of Baroque pieces)
Relaxation
Meditation
Visualization
Creativity
Rhythmic breathing
Slow yoga, especially the Corpse Pose
Tai Chi and other slow-moving exercises
Relaxing walks
Mindless chores
Gazing at scenery while riding in a vehicle
Listening to drumming at eight–twelve beats per second
Attuning to the earth's energies and nature

Your Inner Wisdom

Another way to access alternative consciousness is through your innate wisdom. Using your inner wisdom helps you access your subconscious and higher conscious minds by bypassing conscious mental and emotional loops. This occurs in two ways: your heart wisdom and your body wisdom.

Your Heart Wisdom

Heart wisdom is the wisdom of your true deep Self linked with Source energy. There aren't any concrete-hard facts about heart wisdom. Instead, it holds eternal truths, such as timelessness, spacelessness, unconditional love and acceptance, awareness that everything is made of energy, and the understanding that we are all one.

You can access your heart wisdom not only through deep meditation and ecstatic prayer but also by entering

> ### Resonance with the Earth
> Interestingly, we have a similar brain state to that of the earth. Tesla discovered that the resonant frequency of the earth is around 8 Hz. This is an alpha state! Some people today call it the heartbeat of the earth, or the earth chanting. When we are in alpha, we are in harmony and resonance with the earth.

the sacred space of your heart,[18] a special energetic place within the physical heart itself. Here you can experience eternal truths; learn about your soul's journey; work with the past, present, and future; and determine your new desired universal story. The heart generates the largest magnetic field in the body and responds faster than the brain. It is powerful indeed.[19]

Within the sacred space of your heart there's a tiny space as well, as is written about in the *Chhandogya Upanishad*. You go there by first entering your sacred heart space and then asking to be taken to the tiny space inside. You'll feel movement and then find you're there. Here is the center of your Self. You can ask for your Higher Self to come be present with you and learn from it directly in this tiny space.

You can use imagery to get into your sacred heart space, but once there, look for images to arise, feel sensations, or allow an inner knowing to emerge. Go with the first impression you receive, and stay with it. Remind yourself, "No thinking," and just be with whatever is. Soon

---

18   Allegedly, the sacred space of the heart has been called by names such as "secret chamber of the heart" (*Mundaka Upanishad,* in an addendum to the Torah and by the Theosophists), "secret cave of the heart" (*Katha Uphanishad*), and "pedestal of awareness" by the Buddhists.

19   The Institute of HeartMath discovered that there's a torus around the heart, and that the heart's energy field has measurable effects on other processes in your body, i.e., your physiology and DNA, and on those around you. The brain's rhythms naturally synchronize to the heart's rhythmic activity.

what you experience may morph into another image, sensation, or knowing that eventually brings understanding.

There are multiple levels and layers to this process, so keep following what you see or experience until you feel complete. Understanding may bubble up at that point, or if you need to stop and return to the outer world, it will unfold in its own time. You don't need to know specific details, as that is mental. Instead, allow your heart's wisdom to unfold in its own way and time to reveal what you need to see and experience. Practice will bring you there. Just start with five minutes a day—or several times a day, if you can—and allow it to unfold.

Process to Use Heart Wisdom:

Enter any posture that keeps your back straight.

Ready Your Space

It is best to cover your eyes so you are in complete darkness, as this blocks light to the pineal gland, which activates the brain and mind. Here we want the pineal gland quiet so the sacred heart space can activate. Once you gain experience with the process, you can do it anytime and anyplace, regardless of light.

Set Your Intention

There are two parts to this: one is to set the intention to enter your sacred heart space itself, and the other is to intend what you want to experience while there. This could be as simple as getting to know your sacred heart space or more specific, such as receiving healing, answers to questions, guidance, or another focus. You could also ask something general, such as to be shown what you need to see or what you need to do.

Go to Alpha

It is essential to first enter an alpha state because that opens the door to your sacred heart space. This may be done in several ways. You could see or sense something you love, such as the faces of loved ones, animal companions, or a place in nature. Allow your heart to open and feel love for your people, pets, or place. Expand that love to all life.

The universal way of indigenous tribes is to feel love for the earth and the sky, bringing the returning love from both back into one's self. This is what happens when opening the directions before sacred ceremony. Focus on your breath, and send that with your love to Mother Earth for all she gives. Repeat until you sense her answering love. Now send your breath and love to everything else—the moon, sun, planets, stars, and universe. Continue until you sense love return to you. Expand that love to all of creation.

Dive Down

Once you are relaxed and feel love in your heart, slide down into your sacred heart space. Imagine or sense leaving your head and slipping down to your physical heart (located slightly to your left side and, for our purposes, about level with your nipples rather than higher up in the chest). Enter its outer membrane through the rear of your heart at a sort of "crevice." You will sense movement until you come to a place of stillness. You'll know when you are there, for you will experience love and expansion. If it is dark inside, ask for light to shine.

Observe Your Unique Heart Language

Allow the heart's imagery to emerge. Imagery is unique for everyone, as it encompasses images, sensations, or an inner knowing. One of these will be strongest for you. Remind yourself, "No thinking" as you go. Be patient, and let it naturally arise. Go with what you first receive without question or editing. If you can't, you are thinking. Remind yourself again, "No thinking," and return to witnessing.

Some feel pulsing, hear a sound, see light or colors, have physical sensations, experience an inner knowing, or see images, such as a cave, forest glade, temple, sanctuary, or other setting. The possibilities are endless. Be patient. Go deeper. See what else unfolds. Only when you are ready (and if you desire), ask questions, and wait for guidance to come. If you are uncertain if you are in your sacred heart space, ask to be given an experience so you know you are really there. This inner world holds many places, experiences, wisdom, and connections for you to explore and learn. Take your time, and allow your heart to guide you.

Receive Understanding

After you receive your unique language, you can ask questions for further guidance, such as: "What does this mean? How do I do this? Show me more." Your heart wisdom will lead, direct, and guide you. The meaning and understanding of what you experience may come instantly, or it may unfold bit by bit. If you don't get any obvious answers or direction, take what you do receive and work with it through a tool given in "Tools to Unhook from Your Stories" in section III, such as dialogue, dream work, or gestalt. You may also need to let it percolate over time until it slowly reveals itself. Sometimes the answer comes in the outer world, as the two do merge and overlap.

Your Body Wisdom

When we are confused, upset, bound by limiting stories, or hooked by old beliefs, it can be difficult to access heart wisdom. The body is the next direct way to link with this energy, since like the sacred heart space, it is the communicating vehicle for your soul. Memories, emotions, and images are stored in our bodies. Sometimes just one touch can trigger a forgotten memory, complete with all its senses. Body wisdom bypasses the mind and emotions to link with subconscious memories.

Additionally, you can use your body wisdom if you seem numb, cut off from your emotions, or so jumbled that you don't know where to start. Anytime you don't know what you want, your body wisdom can help you.

Your body will also tell you when you've reached your source story, for there'll be a change in how you physically feel, such as a difference in body posture, alteration of voice, or widening of eyes. It is how you feel physically that is key to the shift; how you feel is what moves you. Body wisdom is so important that it's used in many exercises as well as the Metaphor-phosis process.

Process to Use Body Wisdom:

This process may be done in any posture and in darkness or light.

- Close your eyes.
- Take a few deep breaths.
- What emotion do you feel (or not feel)?
- Where do you feel this in your body?
- Go to that place. How does that area feel?
- You might experience images, sensations, sounds, colors, or an inner knowing. Describe it, using all your senses. Let go of thinking, judgment, trying to figure it out, and other mental stuff. Instead, allow your body to speak.
- Your description might bring you answers and direction or lead you to a memory or another issue. If the latter occurs, repeat the entire process with the memory or issue, starting with what emotion it evokes and then where you feel it in your body. Continue until you are complete.

Exercises

Exercise One: Alpha

Here are different ways to achieve alpha alternative consciousness. Determine which works best for you. If you're not certain you are seeing internally, just imagine you are. Begin by closing your eyes.

- Slowly inhale to the count of seven and slowly exhale to the count of seven for three to ten breaths.
- Slowly inhale through your nose and slowly exhale through your mouth for three to ten breaths.
- Slowly and silently count down from ten to one. See each number as you do.
- Slowly and silently count down from ten to one. See each number flashing three times with the word *deeper* in neon red as you do.
- Slowly and silently count down from ten to one while descending a set of stairs. Climb down a stair with each number. When you come to the number one, you are on the bottom step.
- Starting with your feet, tense and then relax the muscles in your feet, calves, thighs, entire legs, abdomen, torso, arms, neck, head, and entire body.

Exercise Two: Shifting Your Brain State

You can actually change your body just by changing your mind—not mentally but shifting your brain state. Here's an exercise to experience this.

- Ready your space, and set your intention.
- Remember a time when you were very relaxed, such as at a beach, on a couch, on vacation, or in a hammock.
- Use all of your senses.
- As you remember that time, note your body's physical responses, such as your breathing slows, muscles relax, or energy drops from the head down into your body. Note what specifically happens in your body.
- You can use this particular memory in the future to quickly evoke this relaxed state and enter alpha consciousness.

Exercise Three: Imagery

Follow the method for entering your sacred heart space, and set your intention to first breathe with your loved ones and then breathe with all animals, rocks, all of nature, all people, the people near you, and now yourself. What imagery arises? Follow it; make it bigger. What is it saying? What is it trying to tell you? Where did it come from? How did it get there? What does it need?

Exercise Four: Explore Your Inner Terrain

This exercise is actually an ongoing practice that may be done without limit. Follow the method for entering your sacred heart space by setting the intention to explore your inner terrain. Once you dive down into your sacred heart, allow your unique imagery language to arise and show you its many places and possibilities. Allow them to unfold in their own way and at their own pace.

You may also ask to go to the tiny space within your sacred heart space. When there, ask for light to shine and then for your Higher Self to come. Ask questions, dialogue, and receive input as guided.

Exercise Five: Self-Awareness

Follow the method for entering your sacred heart space. Remember that inner seeing is different for everyone. It may seem you are making it up, but do the exercise anyway.

See two trees in front of you. Examine them both in detail and with all your senses. Next, what does each tree say to the other? And what does each tree say to you? Open your eyes and write your experience down. Using this as a metaphorical experience for your inner world, ask yourself questions, such as:

- How do you feel about your internal self?
- Is there any resistance?
- Is there some part you wish was different?
- Do you totally accept yourself?
- Was any conflict present? If so, what was it?

Exercise Six: Tune Into Your Body

Every hour, tune into how your body feels. Sense any areas of discomfort, tension, or irritation. Ask that area what's going on and why the discomfort, tension, or irritation is there. Look for patterns and beliefs.

Step One Metaphor-phosis: Discover Your Conscious Stories

Now that we've learned about the states of consciousness and your innate wisdom, we will use them to discover and neutralize your limiting patterns and core beliefs. First, we'll learn to discover your conscious stories.

How to Proceed

As you discover your stories and beliefs, I suggest you write them all down in one place. Seeing them all together will help you identify emerging patterns. As soon as you discover a key limiting pattern or belief, immediately go to, "Step Two Metaphor-phosis: Unhook from Your Stories" in section III to diffuse its energy.

Keep in mind that as you uncover patterns, you may experience any number of different responses. Epiphanies may spark your energy and fuel your understanding. You may also seem a bit sensitive or have some pretty strong feelings. Realize that you don't have to process your experiences all in one sitting. Be patient with yourself, and take your time. Perhaps work with just one memory, and when you do discover its limiting pattern or belief, immediately neutralize its energy in "Step Two Metaphor-phosis." If you don't discover a pattern, you may still take your issue to "Step Two Metaphor-phosis."

If any emotions get to be too much, you don't have to be sucked in by them. Remember that you are not your story, and you are not your emotions. It's okay to back off if you feel overwhelmed, or better yet, don't let your process go that far. Instead take a break, get some tea, or shake it off in some other way. Read "If You Feel Triggered" below, and go to the "Tools to Discover Your Stories" under "Emotions" at the end of this section for techniques to help transform your emotions.

Remembering past stories is half the work and helps to discharge its hold. They only possess power over you when they are automatic reactions. When you remember a source story—truly understand and see the causes for a pattern or belief and the emotions they evoke—you bring it to conscious awareness. It is then that you can free its grip and take back the energy you lost or gave away.

Afterward, you'll still remember the story, but it won't trigger you because it no longer activates your emotions. Then you are free to transform and create the life you desire. So face your memories; embrace what they have to teach you, and then regain their gifts and power. Your emotions of guilt, anger, fear, and grief feed, empower, and reinforce your memories, patterns, and beliefs, so use them to help you instead.

If You Feel Triggered

While old memories emerge, stories surface, and patterns or beliefs connect, you may feel emotionally triggered. If this happens, try the following two keys.

The First Key: Passive Observer

To be a passive observer means to just observe how you engage in any given moment. It could be when you are with someone else or when alone. It could be when you are emotionally riled up or stuck or when you are calm. Either way, the approach is to shift your focus from what is happening in the moment to just observing yourself and the situation instead. Here are various ways to access your passive-observer self:

1) *Go to stillness.* Close your eyes, and take a few deep breaths. Relax each part of your body, head to foot. Now as if you are standing outside your body, observe yourself, and make note of your feelings and reactions.

2) *Rise above.* Do what one of my teachers, Evelyn Eaton, often said, "Take the elevator up." Mentally soar above to a vantage point where you can look down on yourself and the event from a different perspective. See the scene as if from above so you can separate your true self from your reaction enough to proceed.

3) *Be curious.* Approach your issue from the viewpoint of a detective sleuthing out clues, a tracker following animal prints, or a seeker searching for information. Get curious, even excited, about discovering important information that could positively alter your life.

---

4) Notice triggers. **When you seem emotionally triggered, say something to yourself like, "Here I am once more, reacting to John because of what he just said." Or, "She always gets my goat. I'm triggered again." Just being aware that you are emotionally sparked may create enough distance that you can proceed from there.**

5) Use tools. **Choose a tool given in "Essential Tools for Change" at the end of section I or "Tools to Discover Your Stories" at the end of section II under "Emotions," such as journal writing, movement, or something on your Emergency List to help release the emotional situation. After, return to the passive-observer mode.**

The Second Key: Emotional Reactions

Every emotion you feel has a right to exist. Suppressing your emotions is just as detrimental as indulging them. It's important to honor your emotions. At the same time, you want to move out of a trauma-drama approach, as this keeps you in an endless loop of reacting. Instead, use your emotions to help find the story, pattern, or belief that fuels them.

Emotion is "e-motion," or energy in motion, meaning that emotion gives you energy. Apply that energy to open the door to your stored memories. Start with a triggered emotion, and follow it like a thread through the labyrinth of your subconscious to your hidden cyclical patterns and limiting beliefs.

As you do so, try to be a passive observer. Allow anger to flow through you rather than be the anger or identify with the anger. Rather than saying, "I *am* angry," shift to saying, "I *feel* anger." This subtle rephrasing can be enough to separate your observer self from your triggered emotional self. Use your emotions, but don't let them use you.

As you feel an emotion, ask questions. Learn what originally provoked that repeated emotion or belief. Track backward and find the source memory. As you do so, you don't need to relive the entire event. Just become aware of it and its causative factors.

It can be useful to do this process out loud in front of a mirror or by recording yourself. You can even do this with someone else silently witnessing you as a "shadow buddy." Although it may be scary, it is actually very powerful and empowering.

Example of Using the Two Keys

Whenever Katie felt confronted, she withdrew and left the people or situation involved. This became an annoying problem, as it seemed that more and more people tended to confront her lately, including her boss, partner, and even her mother. Finally, Katie decided to correct this and used her body as a tool.

The next time she felt confronted, Katie withdrew as usual, but this time, she closed her eyes, took a deep breath, and tried to still her mind. She imagined herself floating above her body and looking down at it as a passive observer. She recognized that once again she had fled a confrontation. She focused on the emotion she felt and was surprised to discover that she felt both fear and anger.

Next, Katie tuned into her body. She felt her gut tighten and realized this could be the reason for her recurring stomach pain. She thought back over her life and asked herself when she had felt this way before. She recalled a memory of her stomach frequently tightening in high school when a group of kids she worked with on the yearbook repeatedly confronted her unusual ideas and approach.

Thinking back even further, Katie remembered an incident in elementary school when a teacher confronted her. It had been quite traumatic, as the teacher had badgered her with questions, repeatedly asking her why she had done something. Katie had felt humiliated. All she had wanted to do was run and hide. She had tried to answer, but the teacher kept berating her. So she clamped down to avoid further embarrassment and wouldn't answer.

Katie realized that her pattern of running from confrontation had stemmed from this source story in elementary school, which was when her recurring stomach pains had begun. Katie had now identified a pattern behind her reaction to confrontation and to her recurring stomach problems by using the two keys.

Discover Your Conscious Stories

There are four steps to discovering your stories:

- Ready your space
- Set your intention
- Go to self-inquiry
- Act on the stories

Along with these steps, explore "Tools to Discover Your Stories" at the end of this section. You can work back and forth between these two chapters as you wish.

Ready Your Space

As we just learned in the "States of Consciousness and Stories," it's best to enter an alpha state of consciousness to uncover your stories and beliefs. The steps to do this are described in "Essential Tools for Change" at the end of section I under "Process Preparation." In summary, find a quiet place where you won't be disturbed, set your space so it'll support your process, and take a few slow, deep breaths.

Set Your Intention

Set your intention for discovering your conscious stories. For more about setting intention, see "Process Preparation" in "Essential Tools for Change" at the end of section I.

Go to Self-Inquiry

The following questions can help you access your conscious stories and beliefs. Answering them helps reveal repeating issues that set up cyclical patterns.

1) What self-concepts, ideas, and beliefs do you tell people over and over about yourself? For example, do you frequently tell people that you ask dumb questions or that you aren't good at a particular activity or skill?

2) Do other people repeatedly say the same thing about you? For example, do people frequently say that you are graceful, but you don't believe it? Or do others often tell you that you're reactive, but you vehemently refuse that's true? No matter how much you deny it or think it's another person's gift or problem and not yours, such repeated comments point to something about you.

3) Examine all areas of your life to see what stories the universe reflects back to you. For example, do you live in a place that nourishes and enlivens you, or do you always end up living in small spaces, a house with leaks, or a place with noisy neighbors? Now examine your beliefs and patterns about where you live.

Repeat this for other areas of your life, such as relationships, work, career, finances, spirituality, friends, and creativity. See what experiences you have had along with what you encounter now. Identify your limiting stories and beliefs in all areas of your life, the successful and the unfulfilled parts alike.

4) Do your "buttons" often get pushed, causing you to react in a certain way? Use that repetitive response and follow it like a thread to its story. For example, perhaps whenever your partner covers your kitchen counter with books, papers, and other items, you always feel angry and resentful. Now look to see if there are other situations in which people treat you similarly. For example, do people at work dump stuff on your desk, or does your carpool mate trash your car? If so, you have a pattern of people "dumping" on you, others disrespecting your space, or some other possibility.

5) Do certain words or phrases irritate you or make you react? These words also indicate stories. For instance, if you feel upset, irritated, or angry from any concepts or words in this book, they reflect some belief or story you hold.

6) Do you repeatedly seem like a victim, rescuer, or perpetrator in any area of your life? The role of victim, rescuer, or perpetrator is a clue that there is a story to explore.

7) What roles do you fill or perform? Make a list of these, and see how they each reveal a hidden belief or pattern.

Act on Your Stories

Once you've discovered your stories, there are three parts to acting on them:

- Determine the limiting patterns or core beliefs
- Act on the information you receive
- Close your space, or immediately go to "Step Two Metaphor-phosis"

1) Determine the Limiting Patterns or Core Beliefs

Look at all the answers to your questions and see what new memories bubble forth. Keep going back over your life, revisiting past experiences when you felt the same way or when a similar event occurred until you come to the situation originating that pattern or belief. If possible, go all the way back to your earliest childhood memories. If you don't remember your childhood, go to your earliest memory.

Next, look at all of your memories together and determine their common theme. It could be a similar emotion, belief, or repeated experience, for instance. This is your pattern. If you can't figure out what the limiting pattern or core belief is, ask yourself this question, If you *did* know, what would it be? Then go with that answer.

Once you've identified your source pattern, look at your parents and grandparents to see if they had a similar theme in their lives. If possible, take it back down your family line even further. Sometimes a pattern originated with our ancestors, and yet we carry it and keep it alive, either genetically or energetically.

For example, all the sons throughout your lineage cut their fathers off; all the parents, grandparents, and great-grandparents in your family get divorced; or there's repeated abuse or abandonment, generation after generation.

Questions to determine patterns:

- Have you ever experienced a similar relationship, health issue, or situation like this before? If so, when? Who was involved?
- What repeats over and over?
- What life themes recur?
- What is the core belief you developed about yourself and the world as a result?
- What pattern emerged in your life that recurs again and again (though perhaps only as a hint of the original experience)?
- What emotions tend to repeatedly arise because of this?

2) Act on the Information You Receive

If you receive any information from your memories, stories, and patterns while you identify them, it is essential that you act on it. Usually, such realizations occur when processing the old story, but if it happens now, follow through on what you receive. Otherwise, the old pattern will stay in place. For example, you might realize you need to forgive someone, release a role, or complete a project, just as I learned I had to tell my story to release my old eczema skin (read the Prologue).

3) Close Your Space, or Go Unhook from Your Patterns

After you have determined your limiting patterns or beliefs, you may feel changed simply by recognizing the limiting pattern or core belief. This is definitely possible. If your issue clears quickly, that's great, but if it's a deeper problem, more is needed. It's one thing to identify a pattern and write about it in your journal, but it's quite another to actually shift your life and create a new experience.

If you need to stop now, close your space. Thank any spirit helpers or healers, close the directions, blow out your candle, or finish whatever else is needed to signal completion of your process.

If you are ready to continue now, go immediately to "Step Two Metaphor-phosis" in section III to diffuse the energy behind your old stories. This is necessary because otherwise its energy stays locked in the reptilian brain where it will repeat simply by rote habit. The more you ignore or stuff it, the more it will continue to affect your life.

Just recognizing a core belief or shifting to an affirmation statement doesn't necessarily shift issues. Wanting to change is not enough. You can intend and affirm a new belief or behavior as much as you

> ### Chris Discovers Her Conscious Story
>
> **Chris had environmental allergies and felt stymied by them. She followed the Metaphor-phosis process by readying her space, setting her intention, and completing the self-inquiry questions. As she did so, she realized how impossible her situation felt. Not only couldn't she find a way to heal the environmental allergies, but she also couldn't live with her sister like she wanted because her sister lived with a boyfriend in an open-space studio.**
>
> **Chris then recognized that she often told people, "Everything is impossible for me." Chris took this belief further back in time and remembered that as a child her mother had often said, "You can't do that. That's impossible." Chris had discovered her pattern: that everything was impossible for her. As a result, she couldn't resolve her environmental allergies no matter what she did. She took the pattern, "everything is impossible for me," to "Step Two Metaphor-phosis."**

want, and this can help, but the cyclical behavior or limiting belief will reappear sooner or later. Go to "Step Two Metaphor-phosis: Unhook from Your Stories" to defuse its energy. This is also where you will access your Higher Self, or your spiritual brain, to neutralize your stories.

Our Examples

We will take two examples throughout the entire Metaphor-phosis process in this book, Pattie and Tom. We'll follow them as they work each step of the process to change their lives and how they created what they desired instead. In this chapter, their general stories are given. In the next chapter, their patterns are discovered.

Pattie:

Pattie was very unhappy in her marriage. Her husband didn't see or hear her and laughed everything off. He would be kind to her and then berate her. His lack of support devastated her, yet she couldn't leave her marriage because she felt guilty. He was a great guy after all, and she didn't want to hurt him. Instead, she stayed in the marriage, knowing she wasn't true to her self and felt constantly hurt and angry inside. She knew her life was toxic, but she felt powerless to do anything about it.

Tom:

Tom thought that his boss ignored and disrespected him, that his boss was "out to get him" through his decisions and actions. He also felt his office mates either ignored or denigrated his work. Tom wanted to leave his job, move out of the area, and start over again, away from this boss, office mates, and the entire situation.

Step One Metaphor-phosis: Discover Your Unconscious Stories

Your emotional reactions arise from your hidden stories, patterns, and beliefs. These include such elements as your roles, habits, assumptions, hidden agendas, and values. This hidden stuff has a way of creating lots of drama, blame, and distractions. It also drains your energy and keeps you from experiencing the life you want. Only when you bring this stuff to surface awareness can its energy be released and its cyclical appearance cleared.

It's important to make your invisible stuff visible. This chapter is focused on doing just that—learning how to uncover your unconscious stories so you can determine any cyclical patterns or limiting beliefs that stop you from living the life you want.

You probably already know many of your stories, but most are hidden, since the majority of your brain's activity goes on beyond your conscious awareness. That means the most powerful stories to learn are the subconscious ones that run your life on autopilot.

Your Subconscious

As stated earlier, the subconscious includes hidden feelings; unnoticed perceptions; unaware thoughts; automatic reactions; unknown phobias; concealed desires; forgotten memories; unacceptable ideas, wishes or desires; and traumatic memories. Accessing this subconscious material actually attunes you to your authentic self. It helps you learn how you really feel and what you really want. By accessing your truths, you have the power to change.

All of our hidden stuff is triggered through thoughts, emotions, and images. This is one reason why memories stay locked in the subconscious—to protect us from reliving past trauma and shock. While thankfully you can't easily remember certain stories, at the same time, they are the reasons you developed particular beliefs about the world and yourself. These in turn create patterns of behavior, both for you and for how others treat you.

Your hidden stories may protect you, but they are like a monster that lurks in your subconscious and repeatedly haunts you through limiting beliefs and cyclical patterns. Such monsters have stories to tell about why the pattern or belief was formed in the first place. Only when you face a memory can you regain control and dissipate its hold.

Your Shadows

Jung included as part of the subconscious what he called the "shadow," the denied parts of your personality that you reject out of fear, shame, or ignorance. Because of this, the shadow is hidden, yet it still exists deep within as part of your subconscious mind. Your denial about these parts of yourself gives them energy and power over you.

There are two aspects to the shadow: a dark shadow and a light shadow. People reflect these dark and light parts back to you. You can see them in clients, workmates, partners, colleagues, celebrities, politicians, partners, or friends. What we perceive causes us to resonate with, like, love, be irritated by, dislike, or hate a particular person, whether we know them or not. It is not the person him- or herself we love or hate, but the reflection he or she gives us of our hidden shadow selves.

Your Dark Shadow

Your dark shadow includes the parts you don't like about yourself as well as the manipulative, grumpy, violent, lazy, hateful parts that you see in people you don't like. It is the parts you reject out of shame and guilt.

Your Light Shadow

Your light shadow includes your greatest possible self. It is the "sweet" or brilliant side of you, the positive, talented, and creative parts that you haven't yet owned. When you say someone else can do something but that you can't, or that you're not beautiful enough, skinny enough, smart enough, or talented enough, you disown your light shadow. Believe it or not, the light shadow can be even harder to accept than the dark one.

Collective Shadows

Not only does each of us have a shadow, but cultures, nations, and other groups have collective shadows. The feminine and masculine each has a shadow too.

Shadows and Your Stories

Shadows act in our lives through resonance and coherence by attracting people and circumstances that reflect what they hide. This is seen by any reactions you have to what others say or do. For example, if you deny or are uncomfortable with anger, you may often attract angry people into your life, suppress your angry feelings, or judge people whom you see as angry. Or if you find you're always dating a geek, loser, blamer, or abuser, you are denying the geek, loser, blamer, or abuser part of yourself. Your hidden inner geek, loser, blamer, or abuser attracts others with these qualities until you acknowledge these parts of yourself.

Any parts of yourself that you can't love or embrace are part of your shadow self too. This often appears as a resistance toward, jealousy of, or uncomfortable feelings about anyone with "light" qualities that you don't accept. For example, if you are jealous of Mary because she has a nicer car and better clothes, you aren't acknowledging your own ability to have wealth and prosperity. Or if you belittle Fred because he is always receiving awards for his creative ideas, you haven't fully embraced your own creative side.

Embrace Your Shadow

Expanding your consciousness to cast a "light" on the shadow self makes it visible. This is also why right before you make a leap into the light, the dark shadow often shows up—not to keep you from the light, but so you face it, know its teachings, and receive its gifts. This is what you want to do now, reveal your shadow so it is consciously known.

What if you don't embrace your shadow? What if you leave your hidden subconscious patterns and beliefs alone? What if you think that life is just fine as it is, thank you very much, that you don't need to deal with any of that stuff? Your shadow side will continue to stalk you until you face it. What you don't bring to

Balance of Dark and Light

The dark shadow is not "bad," and the light shadow is not "good;" both are disowned parts of us. There's a concept in Japanese art called "Notan" about the balance of dark and light elements. If the artwork is all light, it floats away or disappears. The dark areas are what anchor the light ones and bring balance to the whole. They ground the work so it is more solid, palpable, and expressive.

The same goes for our dark and light shadows; they are the Notan of our lives. We don't want to express just one or the other or have one dominate the other. Rather, we want to accept both our dark and light sides and acknowledge what they hide.

When shadow parts are unconscious, they run our life and cause problems not only for us but also for others. They then have power over us.

When we embrace and accept our shadow parts, they become conscious and no longer control our reactions and beliefs. We then shine light on them so their hold can disappear.

conscious awareness will appear in your life as fate instead. Then your future will be a predictable repeat of your past.

Discover Your Unconscious Stories

Speaking to the subconscious in its own language helps override its stopgap measures so you aren't triggered to protect yourself. The language of the subconscious is imagery and emotions. Imagery occurs when you "see," know, or sense yourself jogging, lying on a beach, or playing basketball rather than actually *doing* any of these activities. It accesses the subconscious because your brain doesn't differentiate between what you imagine and what you actually see; the same areas of the brain light up with both.

Your emotions act by chemically reinforcing experiences into long-term memory, and so they are directly associated with your hidden stories and images. Your perception accesses your subconscious memories and triggers how you feel and react.

How to Proceed

As you open your subconscious to discover old stories, patterns, and beliefs, get very honest with yourself. No one else has to know what you discover. Get to the guts of your source stories. Seek your deepest truth, and breathe life into it. What part of you needs to come out, be expressed, seen, and acknowledged? Allow those parts to fully emerge.

There are four steps to uncovering your subconscious stories:

- Ready your space
- Set your intention
- Go to your heart wisdom or body wisdom
- Act on your subconscious stories

Along with these steps, read "Tools to Discover Your Stories" at the end of this section for helpful techniques to unlock your subconscious, discover your shadow, and learn your patterns and beliefs.

In the prior chapter, I suggested you write down all the stories and beliefs you uncover in one place. Seeing them all together helps to identify emerging patterns. As soon as you discover a key limiting pattern or belief, you can also move immediately to "Step Two Metaphor-phosis" to neutralize its energy.

As memories bubble forth, they open the door to your subconscious. As they do, you can ask questions and follow their answers to the source story. ***The key to this process is to record the answers you receive. Either write them down or speak them out loud into a recorder.*** If you try to think through this process, you'll stay in a mental loop and never reach the material stored in your subconscious. The process of writing or speaking helps open the door to your subconscious for the patterns and beliefs to emerge. If difficult emotions are triggered, go to "If You Feel Triggered" in the prior chapter, "Step One Metaphor-phosis: Discover Your Conscious Stories."

The Metaphor-phosis process to discover your unconscious stories is very similar to uncovering your conscious stories, except instead of using self-inquiry, you will use heart or body wisdom to discover your unconscious stories.

Ready Your Space

The steps to ready your space are described in "Essential Tools for Change" at the end of section I under "Process Preparation." In summary, find a quiet place where you won't be disturbed, set your space so it will support your process, and take a few slow, rhythmical breaths.

Set Your Intention

Set your intention for discovering your unconscious stories. For more about setting intention, see "Set Intention" in "Essential Tools for Change."

Go to Your Heart or Body Wisdom

How to Use Your Heart Wisdom:

Follow the steps to enter your sacred heart space given in "States of Consciousness and Stories" under "Your Inner Wisdom." As you do so, set your intention to both enter your sacred heart space and to discover your unconscious stories, cyclical patterns, and limiting beliefs.

- Go to alpha
- Dive down and "travel" into your heart
- Observe your unique heart language (such as imagery, sensations, or an inner knowing)
- Receive understanding

How to Use Your Body Wisdom:
- Choose an issue to explore

- What emotion do you feel?
- Where do you feel that emotion in your body (any discomfort, stress, tension or where something is "off")?
- What sensations do you feel? (Use all of your senses.)
- What memories come forth?
- What images arise? Are they in black-and-white or color? Any smells, sounds, tastes, textures? Is it still, or is there movement like a movie?

> ### Working Subconscious Memories
> As subconscious memories surface, you can work with them to help uncover your patterns. Ask any people in the memory questions, such as, How do you feel? What do you want? and What do you need to say? to trigger further memories. Take the responses to your body wisdom again to determine underlying patterns or core beliefs.

- When did you feel/experience this at an earlier time in your life? Keep going back and identify all the times you felt this way in your body.
- What people and places are involved?
- When did you experience the issue and feel this way at an even earlier time?
- What is your earliest memory when this theme occurred?
- Pay attention to how your body feels while you do this, as it will tell you when you have found the originating memory where your source story lies.
- What roles did you play?
- What roles did others play?
- Do you still have this issue today?
- What did you lose that you are trying to get back?
- How have you been behaving because of that loss?
- What is the limiting pattern or core belief you discover?

Act on Your Stories

Once you've discovered your subconscious stories, there are three parts to acting on them: determine the limiting patterns or core beliefs; act on the information you received; and close your space, or go unhook from your patterns. These steps are the same as those given for discovering your conscious stories in the prior chapter.

Close Your Space, or Go Unhook from Your Stories

After you have determined your limiting patterns or beliefs, you may either close your space or go immediately to "Step Two Metphor-phosis."

Our Examples

Here we continue our examples from "Step One Metaphor-phosis: Discover Your Conscious Stories" with both Pattie and Tom. Let's see how they discovered their limiting patterns and core beliefs.

Pattie:

Remember how Pattie felt angry with her husband for his lack of respect and support, and yet she couldn't change the situation because of the guilt she felt? She now reviewed her life from the perspective of this theme. Immediately, she realized she behaved similarly with her friends. She didn't express her true self and needs with them either.

Because she didn't want to hurt anyone, she felt guilty whenever she wanted to say no. She knew what she desired but would surrender to others' needs and requests no matter how much she wanted something or was exhausted and overworked. Her self-assurance was very low, and she was consumed by guilt. She even felt guilty about not expressing or following her own needs.

Pattie tuned into her body wisdom and felt tightness in her chest. As she did so, memories emerged of how her mother had treated her horribly as a child. Through constant verbal abuse, Pattie was told she was worthless, stupid, unwanted, and could never do anything right. She was frequently punished when she didn't do what her mother wanted. Her dad's sweetness was the only thing that helped her survive childhood. Yet at the same time, she realized that he did nothing to protect her from her mom's verbal abuse. Additionally, her mom and dad had a very bad relationship with each other.

Pattie realized she had a pattern of being sweet to others and doing what they wanted at her own expense in order to prevent abuse or punishment. She allowed her husband, children, and friends to walk all over her because she couldn't set her boundaries or say no. If she did, she felt she'd be abusing or hurting others just as she had been abused and hurt. As a result, she also developed a lack of self-confidence and tremendous guilt.

Tom:

Tom broadened his issues about his boss who ignored him and officemates who treated him poorly to his entire life. He did an exercise with his dark shadow and remembered that after his dad abandoned him as a very young child, he wasn't protected from other children's attacks and harassment. He realized that he had decided at that point in his life that men weren't there for him but attacked him instead. This core belief became even more obvious as he thought about other male relationships he had experienced throughout his life.

Tools to Discover Your Stories

The tools given here are diverse. If one doesn't work, try another. If one helps, still try another. Sometimes just doing a process helps you shift enough that energy is diffused and you're no longer hooked. Other issues are so deeply buried that they need further work. If you choose to use external tools, avoid techniques and sessions as platforms to repeatedly emote or relive your stories. This only keeps you stuck.

Process to Find Patterns and Core Beliefs

Use this with every exercise in this chapter as appropriate. To determine patterns and core beliefs, look deeper than the story itself to any repetitive feelings, emotions, or beliefs. Find what affects multiple areas of your life. To do this, ask questions, such as:

- When have you felt this way before?
- What happened?
- Who was involved?
- What earlier times did you feel this way?
- What happened then?
- Who was involved at those times?
- What is the earliest memory you felt this way or experienced this?
- Who was involved then?
- What happened to cause it?
- What decisions did you make about yourself and your life as a result?
- What is the overall pattern or core belief?

Write down all the patterns and beliefs you find in one place. Look at them together to identify common themes in many areas of your life. These are the ones to work with because clearing their far-reaching effects helps you make greater change.

If You Can't Discover Anything

When we're confused or emotional, it can be very difficult to determine patterns. Here are two ways to get unstuck and receive guidance.

Use Your Body Wisdom:

If you don't consciously recognize a pattern or core belief, look for a physical reaction. When you find the pattern or core belief, you'll feel it in your body, such as gut tension, facial changes, labored breathing, or blank mind. Or you won't believe it's true and try to rationalize it. Or your emotions say it's true, but your mind says it's not true. If any of these happen, you've got the pattern or core belief. You might also think there's no way you can give up that pattern or belief. This means it's emotionally true, and you have the right one.

Ask Your Soul:

Write a letter to your soul expressing your feelings, hopes, fears, and longings. Be honest, knowing this is for your eyes only. Ask questions, such as:

- What in my life needs healing?
- What is the next step in my ongoing healing process?
- How can I start the healing process with ___?
- What do you, Spirit, know needs healing in my life?
- How can you help me with ___?
- Show me how to express and realign with my soul purpose.

Address and return address your letter to your soul. Put it someplace safe, such as on your altar. When you "hear" a response from your soul, write whatever comes, stream of consciousness. Keep doing this until your questions have been answered. Then look at the responses together, and see what patterns emerge.

Use Your Inner Wisdom

As you use the following tools, discover your unique meanings rather than adapt other interpretations. Outside ideas can assist your process, but don't substitute them for your personal meaning. There are lots of books and resources, i.e., interpreting dreams, animal helpers, life maps, and archetypes, for instance, however, they come from someone else's ideas. The best meanings come from within; your inner wisdom holds the most powerful understandings.

What's Next?

Once you discover a core pattern or belief, go to "Step Two Metaphor-phosis" and follow the process to diffuse its energy.

Tools To Discover Your Stories

Patterns

A useful way to discover patterns is through self-inquiry. Write your answers to the following questions, and look at them together for any patterns or beliefs.

Exercise One: Self-Inquiry 1

- What needs to shift in your life so you come into right relationship (harmony) with yourself, family, community, country, and the world?
- What part of your life doesn't serve you?
- What keeps you from living the life you want? I should do ___, I want to do ___ but don't.
- What's keeping you back, stopping you, or holding your energy?
- Where do you feel stuck in your life? When does this happen?
- What wants to die out?
- What wants to emerge and be born?
- What life crisis are you in or resolving?
- What repeats over and over in your life?
- What core beliefs limit your life?
- List your dreams and visions. What's stopping you from realizing them?
- What changes do you want to make in your life?
- What's stopping you from making those changes?
- What in your life needs healing?
- What's stopping you from healing?

Exercise Two: Self-Inquiry 2

Use this technique with whatever you are unhappy, such as a relationship, partner, finances, living situation, creative expression, or work:

- Make a list of what you don't like. Use complete sentences.

- Substitute the word *I* for each of these listed items in terms of how you do these to your self.
- Look for and name the overall pattern, that is, how have you experienced this before in your life and when has this happened?

For example, the first statement might be, "My boss doesn't see me" or "My apartment is too small." When substituting the word *I*, the statement could change to, "*I* don't see myself" or "*I* keep myself small." The overall patterns might be, "I'm invisible" or "My needs are never met."

Exercise Three: Self-Inquiry 3

Do you ever say or think any of the following? If so, it points to a pattern or belief. What do you say these about?

- Why does this always happen to me? (Or, that always happens to me.)
- Why does he/she always do that? (Or, he/she always does that.)
- It's a dog-eat-dog world.
- Who gets to live exactly the life they want?
- There's always something to deal with.
- I never feel ___.
- I never have enough ___.
- I need approval for ___.
- I don't accept ___ about myself.
- I'm addicted to ___.
- I'm not healthy.
- I need ___ in order to be okay.
- People don't understand me.
- I can't fully be myself.
- I can't be bothered with my own feelings.
- I can never have what I want.
- I mess everything up.

Known Beliefs, Values, and Assumptions

Beliefs and values point to assumptions we hold. For example, you assume that you aren't good at math. While reviewing your past, you remember a parent or teacher who repeatedly said you couldn't do math, you were teased whenever you did a math problem in front of class, a traumatic event occurred while doing math, or you had a math teacher who was particularly mean. From this, you developed a belief that you aren't good at math.

Take it one step further to find your core belief, such as you aren't worthy, good at things, or valued, or some other belief that affects many areas of your life. This is the core belief to neutralize.

Exercise: What You Already Know

Make a list of all your beliefs and assumptions. Take your time. When you've accumulated two or more dozen, look at them together. See if any are dependent on others. What patterns emerge? Repeat this process with your values.

Emotions

As you determine your patterns and beliefs, emotions usually arise. Emotion is different than feeling. A feeling is a sense of touch or physical sensation, such as hot, cold, sticky, or dry. Emotion is a state of consciousness produced by a thought, memory, or external stimulus. Love, hate, anger, and joy are emotions. Feelings are external whereas emotions are both external and internal. We experience feelings for short periods whereas emotions are usually prolonged.

Emotions are crucial to acknowledge and express. If you hold them inside, they can cause illness, low energy, anxiety, or depression. Writing your emotions in a journal or sharing them with a friend can help diffuse their energy, but they don't necessarily neutralize the underlying pattern or belief that triggers them. Although the words *feelings* and *emotions* have become interchangeable, we'll focus on emotions.

Exercise One: Discharging Emotional Energy

This technique helps discharge enough emotional energy that you can work with an emotion to determine its pattern or belief.

- Bring the emotion alive with all of your senses. What do you see, feel, hear, taste, and/or touch (its texture)?
- If it's in color, switch to black-and-white; if in black-and-white, adjust to color.
- Put a frame around it.
- Move the frame away from you until the picture is fuzzy.
- Turn the framed picture upside down.

By now the emotion might defuse enough that you can uncover the source pattern or belief behind its repetitive appearance.

Example Beliefs and Assumptions

I have to do everything myself.

No one appreciates what I do.

I can't do anything right.

Everyone/everything always sabotages me.

I can't fulfill everyone's expectations.

I can't trust anyone.

I'm lost.

Others aren't there for me.

I'm not safe.

I'm not good enough.

Life isn't fair to me.

I don't exist.

I work hard, but life doesn't support me.

I'm not original.

I don't know enough.

I'm not enough.

I can't make things happen.

I withhold myself.

I don't belong.

I'm not consistent.

I never win.

I'm not worthy.

I'm afraid.

I'm pathetic.

Others don't want what I have.

I can't make things happen.

I don't matter.

I'm unlovable.

The world isn't safe.

I'm always wrong.

I don't deserve success.

I'm a big disappointment.

I'm a failure.

I'm invisible.

I'm alone.

Life is dangerous and scary.

I'm not respected.

I'm abandoned.

I'm not valuable.

I'm disconnected.

I'm bad.

I'm lost in a fog.

I get passed over.

I'm not resourceful.

I'm stupid.

I'm incompetent.

I'm left out.

Life isn't fair.

I'm not valuable.

I'm not worthy of ___.

I'm a loser.

Nothing works for me.

Others are better than me.

I'm not spiritual enough.

I get passed over.

I'm always wrong.

I have to work hard, but I'll always succeed in the end.

I have to work hard to be seen, acknowledged, or ___.

He/she wants me to do well but not better than him/her.

I'm neglected, undervalued, unimportant, different, too much, wrong, a burden, a failure, powerless, ___.

Exercise Two: Emotionally Triggered?

When someone says or does something that emotionally triggers you, try to calmly repeat back what you thought you heard or experienced. This is to check that you interpreted the other person's words or actions as they were intended. Often our perceptions distort what someone else intended. We react according to our perceptions, which points to underlying patterns or beliefs.

Exercise Three: Quick Emotional Change

If you are too emotionally stuck to find your pattern or core belief, discharge the emotion through one of these methods.

- Sweep the unwanted emotion away with your left hand and sweep in the desired emotion with your right hand.
- To quickly shift how you feel, alter your posture, facial expression, or breathing.
- Look at your gratitude journal and focus on what you are grateful for.
- Write a letter expressing your emotions and then burn, bury, or tear it up.

Exercise Four: Emotional Emergency List

When emotionally triggered, it can be difficult to look further for underlying patterns and beliefs. Using tools to diffuse an emotion's energy lessens its hold so you can work with it. The following are covered in this book:

- *Ho'Oponopono*
- Divine Triangulation
- Healing Triangulation
- Sandpaintings
- Refocusing
- Repatterning
- Body Wisdom
- Contracts with Others
- Your Emergency List

Exercise Five: How to Appropriately Express Emotions

When emotionally triggered, it's easy to react. Until you clear their patterns, here are some useful ways to respond instead. They can halt the progression of a potentially harmful situation or prevent emotional reactions:

- "I don't understand what you meant. Please clarify."
- "When you do _____, I feel _____."
- "What are you really asking me?"
- "What are you really saying?"
- "Does that have anything to do with me?"
- "Let me take that in for a few minutes."
- "I regret you feel that way" (and then leave the situation).

Exercise Six: Still Emotionally Triggered?

Rather than dwell on what the person said or did, look for the meaning behind it. What is *really* going on with that person? What is *really* going on with you? This is not a rationalization for what happened, but a way to disengage, be a passive observer, and discriminate your stuff from the other person's. Try not to make yourself right, defend yourself, or engage in the issue. Avoid the blame game. Instead, look for your own patterns and beliefs behind your reaction.

Exercise Seven: Continue to Feel Emotionally Triggered?

Use what happened as a mirror to see what triggered your reaction and uncover a limiting pattern or core belief. When emotionally triggered or stuck, do the following:

- Breathe
- What emotion is up?
- Where do you feel this in your body (such as tension in your gut, emptiness in your chest, fluttering in your heart)?
- Under what situations do you usually experience this sensation or have experienced it in the past? Allow memories to emerge.
- Explore the sensation further and look for an underlying pattern or belief.

Exercise Eight: Get to Know Your Emotions

This exercise helps you determine any patterns or beliefs you hold from repeating emotions.

- Determine which emotions(s) you most frequently experience.
- Focus on it for a month and really get to know it.
- Whenever that emotion comes up, follow it like crumbs through the woods to its source. Say something like, "Oh, you're back. What is it you want to tell me this time? What should I know, realize, or recognize? What do you give me or buy me? How do you serve me?"

Example Emotions

Quite often we have an emotion but can't name it. Pinpointing an exact emotion can help determine patterns and beliefs. Here are some possibilities:

glad	mad	sad
happy	upset	disappointed
overjoyed	angry	crushed
excited	frustrated	sore
ecstatic	worried	defeated
cheerful	impatient	defenseless
lively	troubled	dismayed
enthusiastic	guilty	apathetic
eager	rejected	helpless
proud	embarrassed	powerless
secure	ashamed	lonely
zealous	shocked	deprived
thrilled	afraid	rejected
relieved	anxious	hopeless
fervent	tense	unwanted
energetic	defensive	uncared for
contented	furious	remorseful
alive	disgusted	numb
elated	desolate	sorry
serene	annoyed	overly busy
powerful	humiliated	blue
empty	tired	sympathetic
sympathetic	weak	tender
strong	nauseous	humble
calm	nervous	revolted
refreshed	starved	stupid
satisfied	indifferent	disappointed
full	humiliated	shocked
ardent	aroused	horny
relieved	smothered	furious
reassured	strangled	enraged
passionate	oppressed	suffocated

Exercise Nine: Self-Inquiry 1

Ask what that emotion buys you, gives you, or does for you. For instance, confusion or feeling stuck often masks something else, such as an excuse to stay in limbo or not make a decision or change. Consider that it might buy you attention, help, support, denial, or avoidance. To know which answer is correct, use your body wisdom. Let physical responses be clues that you are on track. Look for patterns or beliefs.

The same can be said for illness. Being sick sometimes serves us in some way. The first time I was to lecture before a large audience, I felt terrified, so I subconsciously "found" an acceptable excuse and got the flu with a 104-degree fever. I had no idea there was a connection until I later remembered a fleeting thought before I got ill. I thought it would be a tremendous relief if I was sick and couldn't go. I was shocked to realize that I had created my flu just to get out of a terrifying situation. The next time I had the opportunity to lecture before a large group, I remembered this and stayed well.

Exercise Ten: Self-Inquiry 2

The following questions are useful indicators for underlying emotional issues. Use them as guides to identify patterns and beliefs. Journal on the following questions:

Do you:

- Have difficulty being present when another person is expressing his/her emotions? Which emotion?
- Have difficulty expressing one particular emotion? Which one?
- Spend most of your time in one particular emotion? Which one?
- Have a particular body part that becomes tense, tight, or uncomfortable when a specific emotion or situation arises?
- Have a particular symptom arise when a specific emotion occurs? Which emotion?
- Have a habit or behavior pattern regularly arise during emotional situations?
- Experience thoughts, memories, or fantasies during emotional situations or when doing nothing? What are they? During which emotions do they arise?
- Experience numbness during emotional situations? During which emotional situations does this arise?
- Overreact to situations? Which emotion arises?
- Feel like a pressure cooker about to explode? Which emotions cause this?
- Feel trapped in a situation? Which emotions are involved?

- Have a specific person, place, or thing you can't stand seeing or being around? What emotion arises when you think about him, her, or it?

Exercise Eleven: Praise List

Create a praise list for the people or problems with which you have an issue. Write down the person or situation's name. What do you like, appreciate, or value about that person, issue, or situation? How have they helped you? If nothing else, maybe they've helped you learn something about yourself. Then when an issue arises with that person, immediately think of something on that list and hold it in mind.

Map Your Life

It's vital to tell your life story. This not only owns it but also honors your life and your self. When you look at your life as a whole, it creates a broader perspective that can reveal cyclical patterns. Most of us live from day to day or move from one drama to the next. Pulling back and viewing all the major events in your life together can bring cyclical issues into sharp focus, help you make connections, see cause-and-effect, identify when patterns or beliefs started, and learn how you got where you are now. Even more, you can identify what's missing in your life, assess unlived dreams, and receive guidance for where to go next. Most of all, this is one of the best ways to determine your soul's journey. Doing a life review is a very powerful experience.

> ### Mapping My Life
> I've mapped my life several ways and many times from a revere style to a childhood autobiography, outlines, timelines, and metaphorical maps. All have been equally revealing. Each time I map my life, I see or realize something different. It's been invaluable not only to identify patterns but my soul's journey as well.

As you record your life story, pay attention to the images and memories that appear and ask why they emerged as opposed to others. Use them to find limiting patterns, beliefs, and themes. If you find this difficult to do, imagine you are sharing it with your most trusted friend, guardian angel, or someone you love. When you complete your narrative, share it with at least one person. This makes it real and establishes a witness for your life.

Once you map your life through any of the following methods, view it as a whole and ask questions, such as:

- What feelings do you have overall?
- What insights do you gain overall?
- What repeats over and over regardless of people, place, or area involved?

- What themes recur throughout?
- What is dying out?
- What is being born?
- What are the highs?
- What are the lows?
- What are the significant areas in your life?
- What stands out to you?
- Where is the most emphasis and in which area? This is your major teacher. What have you learned from it?
- Where are the biggest gaps or holes? What is missing in your life?
- What patterns, rhythms, and cycles emerge?

Exercise One: Life Timeline

Make a brief outline of your entire life, listing all the major areas, such as health, relationships, career, spirituality, places lived, creativity, dreams, finances, emotions, and limiting/supportive beliefs. Create a timeline horizontally and/or vertically with the details. Review your overall timeline with the questions above.

Exercise Two: Autobiography

Write your life story as an autobiography. This does not have to be a book (unless that's what you want) but rather can be a detailed outline. Hit the highlights, such as the events that influenced you the most, what you are most sad about, most fearful of, and has shaped your beliefs and who you are. Write the stories that stick most in your mind, the ones that you repeatedly tell others, and the ones you only tell your closest friends. Include how you felt during these major life events, what happened as a result, and what decisions you or others made. Look for overall patterns and core beliefs.

Exercise Three: Tell the Juicy Stories

Detail two or three of the saddest or most painful stories of your life. Many of us keep our difficult stories buried inside. Start with these hidden stories, the ones you don't want to talk or write about. If you are too scared to do this, you're on the right track. If you don't dare tell a story because you might die, go crazy, or not be able to live your current life, this is the one to write.

You do not need to show it to anyone; you can tear it up or burn it in a ritual if you desire. Remember, you are writing your stories to open your subconscious and reveal patterns. After all, you've probably spent your whole life stopping yourself because of this story, so now is the time to face that monster. Then you can let it go and reclaim its power. Write your most wounded stories, the ones that you would pay a price to tell.

Exercise Four: Family Stories

Write your family stories. If you know where you came from, you know your influences. This helps understand why certain events have happened, why siblings, parents, or grandparents behaved as they did or treated you in certain ways. In addition, it's a great beginning for writing a life story in general because often our cyclical patterns begin early in life.

Exercise Five: Metaphorical Map

Map your life metaphorically rather than literally. Use images to represent different areas and times of your life. For example, one person drew a hammock for all the restful times while another scribbled red lines for painful ones. You can do this as an extension of the exercises above, detailing important events in all major areas of your life and then creating metaphorical images for each. Use a large sheet of paper, and map them together in any way that feels right. You could also make a collage of various magazine images by gluing them together on paper or cardboard until the final image feels right.

When finished, look at the whole picture metaphorically. Look for the following:

- *Colors:* Where is the most color? Least? What is the predominant color? The least used or not used color? What do these colors mean to you?
- *Light and dark:* Where is the most light? Dark? Overall, is the picture dark (heavy, difficult, deep, buried, mysterious) or faint (are you invisible in your life)?
- *Form:* Gaps? Chaos? Crowded? Lively? Linear? Cyclical? Geometric?
- *Shapes:* Remind you of _____? Empty spaces?
- *Activity:* Bland? Some activity? Active? Too active?

Exercise Six: Write Your Desired Stories

Write the stories of who you want to be but can't or what you really wanted to do but couldn't. What is that story? Include why you were held back. Look for the patterns or beliefs behind these.

Exercise Seven: Reversing

As stated in "Essential Tools for Change," reversing is a process of reviewing something, starting with the most recent experience and ending with the earliest. In this case, reverse your life year by year, asking what was most important about that year and what needed to be changed, corrected, or rectified. This can reveal connections, patterns, and beliefs.

Ancestral Patterns

Your history is your foundation. Learning it deepens your sense of self and place. If you know where you came from, you know your influences. You can then choose to keep what you want and clear what you don't. You can also draw strength from it and know you are not alone. Many cultures introduce themselves through their lineage for these reasons.

Repeating issues that don't seem "yours" can actually be genetically inherited. Ancestors inform you through physical traits, words you use, mannerisms, even tone of voice. And you are impacted by how they lived and died as well. These are your hungry ghosts because they subconsciously influence you. Until released, you might continue to relive their themes on all levels throughout your life. On the other hand, after you neutralize genetic influences, you not only don't have to act them out, it can have a positive effect on your descendants too.

Ancestral energy also directs your beliefs and actions. Issues, such as betrayal, abandonment, or loss, and beliefs, such as "I must do it alone," "I have to work hard to earn anything," or "It's not safe to be me," can all be inherited too. You usually don't know how the painful loss of Auntie's, Grandmother's, or Great-grandfather's wealth, for instance, influences your own expectations that you'll lose money.

When you look for ancestral patterns, investigate at least three ancestors and several genetic lines. Sometimes issues skip generations, so keep that in mind.

Exercise One: Family Tree

Make a family tree. List whatever you can about each ancestor. Look for common patterns, such as how your ancestors were born, lived, and died; divorces; health problems; and behavioral issues like abandonment, poor self-esteem, running away from things, cutting people off, and other behaviors. Discover as much as you can, and write it all down. Look at all the information together, and determine the patterns and beliefs that influence you.

Exercise Two: Self-Inquiry

Ask yourself the following questions and record their answers:

- What are the scripts in your family? Look at your siblings, parents, cousins, aunts, uncles, grandparents, great-grandparents, and even further, if possible.
- What drives you nuts in your family about your siblings, parents, nephews, nieces, cousins, grandparents, and so forth? (These are part of your dark shadow.)

- Look at your known cyclical patterns and core beliefs. Which ones are generational? Which ones are yours alone?

Shadow Work

Your shadow includes the parts of your personality that you reject out of fear, shame, ignorance, or lack of acceptance or love. Whatever you don't accept acts out in your life instead. It's important to identify and claim shadow pieces because, if left unconscious, they not only cause problems for you but can hurt others as well. When the shadow piece is conscious, you can make choices about it.

As you do the following exercises, use your body wisdom to note physical reactions. They give a true indication if you can't accept a trait, which makes it part of your shadow.

Exercise One: Discover Your Dark and Light Shadows

Make a list of:

- The people who tick you off and why
- The people you admire and why

Ways the Shadow Shows Up

- Humor
- Snide comments meant to be humorous
- Exaggerated emotions
- Negative feedback
- Impulsive or inadvertent acts (Freudian slips or comments that "pop out")
- Humiliation or shame
- Behaviors that are different or off from what you'd normally say or do
- The person you'd rather not be or are afraid to be
- What you are running from
- Your greatest fears and unexpressed stuff
- When you wonder, "Why did I say (or do) that?"
- When you have questions about others, such as, "Why are they so selfish/ angry/inconsiderate?"
- Feelings that you don't know where they came from, what they're about, or why they're there
- Anything you project onto others
- Any feelings you don't want to own
- Traits of people you don't like
- The parts that you don't like or want known about yourself
- Traits of people you put on a pedestal
- The characteristics you wish you had

- Your favorite story (fairy tale, myth, or other story)
- Your least favorite story (fairy tale, myth, or other story)

For the people who tick you off, make two columns. Label the left column "Negative Traits" and head the right one "I don't like myself when I …" List all the negative traits of the people who tick you off in the left column and to its right fill in the blank with the negative trait you listed in the left column. Consider which traits were difficult or impossible to accept. These are part of your dark shadow.

For the people who you admire, make two columns. Label the left column "Positive Traits" and head the right one "I love myself when I …" List all the positive traits of the people you admire in the left column and to its right fill in the blank with the positive trait you listed in the left column. Consider which traits were difficult or impossible to accept. These are your light shadow.

In the stories, substitute the word *I* for each main character. Reread the story from this new perspective, and look for traits you can't accept.

Exercise Two: Journey to Your Shadows

Journey to your shadows to meet them, ask questions, and dissipate their grip. (For more about journeying, see "Journeying" under "Tools to Ceremonially Process Your Universal Story" in section III.)

- Ready your space.
- Hold your pen and journal or paper in your lap.
- Get comfortable, and take several deep breaths.
- Set your intention to meet both of your shadows.
- When ready, imagine traveling to a special place you know or love in nature. Examine the area with all your senses.
- Now find an opening, such as a cave, cavern, tree, stream, waterfall, or hole.
- Go inside, and travel down into the earth. Keep moving downward, deep, deep down, until you come out in another place.
- Look around, and see a figure or being approach, whether detailed or amorphous. See that it's a composite of all the traits you don't like.
- Talk with this dark shadow to find out why it's in your life and how it got there. Ask it the following questions, and record its answers. Be sure to write something, even if it's just one word, seems unrelated, or doesn't make sense.
    - What am I most afraid of?

- ♦ What do I need to change in my life?
- ♦ What could stop me from changing?
- ♦ What do I not want to tell myself?
- ♦ What do I not want someone else to know about me?
- ♦ What do you have to teach me?
- ♦ What do I need to learn from you?
- ♦ What is your gift?

- Ask your dark shadow to return with you. Travel back up together, going up and up, to your nature spot. Help your dark shadow get comfortable. Say you're going to leave for a few minutes but will be back.

- Now find another opening, such as a cave, cavern, tree, stream, waterfall, or hole (it could be the same one).

- Enter, and go up into the sky. Travel far upward, up and up, to the upper world. You may sense some resistance at some point, but continue pushing through and moving up until you come out in another place.

- Look around, and see a figure or being approach, whether detailed or amorphous. See that it's a composite of all the traits you like. Visit with the composite you admire.

- Talk with your light shadow to find out why it is in your life and how it got there. Ask it the following questions, and record its answers. Be sure to write something, even if it's just one word, seems unrelated, or doesn't make sense.
  - ♦ What am I most afraid of?
  - ♦ What do I need to change in my life?
  - ♦ What could stop me from changing?
  - ♦ What do I not want to tell myself?
  - ♦ What do I not want someone else to know about me?
  - ♦ What do you have to teach me?
  - ♦ What do I need to learn from you?
  - ♦ What is your gift?

- Ask your light shadow to return with you. Travel back down together, going down and down, to your nature spot. When there, take your light shadow over to your dark shadow.

- Have both shadows talk together. Write down the dialogue.

- When complete, have the two shadows hug or have the light shadow hug the dark shadow. Now give thanks to both of your shadows. Hug both shadows or even all three of you hug together.

- See your dark shadow return to the lower world and your light shadow return to the upper world.
- Now return to your body. Wiggle your toes, move your arms and legs, and open your eyes when ready.
- Review everything you wrote, and look for patterns and beliefs.

Exercise Three: Draw Your Shadows

Step into your dark shadow's "shoes," and draw how you look from your dark shadow's perspective. What are the main unacknowledged patterns and issues you see? What wants to be known that is hidden? What memories, images, and meanings arise? What patterns or beliefs emerge?

Repeat this process with your light shadow.

Projections

We transfer our own unconscious behavior onto others so it appears that they express those qualities. What we see in others is what we don't like or accept in ourselves. Projections are disowned shadow pieces that we see other people act out. Because everything mirrors a story about how we believe the universe works, the whole world is a projection. Projections aren't bad or good. In fact, we all project our stuff onto others so we can see it.

The key to projections is to become aware of them so you can alter them and they don't control you. They also impose your version of reality on others and limit your possible experiences with them. When you embrace a quality in yourself, other people with the same quality will no longer trigger you. Even more, you'll see them act in ways you thought impossible before.

This goes for positive projections too. If you deny your positive traits, you perpetuate the myth that others have something you don't possess.

Exercise One: Owning Projections

Choose one of your beliefs and pick out its core words. For example, the core words in the statement "If I don't work hard, I will die," could be *work, hard, die.*

- To own the projection, flip the statement around. For the above example, this could be, "By working so hard, I am killing myself" or "If I work hard, I will die."
- Using the core words and flipped statement, determine the pattern or belief in this projection. For the example above, it could be, "I don't deserve," "I'm worthless," or "I'm lazy."

Exercise Two: Identify Dark Projections

Think of someone who bothers you. Make a list of what bugs you about them.

- Say out loud, "I dislike ___ because he's ___" and fill in the blanks. For example, "Fred bugs me because he's arrogant."
- Now flip this statement, and insert yourself instead. For the example above, it could be, "I don't like my own arrogance" or "I don't like it when I'm arrogant."
- Next, ask when you've been arrogant in the past, are arrogant now, and could be arrogant in the future.
- What pattern or belief arises?

Exercise Three: Identify Light Projections

Think of someone you admire. Make a list of what you admire about them.

- Say out loud, "I admire ___ because she's ___" and fill in the blanks. For example, "I admire Katie because she's patient and kind."
- Now flip this statement, and insert yourself instead. For the example above, it could be, "I don't accept my own patience and kindness."
- Next, ask when you've been patient and kind in the past, are patient and kind now, and could be patient and kind in the future.
- What pattern or belief arises?

Collage

A collage assembles different parts together to create a new whole. *Collage* derives from the French word *coller*, which means, "glue." This refers to gluing together various different objects on paper, cardboard, or canvas to create a new image. It can include magazine pictures, newspaper clippings, colored paper, ribbons, other artwork, photographs, and found objects.

Making a collage is an intuitive process. You could create a collage for one particular area of your life, an issue you want to discover, or for your life as a whole. Choose images and objects that represent how your issue or life story *feels*. Once it's complete, look at the whole picture metaphorically for such items as color, light and dark areas, form, shapes, and activities, and look for patterns or beliefs to emerge.

Word Breakdown

Words that bug, alienate, or trigger you can indicate patterns and beliefs. Most people have at least one word that causes anger, makes their skin crawl, or elicits some other emotional or kinetic response. Such words indicate hidden subconscious issues. To release their control and discover the underlying pattern or belief, deconstruct such words.

Exercise: Word Breakdown

Chose a word or phrase that triggers you. Repeatedly state it out loud while changing its emphasis. Allow the word or phrase to morph into other words. These will uncover any hidden charge or meaning behind the original word or phrase. It's essential to do this out loud and best to do so while moving, which accesses your subconscious. You'll feel it inside when you've found the meaning.

For example, Wendy reacted whenever she heard the word *surrender*. While doing this exercise, she couldn't get past the syllable "sur." She realized it meant "sir" to her, and a memory flashed of a boss who had verbally abused her in the past. After she processed this incident, she no longer reacted to the word *surrender*. She discovered a core memory that sourced her belief "I'm no good" as well.

If you don't have a particular word or phrase that bugs you, choose a concept or action that does and break that down to find its essence. For example, take the word *murderer*. First, ask what kind of person would commit these acts, such as a murderer doesn't value life, is sick, psychotic, demented, and so forth. Keep breaking it down until you find the specific word or quality with the most emotional charge. Then break that word down.

Hidden Assumptions and Double Binds

Assumptions are beliefs that you hold as inviolate about yourself, others, and the world. The words or phrases you use; your opinions about people, situations, and life; anything you say automatically; the roles you assume; superstitions; and your ideas about family, sex, politics, religion, and spirituality are all assumptions that you hold. Assumptions hide in your subconscious and can be genetically passed down. Example assumptions are blondes are dumb, men are insensitive, women talk a lot, other cultures and religions are clueless, and you must meditate every day to be spiritual.

Double binds are endless loops or catch-22s. They are conditional beliefs that depend upon something to happen in order for them to occur. You think they're true, and that there'll never be any other way. They become unconscious assumptions. These limiting beliefs trap you so you can never achieve or have what you want until that condition is met, and of course, that condition can't be met unless you have what you want. Double binds are lose-lose situations because either there's no choice or they result in death, the ultimate double bind.

Exercise: Assumptions and Double Binds

Using the following format, write a statement for at least five major areas of your life, such as work, relationships, spirituality, places lived, creativity, finances, and health. You will end up with five or more statements. Then reverse the statement, and see where that takes you.

- *Statement:* When I am/have _____, I will be able to do/be _____.
- *Reverse:* I can't do/be _____ unless I am/have _____.

Examples:

Statement: **I**f I'm not perfect, I can't have the life I want.
Reverse: I can't have the life I want unless I'm perfect.

Statement: If I work hard enough, I'll have enough money.
Reverse: If I don't work hard enough, I won't have enough money. If I don't work hard enough, I can't support myself. If I can't support myself, I'll die. I'll die if I overwork.

Statement: When I have enough money I can keep my house.
Reverse: If I don't have enough money, I can't keep my house. If I can't keep my house, I'll be homeless. If I'm homeless, I won't be able to earn money. If I'm homeless, I'll die.

Read all five or more statements and their reverse out loud. Which had the greatest impact? Where did you get stuck? What overall statement embraces everything that keeps you from living your dreams? Look for any major patterns. There's no need to figure out an answer to your statement or to understand the situation. It's not about finding an answer, for this is where we get stuck. Instead, choose the main overall statement that shows up everywhere in your life and look for the core pattern or belief.

Roles

We play many roles throughout our lives. Some we want, others we don't. Most of us not only live immersed in our various roles but also identify so strongly with them we think that's who we are. The roles you identify with create patterns or reflect beliefs. Strong identification makes it difficult to see your self clearly let alone be authentic.

If you think you don't identify with any roles, imagine this: Who would you be without your current activities, schedule, or life demands? Who would you be without your job or identity as a mother, father, worker, boss, student, breadwinner, caretaker, adventurer, artist, politician, activist, or musician? If all your roles were stripped away, who would you be?

If you are panicked, feel the bottom falling out, or are disoriented from this idea, you are identified with a role, and it's defining you. Without it, you don't fully know who you are. On the other hand, if you are calm, centered, and peaceful when those roles are stripped away, you are not identified with them. Realize that roles are what you *do*, not who you *are*.

There are many reasons for identifying with roles. Usually they give us something in return, even if we claim to hate them. It could be a known routine, security, being in control, or receiving acknowledgment. Whatever the reason, it's a story that has you hooked.

Sometimes we take on roles because others want or expect us to and we don't want to let them down, fear loss of others' approval or love, or have cultural, religious, racial, or gender expectations to fulfill. If you have a "good" excuse ready, you are trapped in a story. That role is then "buying" you something. The most negative roles still give you something in exchange, even if just to feed an emotional addiction.

Releasing a role means you no longer identify with it. You can let go how you hold the role and how the role hooks you and instead *choose* to fulfill the actions of a role, such as to have pets, help the earth, or be a mom. This is being the playwright rather than the actor. Switch "I have to" to "I choose to." When you release roles, you also free others from their part in them.

Exercise: Identify Roles

Make a list of all your roles. There are usually dozens of them. Begin with the obvious, such as man, woman, child, husband, wife, father, mother, sister, brother, student, accountant, and painter. Include any identification with groups, organizations, sports teams, and places you live. Next, list the symbolic roles you hold, such as pet owner or light-bearer. Take your time, and identify as many as possible.

When you have a complete list of at least two or more dozen roles, look at them together. Which depend on others? Which stand out? Which carry the most energy, are unrelated, or are separate but really connected? If you didn't have one role, would another be unnecessary? Ask similar questions to learn more about your roles and how they impact your life. Gather any insights or new information that might come. Identify which roles arise from beliefs or create patterns.

Routines and Habits

Like roles, we each engage in repetitive routines and habits. Some are rituals that sustain us like going to a weekly religious or spiritual gathering, participating in a book club, or brushing our teeth every night. Other routines and habits bind us to limiting stories, such as driving the same route to avoid a person or always volunteering to head a committee even though overwhelmed and tired.

Exercise: Indentify Routines and Habits

List your routines and habits, looking for patterns and beliefs. Which ones:

- Support you?
- Hold you back?
- Drain you?
- Can you do differently but don't?
- Can't you live without?

Messages from the Universe

Many spiritual and indigenous traditions around the world have long used nature as a macrocosmic reflection of one's internal microcosm. This is quite revealing and powerful. You can even set an intention or question and look for your answer through an experience or nature. I call these messages from the universe.

For example, one month, I saw or heard a police siren or fire engine every single day, which is highly unusual for where I live. At some point, it caught my attention, and I wondered what was going on. I asked my inner wisdom and heard, "You are moving too fast. You need to slow down, or you'll have a life accident." When I heeded this advice, I didn't hear any more sirens! Your message might be different for the same experience, such as there's a fire in your life to be put out, be more alert, give thanks for your health, or some other interpretation.

Whatever you see or experience that stands out can be viewed as a personal message. This can help you solve problems, find solutions, and get unstuck. You might open a book and a line jumps out that gives a perfect message for your current situation, or you might see a yield sign that tells you how to handle your next meeting.

I knew a woman who used to find messages in license plates. Others use seemingly random signs, symbols, or natural objects that "suddenly" appear in their path or even literally fall on them. An eagle in the sky, a rabbit in a field, bugs hanging on strings, or a raccoon on your deck can give messages or teachings if you tune in and ask as well. It's the next book you open, the next person you talk to, the next story you hear, the next conversation you overhear, or the next whispering tree that might hold an important message.

> ### As Above, so Below; As Within, so Without
> **In the ancient work,** *The Emerald Tablet,* **claimed to be the work of Hermes Trismegistus (a legendary Hellenistic combination of the Greek god Hermes and the Egyptian god Thoth), it states: "That which is above is the same as that which is below; as without, so within."**

Exercise: Messages from the Universe

Purposefully set an intention or ask a question, and look for messages from the universe to bring your answer.

- Find your own wisdom teachers. For instance, try reading road signs or license plates, opening a book at random and reading a passage, or looking for signs in nature (animals, clouds, weather, or plants).
- Dialogue with the sign you receive to learn its message and teaching. Look for repeating themes and identify any limiting patterns or beliefs.

Mirrors

You can use most anything in your life as a mirror for patterns and beliefs. I've used my cars, handwriting, animal companions, and places I've lived as reflections. All can be teachers for what needs to be cleared or developed. If any of your basic processes are "off," such as your ability to eat, digest, eliminate, sleep, love, work and play, this indicates something big is trying to get your attention as well. Use such reflections to discover patterns and beliefs.

Exercise: Identify Your Mirrors

Choose one area of your life, and look at how it has been expressed throughout your entire life. Look for changes. Note what these are and what was happening in your life at that time. This is a great exercise to do with a life timeline. Examine such areas as places lived, work/careers, schools, friends, family, vehicles, finances, handwriting, studies, creative projects, and relationships. Now determine what patterns or beliefs they reflect.

> **Nature as Your Guide**
> One of my teachers, Grandmother Eve, always said that when you attune to the Source of all life, nature shows up to participate. I've found this to be so true. Use nature as your mirror, and ask how it reflects your patterns and beliefs. You'll know the message is yours when you feel your body respond.

Contracts with Others

What if before you were born you made contracts with people to help you learn? What if someone who pushes your buttons isn't doing it *to* you but *for* you?

As an example, before you were born, you wanted to learn self-respect. You needed help, so you searched for someone with such intense love that they could treat you in the opposite way so it would motivate you to learn self-respect. Let's say your dad-to-be stepped up to make this contract.

After birth, your pattern began to emerge. Your dad repeatedly criticized you so you never felt good enough no matter what you did. You began to experience lack of self-respect. Eventually, you internalized your dad's harsh voice, so you criticized yourself. As a result, you pushed to accomplish more to prove you deserved respect. You did this so long that you developed high blood pressure.

Then you remembered your contract. You had to first learn lack of respect so you'd be motivated to develop self-respect. You realized that your dad did such a good job acting his part that it beautifully set you up to seek the respect you so deserve and desire.

Instead of being angry with your dad (or whoever helped), thank him for doing a great job. Acknowledge that he taught you to seek self-respect. His part is now complete, and you can release negative feelings about him. He probably has no memory of creating this contract any more than you do, but that doesn't matter, for the job is now done and done well. You can discharge the chronic anger, hurt, grief, or pain you've carried because of how your dad treated you. Now clear the energy behind this belief through Metaphor-phosis.

There may be multiple people involved in your contract, such as partners, bosses, or siblings, as this brings the pattern into sharper focus. Rather than be angry with or blame the people involved, look at the pattern itself. What happens to you over and over again? What is it teaching that you want and need to learn? How are you not giving these things to yourself or to others? When you respect yourself, you will project this outward and draw it back from others. It then releases the contracts and allows everyone to step off the pathological triangle.

Your own belief system might call such contracts fate, karma, or a classroom where you choose to learn all facets of life so you can gain experience and compassion. Whatever you call it, viewing issues with others as a contract can help shift your perspective so you discover the underlying pattern or belief.

Exercise: Identify Contracts

If you have an issue with one particular person, assume you made a contract together. In your imagination or through a journey, do the following:

- Go back to the time when you made the contract.
- Give thanks to the other person for making that contract with you.
- Say it is now complete.
- Release that person.
- Release yourself.

- Destroy the contract.

Dreams

Dreams are powerful windows into the subconscious and superconscious minds. They are a direct communication from hidden stories. Remembering and working with your dreams is a powerful way to access patterns and beliefs. Dreams give much information about what's happening below surface awareness. We often process unaddressed emotions and issues in our dreams if we don't deal with them during the day. This can lead to restless or poor sleep, even chronic insomnia.

Exercise: Remember Your Dreams

The first step to dream work is to remember your dreams. We all dream but not everyone remembers them, or we remember dreams some times but not others. In time, you'll begin to remember your dreams and more details will emerge. Here are techniques for remembering dreams.

- Put pen and paper/journal by your bed at night.
- Place a glass of water by your bed, and sip before sleep and whenever you awake (this awakens you to go to the bathroom, which helps dream recall).
- Set your intention to remember dreams during the night before falling asleep.
- When you first wake up after a dream or first thing in the morning, immediately write it down.
- When writing down a dream, get in the same body position as when you had it. This helps access it.
- Write down anything you can remember about the dream, even if it's just a feeling, glimpse, or short memory. As you begin to write, more will come.
- Ask yourself, "If I did dream, what would it have been?" Write that down.

Once you've remembered your dreams, there are several ways to work with them and learn their messages as given in "Tools to Unhook from Your Stories" at the end of section III. However, try one of the following now to uncover any hidden patterns or beliefs:

- Cluster parts of a dream together to see how they interrelate. What does this feel like in your life? What patterns or beliefs emerge?
- Look at dream images as a masquerading emotion. A spitting dragon might be anger; an old hag, spitefulness; a greenish blob, indolence or jealousy. Take your major dream images, and see what emotions each represent. Do you frequently feel

that emotion? What usually happens to evoke it? What memories or stories arise? Look for patterns or beliefs.

Death Work

We experience all sorts of death throughout life—physical death, death of an old story, death of a fear, death of a way of being, and symbolic death to who we've been. When we take the sting out of death, we can make it an ally instead. Death is an archetype with lots of cultural beliefs that evoke fear. When you fear death, it holds your energy. Preparing for death releases fears and teaches us how to live.

Some religions believe preparing to die is paramount for life. It can teach you how to die consciously and give you the opportunity to say, "I love you," "I forgive you," and "I apologize" before death. This is an incredible gift for all involved and helps you release limiting patterns and beliefs.

Exercise One: Self-Inquiry

Answer the following questions, and take the indicated actions.

- Who would you like to have talked with that you didn't? Talk with them now.
- What needs to be completed in your life before you die? Start now.
- Who have you wronged or need to tell "I love you," "I forgive you," or "I apologize"? Tell those people now. If not possible, do *Ho'Oponopono* with them.
- What are the changes you want to make in your life? Make them now.
- What do you want to do before you die? What are the books you need to write, the places you need to visit, or the people you need to see? Do so now.
- Look at your ancestral patterns around death. How have people in your family died? Clear any patterns you discover.
- If you had your life to live over again, what would you do differently? Who has wronged you that you have not forgiven? Clear those issues now.

Exercise Two: Chakra Cleansing

Many spiritual traditions believe that our chakras hold heavy energy that can affect how we die and what happens after. Cleanse your chakras regularly to release such energies. This not only assists you in detaching from the physical body at death but also improves your health. If possible, cleanse them every day.

To cleanse your chakras, unwind them one by one from the bottom up and close in the same order. Rinse your hand or fingers in between. To unwind chakras on yourself, move your hand down, counterclockwise, to the left and then circle up and to the right. To close them, move your hand up, clockwise, to the right, and then circle to the left and down.[20]

The seven main chakras are located at nerve plexus in the body. The first is at the base of the pubic bone; the second, two inches below the navel; the third, two inches below the breastbone in the center of the stomach; the fourth, on the center of the chest; the fifth, at the throat; the sixth, the center of the forehead above the eyebrows; and the seventh, at the crown of the head just behind the top of the skull.

Exercise Three: Gift Now

Gift now what you want to give away. Tell whomever you are gifting what you have for them. If you can't, there may be a pattern or belief to uncover.

Exercise Four: Your Will

Write your will now if you haven't already. If you have written it, review it periodically to make sure it reflects your current wishes. As you write or read your will, make note of any physical sensations or emotions that arise. Determine any hidden patterns or beliefs to identify and clear.

Exercise Five: Your Eulogy and Tombstone

Write your eulogy and tombstone for how you want to be remembered. For example: "On (today's date), I (your name) died and was buried." Now continue with how you lived, loved, died, and other ways you'd like to be remembered. Read this to your family and friends, as appropriate, or to at least one other person.

Exercise Six: Unlived Wishes

Seriously consider this: Imagine you are truly on your deathbed and will die tomorrow. Was your life a complete success? If the answer is yes, skip the rest. If the answer is no, answer these questions, and use them to discover your patterns. Act on your answers as well. If you can't, that indicates a pattern or belief.

- Why was your life not a success?
- What areas have you not lived to your full potential?
- What would you like to have accomplished that you didn't?

---

20   I learned this technique from Alberto Villoldo. It is also in his book, *Shaman, Healer, Sage: How to Heal Yourself and Others with the Energy Medicine of the Americas.* Crown Archetype. New York, NY, 2000, pages 54-55.

III

After I determined the main patterns behind the insomnia issue, I realized that sleep was a method I had used to not deal with my feelings. If I went to sleep, I knew I'd feel differently in the morning. However, years of bottling up my emotions could no longer be ignored. My subconscious was too busy handling issues at night, so restlessness woke me.

To ceremonially process all these matters, I used many tools, such as ritual, metaphors, archetypes, myths, imagery, dialoguing, dream work, journeying, vision quests, reframing, power walk, shadow and death work, soul retrieval, messages from the universe, and body wisdom. And as I used them, my soul's journey began to surface.

To work on the issue of feeling unloved, I did several journeys and rituals. As I did so, I felt anger rise at being unprotected from my sister. I realized that because of that I had set stiff boundaries that were actually inflexible, hurtful, and imprisoning walls. My shoulder twitched then, and I abruptly understood they hunched forward in an attempt to protect myself. Now they wanted to relax and fall back. Just realizing all this was enough to help me let go. I heard a voice say, "Trust the universe," and saw an image of me lying cradled in the palm of Spirit. As I followed that image, my shoulders relaxed back again.

I further realized I didn't let love in because I felt undeserving. I knew people loved me, I just couldn't take it in or feel it inside. After all, as a child, I felt I was either alone, left behind, or taken away from what I loved, so how could I be worthy of it? This feeling of unworthiness extended to the divine Source energy as well. Somehow I must have done something wrong to have these experiences, and so I didn't deserve love. That meant it would always be taken away no matter what I did.

This pattern resurfaced as I focused on my recurring sore throats. I journeyed into my throat and learned there that it closed down whenever I didn't speak my truth. Until I found my voice, not only would sore throats recur but also sleep would continue to elude me. A memory arose then of being a little girl and never hearing my dad say, "I love you." When I processed the journey, I understood that I had thought I didn't deserve love due to my childhood losses and the types of male relationships I had chosen. Apparently, I felt unworthy of love. As a result, I believed I had to earn love or do something to deserve it. In other words, I presumed I couldn't be loved for who I was, so I protected my heart by shutting it down.

I again thought of how my dad's parents divorced when he was twelve and that he rarely saw his mother afterward. It seemed he also didn't have the love he needed. I knew then that it was an ancestral issue too. I did a journey and learned that first comes the self-trust and self-love and the rest would follow. Most major relationships I had chosen in my life were with people who didn't see or support me because I didn't support or speak up for myself, so how could anyone else? I understood from this that I needed to fully love and accept myself first before I'd be able to let love in from other people, friends, and the community.

To ceremonially process all of the above issues, I did two vision quests. The archetype I chose for both quests was that of the Quester, or Seeker. The first vision quest I did alone on a friend's land. I hiked the wooded mountains, wrote in my journal, charted my dreams, and reflected on my life.

One of my most powerful experiences occurred when I felt prompted to hike in a direction I didn't particularly want to go. However, the urge was so strong, I followed it anyway. When I did so, I arrived at a spot where an entirely new vista opened up. Not only was the path from there obvious, but I also saw new possibilities. This experience repeated several times throughout that quest.

During my second vision quest, I again searched for my power spot and learned that my gut reaction ultimately determined its location. I needed to follow my inner guidance no matter how things looked, for my internal urges always led me to the perfect position. I now knew this was how to find my place in life. A year later, when I returned to do my vision quest renewal, I immediately found my site with no problem. This was a perfect symbol for the inner change that had begun from that vision quest work.

That second vision quest also sparked a wake-up call to continue working on all my issues in general. I had become aware of my limiting stories and core beliefs and felt ready to transform my life. A stream of dreams flooded my nights, many about rooms and houses. They started in the basement of my first childhood home, moved through that house to its attic, and then across the street to my second home, where again I started in the basement and later moved upstairs. I knew these meant I was processing subconscious, conscious, and higher conscious material in my youth.

As I worked these dreams through dialoguing, gestalt, and journeys, they began to change. Soon I dreamed of huge houses, mansions filled with desserts, my ultimate dream house, and creating or rearranging house structures. All of them reflected the increased nourishment I experienced along with finding my place in my outer life.

After processing these old childhood issues, I began to experience more openness, empowerment, and self-confidence. I recognized that my heart had first started closing down after my family moved in my teens and then during my first marriage. Additionally, I realized that my Journey West had been a ritual to help free and open my heart, and as a result, I experienced completely different worlds and possibilities. I knew I was still finding my place and was getting closer, as I dreamed that I inherited my second childhood home where my life had blossomed.

At this point, I felt compelled to create a more formal ceremony in order to launch my new self into the world. To do so, I planned a ritual on my birthday. I invited a group of very close friends and family to come witness and support this process. During it, I read aloud my old core beliefs one by one and burned the strips of paper upon which they had been written. Afterward, I wrote my new core beliefs on slips of ribbon, read these aloud, and tied them into the branches of our blossoming apple tree. Like prayer flags, the ribbons stayed in the tree for months after to strengthen my new beliefs every time I looked at them.

To focus on the pattern of lack, I drew a tarot card and got the Wheel of Fortune. I used this with a gestalt process by "stepping" into the image and speaking back from that place. As I did so, I realized it was exactly how I felt, like a Wounded Healer strapped to a wheel and revolving over and over through her old patterns, unable to release the alternating victim and rescuer roles. I further worked this through several dreams that occurred later. Over time, it became evident this old universal story was part of my soul's journey. I continued to process this with several new series of dreams that arose after my second vision quest.

Dreams became major teachers for me then, like a crack between the worlds that opened and merged all levels of my consciousness. Some were teaching, restorative, or prophetic dreams while others revealed inner issues and wounds or prompted stories that I wrote. All brought me guidance, solace, and healing. Several of these dreams repeated and so became serial dreams that strongly influenced my life. They helped identify and transform my major life patterns, but even more importantly, they directed me to my soul's journey.

The first dream series actually started before my second vision quest. It also lasted the longest, almost twenty-two years. The scenarios and events were always different, but the theme remained the same: I would meet a man whose energy matched mine. When I ceremonially processed these dreams through dialoguing, journey, or dance, I knew they indicated the need to foster male qualities inside so I could match and balance my female self. I called these dreams "Inner Man."

The next dream series, the "Key" dreams, began after my second vision quest. In these, I'd either end up with a key that would open a treasure trove or else prevent world domination by evil. In all Key dreams, there were obstacles to overcome and rewards at the end. When I processed them through gestalt or dialogue, I ultimately understood the key reflected my personal transformation. I learned that the key was in me, that *I* was the key, and lastly, the key opened the door to my room, which became the door to my Self in my heart.

As I processed these dreams, I realized something interesting had happened after my second vision quest. My world seemed to split into an outer life path where things improved and an inner one where I continued to descend deeper into my core issues. In my outer life, I claimed my place through a new clinic, publishing books, and more teaching. Yet despite this, my inner life became the navigator and drove my outer life in the direction of my soul's journey, which has become the greater theme that has continued throughout my entire life.

This became particularly evident with a spirit dream I had three years after my second vision quest. In it, a harpy flew onto the hood of my car and stared at me. It was so vivid and real, I couldn't forget the harpy's energy as it challenged me to face it. When I journeyed to the harpy, I learned she came to help me see my dark side and what I wouldn't look at. She then flew me to a stump that had been inhabited by a magician and told me to turn it into my own alchemical laboratory. I was to use it to bring my authentic self into manifestation.

After this journey, I chose the mythical archetype Inanna as my universal story and consciously chose to make her descent. Examining my life thus far, it seemed that through giving up so much due to poor sleep, I was descending anyway. Besides, I wanted to knowingly embrace my dark side. Little did I know what I was signing up for. Still, it felt like I had no choice, for I was already on this path.

Inanna, the ancient Sumerian goddess of love, fertility, grain, war, sexual love, emotions, and the morning and evening star, is the Queen of Heaven and Earth too. Like all archetypes, she encompasses many qualities, including being a healer, life giver, composer of songs, and a symbol of youth, independence, and the powerful feminine. As well, she was always wandering, searching for her home and her power. This last part at least seemed a perfect fit.

As with most myths, there are many versions of the Inanna story, but the one that most encompassed my experience dates back 3,500 or more years ago. Called Inanna's Descent to the Underworld, in this version, Inanna feels called to visit her sister, Ereshkigal, the Queen of the Underworld. To prepare for this, she girds herself with all her powers, yet as she descends, she is stripped of each one at seven successive gates. Finally naked, she greets Ereshkigal, who fastens on her the eye of death, turns her into a corpse, and hangs her on a meat hook to rot. After Inanna's flesh falls off, her bones are tossed into the fire.

When Inanna died, so did nature, and nothing would grow anymore. Inanna's maternal grandfather, the god of wisdom, Enki, intervened by fashioning mourners to moan with Ereshkigal, who also grieved the loss of her sister. Ereshkigal then agreed that Inanna could be reborn if another person shared her time there. As a result, Inanna was regenerated in the underworld.

Unlike the others, Inanna's consort, Dumuzi, did not mourn her but lived lavishly and relaxed instead. Displeased, Inanna chose him to alternately rule with her every half-year. In some versions, Dumuzi tries to escape his fate, but ultimately, his sister, Geshtinanna, volunteered to go in his place. This allowed Inanna to ascend and unite with her consort.

This myth is a story of the heroine's journey into the mysteries. Here she gives up all that is not true to her life path, faces her dark shadow, is crucified on the underworld peg, and then resurrects to join with her masculine self in full conscious awareness of her dark side. This is a beautiful metaphor for what occurs when we release old patterns, for it is through our fully embracing them that we achieve transformation and new life. This is truly alchemy of the soul.

As I reflected on how sleeplessness had stripped so much away from me, it actually felt like I enacted this myth in my life. I realized that the threshold of my own Inanna descent to the lower world first began in my late twenties with a numinous dream while living at Mariah's house in Montana the spring before I went to Astara. In that dream, I flew through the air to celestial music while being guided to a mountaintop. There I was shown an opening in the mountain with stairs leading down and told to follow them. Since then, I had definitely begun the descent, but after the Harpie dream, I consciously chose to do so.

The descent theme continued with a new dream cycle, the "Hanged Man" series. The first of these dreams began two days after my second vision quest during the night before I was to share my experience with the group. I had spent the prior two days listening to everyone else's experiences while also processing my own. I had wanted to speak earlier, but one way or another, everyone else kept jumping in. This challenged my newfound ability to claim my spot, so I felt conflicted. The first Hanged Man dream occurred then.

In it, I was to meet someone in a huge cathedral. As I waited in the dark, an urgent force like a wind yet not a wind grabbed me so firmly that I couldn't move and soared upward. As I rocketed up, I lost sight of all surroundings. Interestingly, I wasn't scared but just surrendered, for I knew a cosmic force held me.

Then suddenly, the great power turned me upside down, held me by the ankles, and pushed me downward with great speed. It felt wonderful to let go, allowing the cosmos to hold and move me wherever it willed—until I saw the cobblestone street below. Now fear raced through my veins as I thought I'd be crushed on the rocks. As I came closer and closer, I began to chant, "Om, om, om," until the force abruptly slowed, turned me head side up, and gently placed me on my feet.

This experience seemed much more than a dream but rather a cosmic event too. After it, I felt fully supported by the Divine. I knew it, I felt it; it was in me now. I was a babe in the hands of Great Spirit. When I processed this dream, I realized that I had copied the reversed position of the tarot's Major Arcana card, the Hanged Man. In that hanged position, I felt totally held and suspended by the universe. I didn't have any influence but could only surrender to the will of the cosmos and, as a result, felt enormous peace. The next day, I claimed my spot when I told everyone I would go last. This felt like a powerful choice, which only occurred after my Hanged Man dream.

This magical dream repeated almost to the day a year later during my vision quest return. It was similar in that the force grabbed and moved me beyond my control. Yet this time, it almost smashed into the ceiling above as well as almost crashed below. Again I surrendered, and the force kept me safe. Both dreams felt like gifts, messages, and a direction all in one.

The Hanged Man dream repeated many times over the next twelve years. (Interestingly, the Hanged Man is card number twelve in the tarot deck!) In retrospect, I realized this dream of divine support and guidance occurred during the most difficult years of insomnia and into my meltdown period.

This dream series almost viscerally reminded me to surrender and let go. I knew this position meant to see things in a different way than the norm; for me, it meant that there was no way through my unraveling process but through it. I must let go and trust the course, for the cosmos had my back (or ankles as in my dreams). I just needed to let go along the way. For days after the dream, I felt comforted and guided, but it never erased the increasing pain.

The Hanged Man dreams also helped me to release the Wounded Healer roles of victim or rescuer. I understood that who I had been was dissolving so I could be reshaped into who I was becoming. The journey of Inanna is truly about surrender and trust that from dissolution comes new life, much like what the caterpillar must go through in its chrysalis to become a butterfly.

About six months after the first Hanged Man dream, I had a second pivotal spirit dream in my descent course. Short and simple, the dream was quite cryptic. In it, two of my spiritual teachers appeared, Baba Hari Dass (Babaji) and Sai Baba. Babaji told me that Sai Baba said, "Red oaks grow over black pillars on dark ground." As he said these words, I saw Sai Baba standing in a nearby shadow. He stepped into the light and stood out in his normal orange. After he left, Babaji repeated, "Red oak trees grow over black pillars on dark ground."

More than four years passed before I could ceremonially process this dream. At this point, I had already completed my birthday ritual and was claiming my place in outer life. Now my inner life drew me further into my descent as I worked with this dream.

To do so, I first drew it in my journal and then danced it, repeating the phrase out loud over and over. Dancing the dream helped tremendously. It opened me to an inner essence that slowly took over. I felt the power and rhythm of the red, the hardness and strength of the tree, the fluidity and flexibility of growing, the straight and solid black pillar, and the vast mystery of the void and unknown. That is when what I call the "Gates Work" started, a major part of my soul's journey.

The gates journey began as I felt compelled to journey further with the dance. I don't know why; I just knew I had to obey the call. I followed it and saw a door leading to the hollow interior of the tree. I entered and found a set of stairs over dark ground. I climbed downward until they disappeared into an inky black pool. Somehow I knew I couldn't return the way I had come but must go on. I realized that if I followed them, however, I would sink and drown. Terror struck my heart.

And yet, I slowly followed the stairs anyway. There was no preparation, no preamble, but only immediate submersion, for in that instant, I knew I had to give everything up. I could not go back even if I wanted to, as the door was locked behind me. The immediacy of the drowning was overwhelming, for it demanded that I let go of all I knew.

That is when the realization of the meaning of this descent shocked me. I must willingly lose myself and die in order to continue. I must give up all parts of myself, all powers, and all illusions of who I think I am and what I can do. I must continue downward and give up everything until I stand naked in the depths and have my ego stabbed upon the sacred spike. Then I must burn in the fires of transformation until the Divine spark resurrects within. I shuddered at the thought of what lay before me, a descent into the murky depths where pain, sorrow, sadness, heartache, terror, loss, and, ultimately, death lurked.

And yet I could not go back. I realized the descent must be made voluntarily, and I must willingly give up my all. And so I moved down the stairs into the inky pool and drowned. As I did, I genuinely felt a part of me die. I grieved the pain, the loss, the emptiness, and the fear of the unknown. Although I tried to resurface, I couldn't go further at that point and had to stop the journey there.

When I recorded this journey, I suddenly remembered a recent dream where I was in the basement of my beloved second childhood home. In its dingy and murky depths, someone was trying to kill me. From this, I knew that in my dreams I was already making this descent, and that the old subconscious patterns and beliefs must die before I could create new life. If I didn't follow this descent, my unaccepted subconscious stuff would kill me anyway, and I'd join the ranks of the living dead. It seemed that no matter what I did, I'd be stripped bare and die anyway, so I knew I must continue.

As with the Hanged Man dreams, I had to surrender control. I had to give up trying to understand and to know who, what, where, why, how, or when. Instead, I needed to just follow the cosmic energy as it led me into the depths of the lower world, step by step. I didn't need a reason or explanation, for the Divine has its own ways. I only needed to surrender and follow its guidance through my inner direction.

After that first gates journey, I researched red oak trees and discovered they grow where I was born and raised. That reinforced this experience as part of my soul's journey and so helped me surrender even more. I intuitively knew this "water" gate was the first of many to come. Indeed, later that month, I felt an urge to repeat the journey. This time I emerged from the inky pool and climbed onto dry earth. Much relieved, I followed a short path until it ended at a wall of earth. There I stayed, unable to go farther. Interestingly, a few weeks later, I had a dream in which I drowned, but this time, I did not struggle and had no problem with it.

Seven months passed before I could attempt the gates journey again. I started by entering the door in the red oak tree over the black pillar on dark ground. This time, though, I quickly moved through the water gate, came to the earthen wall, and easily passed through. I felt no resistance or difficulty, just thick, dark dirt everywhere. I was thankful it didn't constrict or bury me. But still not knowing what lay ahead, I had to surrender to the process. I continued moving through the dirt and, at some point, started sliding down a tunnel. I slipped and slid around curves and corners, descending deeper into the bowels of the earth.

The end didn't come, and so I stopped the journey. I knew I had gone far into the earth gate but must compost until I was allowed to move forward again. As I processed this journey, I realized the earth element of my body, digestion and assimilation, was my current focus in the outer world. I also knew that it was good I had started gardening again that summer, and that I should continue to put my hands in the dirt and feet on the earth.

Three months later, during the cold depths of winter, I thought about the gates and laid down to journey. I was so tired from lack of sleep that I could barely see the images. Eventually, two sphinxes came and flew me into the red oak tree, down its stairs, through the pool, and back into the earth gate. Again I traveled a long time through the dirt wall and, after a very long descending slide, slipped out and into a small pool of water.

The sphinxes led me into the next room, where they set me in a tub filled with warm water. Dancing fire elementals surrounded me, but I barely noticed their flames or heat. I rested and slept a long time before I became aware of my surroundings again. That's when I saw a long, curving staircase descend from the center of the tub and into the fiery cavern below.

I stood and followed the narrow stairs into the yawning pit. It seemed to extend thousands of feet down, as I couldn't see its bottom. Everything around me burned with fire and danced with flames. I kept descending but found no end. I stopped the journey, realizing I must now ripen in the fire gate for a while.

Indeed, it was two years until I could continue the gates journey, which occurred spontaneously as I lay in bed one day, feeling a painful, gaping hole in my chest where my heart should have been. Rather than starting at the red oak tree, I immediately found myself at the top of the fiery cavern. The dancing flames now formed fire elementals that beat a huge mother drum in their center. This heartbeat of Mother Earth matched that of my empty heart. I then knew I could pass through the fire gate this time. I headed down the narrow stairs suspended above the cavernous depths of earth's fiery bowels and descended far downward.

Eventually, I spotted the churning sea of molten lava below. It spurt and bubbled, hissed and spattered. Searing heat raked my body, and sweat trickled down my skin. The rumbling drums grew louder and beat harder, their rhythm more urgent. I reached the bottom stair and stared at the roiling mass. Once more I needed to yield, only this time to a molten pool.

Although drowning had been difficult, still I loved water and could accept it. Fire was another matter altogether, and I was frightened indeed. Yet I had already delivered my all at the drowning and had survived the smothering earth. I had to trust that fire would demand no more than what I had already given. My feet carried me toward the lava until I was suspended midair and then slowly submerged. I cried inside although my inner wisdom knew that it would be all right. And so I surrendered again and let myself be carried under—head, body, mind, and all.

As before, I felt no searing pain but instead great peace. I surfaced like a dolphin in the deep blue sea and splashed with joy. I discovered that I loved the fire and its burning light. I even craved and needed it around and within me. I swam in the lava, did synchronized tricks, and sat under a molten waterfall, letting it flow through the hole in my chest. I knew eventually I'd need to move on, but not yet. Only when I truly felt ready did I turn onto my back and rest.

I floated a long while, letting the current carry me as it willed. Eventually, I drifted toward the other end of the cavern, and the current, strong now, slipped me through its wall and into a dark tunnel. Again I floated while the lava cooled. Mud and then water blended, and this soothed me. I remembered that after I passed through all the other gates, I had entered earth and then water. Here it was again.

As the stream carried me through the tunnel, the fire in my chest died, and my entire body cooled. I felt at peace. Then a light appeared at the end of the tunnel, and the stream soon swept me outdoors. I was delivered head first into a mud pond and then a pool with waterfalls. Completely cleansed, I had finally survived the transformative fire into new birth.

Several figures in white robes appeared, dried me off, and put me in a white, flowing robe with wing-like sleeves. Then a gorgeous goddess arrived, and with a jolt, I realized it was Aphrodite. She was radiant with long, curly hair banded with jewels and a white sheer dress studded with flowers. Putting one hand on my chest and the other on my back, she sent beautiful love energy through me.

I did not know much about Aphrodite except how the patriarchy painted her as a sex goddess. But she taught me then that she is love itself and understands all levels and types of relationships. After a moment, a realization flashed when I understood that her consort is Vulcan (Hephaestus), the fiery god of volcanoes and lava, from where I had just come! Fire and water, water and fire; they balance, cleanse, and purify one another. The fire of passion and balm of dew, united.

Now Aphrodite was a balm to my heart, and her healing hands filled me with her love and nurturance. She took me from the pool and to a forest glade where she bade me lie down. The spirits surrounded me again and poured mud into my chest hole to fill it. Mice came and created a flower shape with a garland, placed it on my chest, and filled it with mud and gold. Aphrodite poured liquid gold into this flower heart, and the spirits worked the mud and gold together to form a new heart in my chest. The physical pain in my heart instantly disappeared.

I saw tiny wings sprout from the sides of this new heart. Aphrodite along with the mice and spirits showered me with exquisite white flowers until I was buried. The flowers smelled so sweet and pure, so simple and innocent, that my heart felt full again. I had no need to move or seek more; I only wanted to rest in peace and stillness. I slept for I do not know how long.

When I rose from this journey, I knew I had been birthed into the air gate. The spirits blessed me with flowers, and Aphrodite initiated me into a new relationship with myself. I felt the tiny wing buds on my heart and knew that someday they would help my heart fly and maybe even soar. After that gate, I felt completely renewed and reborn. My heart felt whole again. I could see its doors open and light shine within.

I journeyed through the gates several times after this but was never able to go farther than fly in a clear sky. Exactly two years later, I finally entered the next gate. This journey began with no intentions to go through the gates at all, but as I started, a snowy owl took me to the red oak tree, and I found myself passing through them again.

This time, when I entered the air gate, Aphrodite directed me into the sky. I flew upward and forward, pulled toward some unseen destination. Eventually, I saw an archway, and as I flew through it into an area filled with golden light, I heard that I had just entered the ether gate. This amazed me, as I hadn't even conceived of another gate beyond the first four elemental ones. Yet here I was.

I walked down an aisle and saw light beings everywhere. A large fountain stood in a central area that I felt guided to step into. I did so and was bathed by warm, golden light. The journey ended there, and that was the last of my gates journeys for over twelve years. No matter how many other times I journeyed, I could never move or see beyond the ether gate. I knew there was nothing more I could do, nowhere else I must go.

As I now reviewed my journals and all the pieces of the descent process throughout my life, I saw how poor sleep and its resulting symptoms felt exactly like these journeys. I had passed through the gates and been metaphorically drowned, buried, burned, and held in limbo. I had hung on the meat hook for my flesh to rot and fall off and then burned in the fire until every last bit of my old patterns was seared away and I was just bleached bones buried in the earth with nothing left to give as I developed a new relationship with myself.

In my outer world, I even felt dead during this phase. I had journeyed so deeply into the underworld in my life that I hadn't recognized how dead I had become, how much was missing from my life, or how much I had given up. All I had left was the spark of my spirit to renew me. The gates occurred during the worst years of insomnia, when I felt so much being stripped away. Even when I began to ascend with the ether gate, I still continued to lose more of myself until I hit meltdown during menopause.

This Inanna journey was so completely encompassing that it has been a major part of my soul's journey. Identifying with this myth gave meaning to my experience, helped me accept the process, and offered hope that someday I'd ascend to normalcy again if I could just "hang in there" and gain emotional distance.

As I underwent this myth and journeyed through each gate, the middle of night railings and breakdowns became fewer and fewer. Even if I was awake much of the night, I wouldn't be very affected, except physically. I'd listen to recorded books, write children's stories in the dark, adjust my plans for the next day, and in general surrender to what was happening. But I wouldn't be angry, sad, depressed, or emotionally overwrought as before. I was unhooking from my stories.

While I ceremonially processed all my different dreams and journeyed through the gates, I realized why it had been so tough for me to accept something that was quite obvious to most others about their lives, that my path and place in life was different. I had spent so long trying to fit in that it took great effort for me to turn aside and accept my unique journey, even as I was obviously following it.

Additionally, I had learned at a formative age to be a good girl, both as a midwesterner and also as a lonely child who didn't want the negative attention my sister received. I suddenly realized that she was probably trying to follow her own path and, since it was quite different from everyone else's, had gotten lots of flack for it. This helped me sympathize with her and release much of the anger I felt toward her.

I completed the formal processing of the Inanna descent during my croning ritual, when I marked the transition of mothering to that of baby crone. During it, I walked a labyrinth and at its central fire gave thanks to Inanna for helping through so many difficult years. I burned a doll made of paper slips naming the issues I wanted to release. After walking out, I crawled through a "birthing canal" created by my close friends to symbolize new birth and mark the transformed woman I was becoming.

My soul's journey led me to the depths of the underworld to face my dark side. From my birth through my childhood losses, our family's move at age fifteen, all of my relationships, and the dreams, I had melted into goop in my chrysalis where I faced the dark shadow of my limiting patterns and core beliefs. When I finished transforming the marrow of my being, I could start my journey again.

Through all these experiences, I learned that in the wound lies the gift; in the wound lies the power, the understanding, and the light. Our running from our wounds and resisting them causes our pain.

Starting with the Rooms dream, all my ceremonies, rituals, dreams, and journeys ultimately taught me to stop looking outside myself for my place in life. Originally, I had taken the Rooms dream literally and acted on it literally, whereas it really meant for me to find my place in relationship to myself. The Key dreams taught me that my room, my place in life, is inside of me, and ultimately that's in my spiritual heart. That's what I had really seen when the light shone forth from my room in Rooms.

Hanged Man taught me to surrender to what was happening in my life, from poor sleep to having to give up so much to being stripped bare and left in the fires of transformation for as long as it took. It further reassured me that I was held in and guided by the hands of Great Spirit. The Inner Man was not just a metaphor for my masculine self but also gave me impetus and perseverance to search and find what I needed for my transformative growth.

Two years after my croning, I broke free of my chrysalis. At the same time, the house, Inner Man, Key, and Hanged Man dreams all stopped. I had linked with my masculine self, used the key to find my room, and survived the death of my limiting patterns and beliefs on the meat hook in the lower world. Now I could learn to soar free and create my new life. One year later, that's exactly what I began to do.

This is my meaning for what happened to me, the work that fit all the pieces together, and the myth that matched my soul's journey. We each hold our own meanings to our unique life experiences. Other sources are but guideposts to the truth within. Ceremonially processing the universal stories that best fit me was what greatly helped to transform my life. This process can help you transform your stories of pain into those of power as well.

Universal Stories

Now that you've discovered a limiting pattern or core belief, how do you discharge its energy so it no longer hooks you? It's one thing to write about it in your journal or share it with a friend, but its quite another to shift its energy and create a new experience.

We know what doesn't work: If you try to "resolve" cyclical patterns or change limiting beliefs, you just exchange one story for another; if you work on the patterns over and over, you continue to feed them; or if you try to correct any deep-seated emotional issues, you just keep them alive. All of these approaches continue to inform your life with the old patterns and beliefs so you collude with their messages. This is truly staying stuck in the chrysalis "goo," never transforming into a butterfly that soars free. To unhook from your patterns and beliefs, you have to neutralize their energy.

Shifting to Higher Consciousness

To diffuse the energy of your stories, it's necessary to shift your level of awareness to a different state of consciousness. Einstein made the wise observation that problems cannot be solved by the same level of awareness that created them. This is true of our limiting patterns and beliefs as well. Since they reside on the physical, emotional, and mental levels, we must take them to a different level in order to neutralize their energy and shift our perspective. And that is the level of the universal story. It is only on this level that you create a core shift in your being so your life changes.

Working on the soul level with a universal story is where you design your entire garden. It's the place where you dig up roots, till the soil, and landscape your desired patterns. The mythic level embraces all the others—the mental, emotional, and physical—but in a universal way. It is greater than you are. On this level, you rise to a larger vantage point so you get "out of the trees and see the forest." This is where you make the big, lasting changes in life.

Universal Stories

The level of the universal story is the place of metaphors, myths, archetypes, fairy tales, folk stories, and images. These are universal because they contact forces common to everyone regardless of gender, culture, race, religion, politics, or nation. They are original models of something, pure essence of energy, and enduring, elemental ideas and universal principles from which others are copied. And they contain multiple layers of meaning from which we individually garner our own interpretation and meaning too. All tell a larger account of enduring truths and teachings and are timeless and transcendent. They are truly the language of the soul.

Metaphors, myths, archetypes, fairy tales, folk stories, and images are different from a symbol, which is a sign, shape, or object that is used to represent something. For instance, a heart shape is the symbol of love, a dove means peace, and a dollar sign (or euro, etc.) indicates money. You probably even have your own symbols to represent things unique to you. However, symbols vary over time while metaphors, myths, archetypes, fairy tales, folk stories, and images are not personal but unchanging ancient universal principles or dynamic patterns.

You live various metaphors, myths, archetypes, fairy tales, folk stories, and images at different stages of your life. Each part of you connects with some archetype. Likewise, each character in a story represents a separate part of you. When a metaphor, myth, archetype, or image is active in your life, it calls forth its particular energies, stories, themes, or plots. It also gives a unique gift and challenge to explore. The ones active in your life determine the stories you repeatedly experience based upon the core beliefs rooted in your subconscious.

Universal Stories Live Inside of Us

Metaphors, myths, archetypes, and images live inside of us—all the heroes and heroines, all the villains and victims, all the gods and goddesses are within us all. They are vehicles of universal energies, not their source, and so access the sacred power or divine spark within. Each of us has our inner Zeus, Hathor, Odin, or Sita. Each is already a part of your deepest self.

The gods and goddesses of old were not seen as separate living entities but were the names for natural powers of the world. For example, Gaia encompassed energies of the earth; Mars, wars; Ceres, grain; and Vesta, sacred fires. They were powers of nature to be honored and invoked for their specific qualities. They were personified so that people could relate to them. It is only when taken literally that they became idols.

Why Shift to a Universal Story?

There are three major reasons to shift your cyclical patterns and limiting beliefs into universal stories. The first is that they take you out of the place of reactivity, either emotional or mental; the second is that they bypass the mammalian brain of fear, or fight-or-flight; and the third is that you connect with your soul and Source energies where you link with your authentic self.

The result is that when you switch to a universal story, the reptilian brain doesn't react and go into survival mode. Instead, you link with energies greater than you are. In addition, when you connect with your Higher Self at the mythic level, you are empowered to create lasting change. This is one of the unique steps that activates the Metaphor-phosis process.

Transforming your personal story to a universal one also:

- Aligns you with your soul's journey rather than your day-to-day story
- Takes you out of a personal experience and broadens your perspective
- Provides tools to access inner energies in conflict with one another
- Liberates you from culture, race, and gender
- Eases your heart and decreases anxiety
- Harmonizes your mind and emotions
- Inspires you to the adventure of life
- Calls you to live life at a new level
- Teaches acceptance of your journey and tolerance of others' as well

Going to the universal story reframes your experience in a larger context, takes you out of the place of trauma-drama, and sets you as cocreator with the universe. This type of lateral shift sets you free and cracks open all possibilities. Rather than "me and my problems," universal stories work with grand and sacred energies that impart insight, understanding, and realization. These then alter your perspective and neutralize your patterns, catalyzing real change. This is how you transform from a pupa in the chrysalis to a butterfly that soars free.

Example Metaphors, Myths, Archetypes,
Fairy Tales, Folk Stories, and Images

Universal stories link with Source universal energies. They teach us how to understand the powers of nature, how to deal with what happens, and how to live under any circumstances. They help us put aside a passing moment of anger, fear, grief, or sadness and give us direction in life. They instill compassion for our selves as well as for others. They show that we are not alone; other people experience what we do—similar hurts, losses, betrayals, or abandonments. In sum, universal stories speak of our humanity and show us how to live.

Metaphor: Water is a metaphor for our emotions and the subconscious while a tree is a metaphor for the different stages of life. Physical conditions often have the potential for being used as metaphors. For instance, being overweight could be a metaphor for carrying the weight of extra responsibilities; neck pain can be a metaphor for someone who's a pain in the neck; and constipation might be a metaphor for holding onto something (or someone) instead of letting it (him or her) go.

Myth: European dragon myths are usually about greed and violence while Asian ones involve good fortune, and the Chinese dragon is about strength and power. Jonah and the whale is a myth about how transformation occurs within the very belly of our beings.

Archetype: The jock, mystic, warrior, caregiver, magician, ruler, sage, jester, hero, maiden, wise woman, seeker, feminine, and masculine are only a few of the many archetypes available to us all. Time, fate and death are familiar archetypes as well. The philosopher's stone represents the quest for spiritual illumination: mountains of wisdom and transcendence; caves of the womb and mystery; fire of transformation and purification; water of intuition and emotions; eagle of seeing the bigger picture and connecting with spirit; and snake of transformation.

Fairy tale: *The Emperor's New Clothes* explains what happens when we go along with other's ideas and opinions rather than express our own truth.

> *Folk story:* **Vasilisa tells us that when we listen to our intuition (her doll), we can overcome danger (Baba Yaga).**
>
> *Imagery:* **Salvador Dali's painting** *The Persistence of Memory* **portrays a melting pocket watch to depict the relativity of time and space. Myriad tarot decks are filled with interesting and provocative images. (You do not have to use or know the tarot itself to employ its images.)**

Your Soul's Journey

Universal stories take you out of the reptilian, limbic, and neocortex parts of the brain so you work on the level of the sacred and your soul. This is the place that informs all parts of you, that sends "instructions" for how to live your life so you have particular experiences and learn specific lessons. Your soul is like the conductor or director of your life, organizing the various plots from beginning to end into one majestic play or interweaving the major themes into one grand symphony. It charts your life journey through universal stories.

The archetypes that are active in your life determine the stories that you live. Over time, you can recognize one or two universal stories that give central meaning and purpose. They are usually long-standing; relate to your sense of identity, calling, and purpose in life; and are the way you see the world. These then comprise your soul's journey. This is where your soul's director and conductor live and where you make lasting changes.

> ### Physicality and Imagery
>
> **Imagery is powerful. It comes first, is followed by thoughts and words, and only then does what is seen come into form. It's like preparing a meal or building a shed. You first "see" what you wish to eat or the finished shed, and then thoughts arise about how to prepare the food or build the shed, what materials are needed, and other tasks. We all have these images, but we may not be aware of them, like not remembering your dreams even though everyone dreams several times a night.**
>
> **Imagery can create physical responses in the body. Try an experiment right now to experience this for yourself. See something in your hand, such as an apple, a piece of bread, or a chunk of chocolate. Now notice how your body responds. Or imagine the faces of your loved ones, and note how you feel as a result. Or envision yourself in a beautiful place you love in nature, and sense what occurs. The experience you have is your body responding to imagery generated within.**

Working with your soul's journey is like going to the source of a river to unblock a huge obstacle. Rather than fix your life by clearing out dams of problems or opening channels of attempts, we want to go to the source where the water first springs forth and free any blocks there. Once we do so, the water flows stronger and clears the jams downstream. Working with your soul's journey creates the greatest and farthest-reaching impact on your whole life.

Step Two Metaphor-phosis:
Unhook from Your Stories

The Metaphor-phosis process has specific steps for dissolving the hooks of your limiting patterns, beliefs, stories, and issues. Just as the pupa in a chrysalis dissolves to feed its newly forming butterfly body, there is a specific way to compost your old patterns, beliefs, stories, and issues so they form a new you.

Start with any beliefs that could limit your progress, such as "Nothing works for me," "I never get better," "I'm always stuck," "There's nothing there for me," "I can't do anything," or "I don't have enough ___." Such limiting beliefs sabotage your process. Neutralize them first so you'll succeed with other issues. When you are ready, work on a bigger subject. Each pattern and belief you process affects everything else. This means it may lessen other patterns so they are easier to clear or become nonissues entirely so you won't even have to work on them.

How to Proceed

If you just discovered a limiting pattern or core belief, you have already readied your space. Go to the second step, Set Your Intention. Otherwise, follow these steps from beginning to end. See "Essential Tools for Change" at the end of section I for specifics.

There are four steps to the Metaphor-phosis process: ready your space, set your intention, go to a universal story, and act on it through ceremony.

Ready Your Space

If your space is already open from "Step One Metaphor-phosis," proceed to setting your intention. Otherwise, start by creating a safe space where you won't be interrupted. You may want to call in your spirit helpers and healers, and breathe deeply. Then go to an alpha state of altered consciousness.

Set Your Intention

Set your intention to determine your universal story and realize how to best ceremonially process it.

Go to a Universal Story

To shift to a universal story, find the metaphor, myth, archetype, fairy tale, folk story, or image that embodies how your pattern or belief physically *feels* inside your body, and work directly with that. **Somatic feeling is key here.** It's not about mentally or emotionally choosing a universal story; it's about finding what resonates in your body that matters. The body never lies; it is a true reflection of your subconscious thoughts and feelings.

There are thousands of possible metaphors, myths, archetypes, fairy tales, folk stories, or images to choose from. In general, choose the universal story that best encompasses the elements of your personal pattern or belief and how it physically feels inside your body. Several possibilities and resources are given in "Tools to Unhook from Your Stories" at the end of this section.

Example Universal Stories

- **Do you feel you are carrying the weight of the world on your shoulders? This might be the metaphor for your chronic recurring shoulder pain.**
- **Do you feel you are the rebel, the boy from the wrong side of the tracks who is charismatic, street smart, hates authority, and doesn't buckle under pressure? You are living the Bad Boy archetype.**
- **Do you always feel you are on a quest, achieving task after task but never really stopping, only seeking something else instead? Parsifal may be your myth.**
- **Do you feel asleep in life, like you are just drifting through it while waiting for your one big moment or special true love to come along? Sleeping Beauty fits here.**
- **Do you feel that everyone around you treats you poorly—partner, family, boss and coworkers alike—that none of them understand you, or see the true you? If only someone would see who you truly are or give you a break. Sounds like Cinderella, doesn't it?**
- **When you imagine a mudslide burying a tree, does it resonate with how you feel at your job? This could be your image.**

Find Your Own Image

You don't have to be versed in mythology to do this process, but can use your heart or body wisdom. Let an image arise that encompasses how the pattern or belief feels and work with that. You will know it when you feel it, for its universal message will ring true within about your life experience. However, it's important the image is not literal and does not include people. Look for a universal image that encompasses how you feel in your heart or body.

Use Your Heart Wisdom:

Follow the steps to enter your sacred heart space under "Your Inner Wisdom" in "States of Consciousness and Stories" at the beginning of section II. As you do so, set your intention to both enter your sacred heart space and to discover the guiding image.

- Go to alpha
- Dive down, and "travel" into your heart
- Observe your unique heart language (such as imagery, sensations, or an inner knowing)
- Receive understanding

Use Your Body Wisdom:

To determine your universal story image through your body wisdom, ask yourself the following questions:

- What is the pattern, belief, or issue?
- What emotions arise?
- Where do you feel this in your body?
- Go to that place. How does that area feel? Describe it with all of your senses.
- Now allow an image to arise that encompasses how the area feels. Go with the first one that comes to you.

If you don't get an image, you might have a sensation, knowing, or description, such as tight as a knot, a deep hole, or an empty desert. These descriptions are images, too, and metaphors for how you feel inside. Use that metaphor as your universal story to ceremonially process.

Act on Your Universal Story Through Ceremony

The last step is to act on your universal story through some form of ritual or ceremony. This is key because ceremony is the language of the soul and directly accesses your spiritual brain. When you participate in ritual or ceremony, you don't dwell on daily life but engage with transcendent universal energies instead.

The original wounding has some reason or meaning for being in your life. You develop gifts or powers as a result. Ceremonially processing your universal story enables you to acknowledge what the pattern or belief has taught and given to you. This helps you come into "right relationship," or harmony and balance, with it so you understand its greater energies at work in your life and your path to greater freedom. The key here is to not fall into the trap of trading one illusion for another but to use ritual and ceremony as a tool to move into another state of awareness. Ask your universal story questions to determine its teachings and gifts, such as:

- Why are you in my life?
- What do I need?
- What do you want me to know?
- What do you want to share with me?
- Do you need anything?
- What are your lessons?
- What do you want to teach me?
- What are your gifts?

The larger, more encompassing, and longer-lasting the pattern, create a larger or more meaningful ritual. Or if a simple ritual doesn't create your desired shift, perform a larger ceremony. For example, if dialogue, journey, or gestalt doesn't work, perform a ceremony with friends, or do a vision quest, walkabout, or earth power walk.

Sometimes as you ceremonially process a universal story, a larger issue or pattern is revealed. If this occurs, switch to the larger pattern, determine its universal story, and ceremonially process that.

Focus on what the universal story cost you, the lessons you learned, and what new skills and capacities you developed as a result of your old patterns and beliefs. Did it cost you lost opportunities, a loving relationship, or the body size you desired? Did you learn leadership, inner strength, or self-respect? Talk to that warrior voice in your head, to that judge in your heart, or that caregiver in your hands. Respectfully acknowledge it, and see what it wants to share.

For example, Alex felt invisible or invaluable to others and so made decisions based on this by withholding himself, not standing up for himself, and not contributing his gifts to the world. This was the price he paid for that old belief and story. On the other hand, this separation allowed him to delve deeper into his passions and create his own path until ultimately he learned to acknowledge and value himself. He also became an expert in his field. These are the gifts he received from his story.

Fully embrace your universal story as well. Own it, feel it, and process it. Put on its clothes, arrange your hair and face according to its mood, add a chain around your neck, or stick your feet in the mud as appropriate. Do all that's needed to *feel* that universal story, go into it fully, and know every aspect of it in all its ways. Let the universal story tell you how it feels, how it views life, and how it operates in the world.

You cannot change your past; instead, you learn from it to discharge it. Everything we experience—patterns, people, and events alike—has lessons for our spiritual development. Ceremony opens us to receive these lessons and gifts. Gratitude for these hidden gifts diffuses any negativity from our old experiences and can turn them into our allies, like the princess who kisses the frog that then turns into a prince.

As you ceremonially process your cyclical pattern or core belief, ***it's extremely important to just work on the pattern itself and not how the pattern manifests in your life. In other words, ignore the specific details,*** such as the people involved, what she said or he did, or what happened. Just focus on the general pattern.

> ## Sample Ceremonies
> **Examples of ceremonies and rituals include drumming, dancing, or dialoguing with your universal story; setting up an altar; creating some form of art with it, such as a poem, painting, or song; doing a ceremony with fire, water, earth, or air; taking a power walk or night walk; cutting, burning, tearing up, or burying; anointing with oil; bathing in flower water. Go to "Tools to Unhook From Your Stories" at the end of this section for more suggestions.**

Act on What You Receive

It's extremely important to follow through on any information or guidance you may receive. This honors the story so it can fully release. For example, you might realize that you need to tell someone something, complete a project, change a habit or routine, or do something else. It's crucial to follow through on whatever you learn because your old story will repeat or the issue won't resolve if you don't.

Don't Close Your Space

When you are complete, don't close your space but immediately go to "Step Three Metaphor-phosis" in section IV. If you aren't complete or want more time, close your space and, when ready, ceremonially process your old universal story again as needed.

If You Feel Stuck

Usually when people feel stuck, it's because they are approaching their issues the same old way. To get unstuck, it doesn't work to try and figure things out (the mental level and neocortex) or wrestle with the feelings (the emotional level and limbic system). Instead, you need to make a lateral shift to the universal story (the spiritual brain), as this is the perspective served by ceremony. If you get stuck in any way, return to ceremony and honor the stuck stuff. Go *into* it and *through* it rather than want it to be done and over with. There is more to learn and gain, more gifts to receive. Keep going back to your universal story.

Sometimes being stuck *is* the pattern, so then ceremonially process being stuck. Some people believe that nothing will work for them, and so they try dozens of methods, but still nothing works. In this case, the belief that nothing works is the pattern to process. Other people seem numb or apathetic to everything no matter what they do. The pattern here is numbness, so ceremonially process the numbness itself.

In Chinese medicine, two of the best ways to get unstuck are to either physically move or engage in some form of creative expression. While these don't alter the core issue, they can help shift how you feel enough so you can return to the ceremonial process. Remember to use the techniques given earlier in "Essential Tools for Change" at the end of section I. These are designed to help you discharge enough emotional and mental energy so that you can return to ceremonially honor your universal story again.

Our Examples

Pattie:

Pattie's initial anger at her husband for his disrespect and lack of support had turned into a pattern of her being kind and doing what other's wanted at her own expense in order to prevent abuse or punishment. She identified her core beliefs as no self-confidence and tremendous guilt.

She tuned into her body wisdom again and felt enormous tension around her solar plexus. She noticed how the pattern and belief had made her feel invisible. Tremendous anger arose and an image came of a pressure cooker ready to explode. This picture and metaphor became her universal story.

Pattie tuned into this image and "talked" with the pressure cooker, using dialoguing (her form of ceremony). She asked what it wanted to say and listened to its answers. The pressure cooker told her not only how angry it was, but also that she either needed to change or "die." It said that every time she ignored her own needs and desires, she was actually abusing herself.

This realization shocked Pattie. She now understood that allowing others to take advantage of her was actually perpetuating her mother's abuse and father's lack of protection. She had internalized them both so they still controlled her life. She also realized that this pattern had made her incredibly strong as a person, even to a fault, so she could survive anything.

After these revelations, Pattie felt quite different inside. The pressure cooker image disappeared and the tension in her gut dispersed. Pattie's perspective had shifted. Now she was ready to choose a new universal story through "Step Three Metaphor-phosis" in section IV.

Tom:

Tom took his core belief that men weren't supportive of him but attacked him instead and shifted it to a universal story. He did this by drawing how he felt. The result looked like a stack of boxes, each one representing different areas of his life, yet all disconnected from one another.

As he looked at his final drawing, he realized how he had compartmentalized his life. The box with the most objects and colors represented his personal life. As he looked at this, he realized that ever since his dad had left, he had become a self-protective and self-styled man, very strong within himself. Yet these tremendous gifts hadn't extended to the rest of life. Tom now knew he deserved respect externally as well as internally, and so he chose the new belief, "I am respected."

Tools to Unhook from Your Stories

The tools in this section are divided into three sections: one to help you determine your universal story, one to determine your soul's journey, and one to process your universal story ceremonially.

Tools to Determine Your Universal Story

The tools in this section help you choose a universal story from your limiting pattern, belief, or story. Search for the metaphor, myth, archetype, fairy tale, folk story, or image that feels right emotionally and physically.

Universal Stories

We all love myths not just because they're stories but also because they represent universal truths and principles common to us all. As the language of the soul, they are larger than life and so inform our mental, emotional, and physical parts. They reveal the inner landscape of our psyches too. The same is true for metaphors, archetypes, fairy tales, folk stories, and images.

To determine your personal metaphor, archetype, myth, fairy tale, folk story, or image, look at the major triumphs and challenges throughout your life. How did you approach and meet them? There are many books and resources for all of these, and sometimes just reading or even hearing of one will ring true for you. What was your favorite fairy tale as a child, the one that spoke to you over and over? What religious or racial stories do you identify with? What image speaks to you and encompasses how you feel in your pattern or core belief? This is the one to use.

What's important is to pick the metaphor, myth, archetype, fairy tale, folk story, or image that feels right to your body. That is key to this process. Get to know how it manifests in your life. Then take it to ceremony or ritual. If you don't find a specific metaphor, myth, archetype, fairy tale, or folk story that fits you, choose an image.

Metaphors

A metaphor is a comparison between two unlike things that actually have something in common. There are many different types of metaphors from simple language to complex ideas. For example, comparing anger with heat evokes metaphors of simmering, kindled, flaring up, slow burn, and outburst. Metaphors are fundamental to our lives. We use them so often that we don't even think about them, such as her life was a prison, he's a bull, dig up evidence, and my head is spinning with ideas.

Anything can be looked at metaphorically and so used as a mirror for your life. Consider that you live in the everyday outer world and an internal world. Outer issues may be looked at within your internal universe to find and process patterns. That means that not only external experiences can be used metaphorically but also different parts of your self too.

For example, if you don't seem heard by your brother, what part of you is not hearing another part of you? Or what part of you doesn't listen to another part of you? Identify these parts and process them by asking questions, such as when have you felt this way before, how do they act out in your life, and what belief or pattern is behind them? Then ceremonially process the metaphor.

The following metaphors are only possibilities and suggestions to trigger your own revelations from your inner wisdom.

Physical Metaphors:
Ear: hearing or not hearing others or yourself
Eyes: seeing or not seeing others or yourself; using your inner vision; insight
Shoulders: taking on others' problems; not minding your own business; carrying too many responsibilities ("the world on your shoulders")
Lungs: what you take in from the world; inspiration or lack of it
Digestion: how you digest what you take in from the world
Knees: What stops you from moving or makes you bow or kneel to something?
Ankles and other joints: your ability to be flexible in life
Feet: energies being grounded
Skin: emotions erupting

Metaphors for Illness:
Illness can be a useful metaphor for uncovering what's actually going on deep within you. Both the illness and where it is located can give clues to underlying issues needing attention or correction.

For example, poor digestion may actually be due to an inability to handle, or "digest," certain things in your life. When these "indigestible" issues or activities are identified and rectified, physical digestion usually improves. As another example, frequent bladder infections often signal the person is "pissed off." When these angry feelings are identified and released, the chronic bladder infections disappear.

<u>Example Metaphors for Illness</u>
High blood pressure: succumbing to pressures
Diarrhea: difficulty collecting your energy; letting go too easily or frequently
Bladder infections: "pissed off" at or about something or someone
Cough: rejecting someone or something unwanted
Poor digestion: difficulty taking something in ("digesting" or assimilating something)
Asthma: congested life with difficulty in receiving and letting go; fear around loss; feeling suffocated or smothered by someone or something
Frequent urination: wanting to empty out
Migraines: frustrated; plans not being made or followed
Fibroids: knotted emotions. What wants to be birthed?
Bulimia: What or who needs purging from your life (ex. a controlling, demanding person or situation)?
Cancer: chaos, toxicity, or malnourishment in some way or part of your life

Exercise One: Life Metaphors

Look at an overview of your life or a time period and choose one aspect to look at metaphorically. For example, look at:

- Handwriting shift
- Hairstyle changes
- Different cars
- Dream themes
- Words you use
- Places lived
- Relationships
- Careers

Exercise Two: Inner Metaphors

Use an outer situation or a health condition and look at it as parts of yourself. For instance, a skin condition. What parts of you are inflamed? Angry? Itching for attention? In your face? Wants to be seen? What part of your invisible self is talking to you and wants to be acknowledged, and which self is that?

Myths

Myths convey the highest truths and teach life lessons. They convey our values, hopes, aspirations, and disappointments. Found in all societies throughout the world and during all times, myths explain why the world came to be and how to live in it. One of the best ways to explore myths is through books, such as those given in the bibliography at the end of this book. Both Joseph Campbell and Clarissa Pinkola Estes wrote extensively on myths.

Perhaps there's a cultural or racial myth that has always spoken to you or one you heard as a child that repeatedly returns to your thoughts. That is the one to use. As well, books, plays or movies can be used as myths. Otherwise, read various myths until you find the one that resonates with your heart or body, or from which you have a definitive physical response.

Archetypes

An archetype is a prototype or model of a person, personality, or behavior. Ancient myths, and fairy and folk tales are loaded with archetypes. It may be people; gods; goddesses; animals; elements of nature; concepts, such as Time and Death; numbers; and colors. Archetypes may also be discovered through taking one of the various tests available, such as Enneagrams and Meyers-Briggs personality types; investigating personality patterns, such as Chinese Five Elements and Ayurvedic Tridoshas; or studying Jungian behavioral archetypes.

Example Archetypes:

Mother, father, hero, rescuer, victim, maiden, medicine person, seeker, jock, mystic, prostitute, actor, celibate, alchemist, addict, wounded child, orphan, coward, sleuth, knight, damsel, jester, healer, judge, clown, Parsifal, the Fisher King, the feminine (goddess), the masculine (god), the dark goddess (such as Kali), the dark god (such as Shiva), preserver, creator, destroyer, the Wounded Healer, the Shadow, Mountain, Water, Fire, Earth, Air, Dragon, Death, Time, the Shadow, the Natural Woman, Virgin, Wild Woman, Wild Man, Green Man, The Wise Man, The Wise Woman, Crone, Hag, Wizard and the myriad of gods and goddesses throughout all cultures, archetypal events, such as birth, death, marriage, separation from parents.

Exercise: Find Your Archetype

Use these examples to determine both your old or new universal story by finding the part of an archetype that best fits you.

Artist/Creator

Dark Shadow: Self-absorbed in own creations; believe own creations are more important than others' or anyone else; too many projects rob joy from life; overly critical of or lack confidence in own creations; won't compromise and so suffer as a result; not good enough to create own visions; unappreciated for talent and so struggle

Light Shadow: Gifted in perception and expression of beauty and the eternal truths to the benefit of others' and your growth and awareness; your art/creativity is supported; balance creativity with responsibilities, rest, and play; fulfill your potential; avoid the ordinary and create your own life; have trust in own creativity regardless of what others think; give form to vision

Examples: Beethoven, Van Gogh, Leonardo da Vinci, Mozart in *Amadeus*

Caregiver

Dark Shadow: Give with expectation or strings attached; over-give to the point of losing part of self; sacrificing self to serve others; codependent; helping others because it's expected, means you are "good" or to receive something in return, such as recognition or gifts; control and manipulate because you think you know what is best for others or a situation; smothering; hard to assert own needs; martyr; enabler; guilt-tripper; can't say no

Light Shadow: Take nothing for self but give to oppressed; save people from injustice; kind, caring, compassionate, genuinely giving, humanitarian; help others to make a real difference; nurturing, altruistic, generous; can say no when appropriate

Examples: Demeter, Heidi, Florence Nightingale, Princess Diana, Mother Theresa

Clown/Jester/Joker

Dark Shadow: Joke, play tricks, create humor, make fun to cover up own sense of inadequacy or powerlessness or to create an appearance of strength and control; make fun because of nonacceptance; tell the truth in comic but harmful ways; ridicule or put others down; overindulge in seeking pleasure; don't take self seriously enough; fool around rather than appropriately serious; self-indulgent; irresponsible; waste life on trivial things

Light Shadow: Freely express emotions and feelings no matter what others think or say; speak the truth honestly; make mundane tasks fun; enjoy life through humor; make visible what is hidden; laugh at self and help others laugh at themselves; tell truth in comic but kind and harmless ways; don't take self too seriously; help others take themselves less seriously; make experiences fun for self and others; live in the moment; lighten up those around; joyful

Examples: Lucille Ball, Kokopeli, Laurel and Hardy, wise fool in *King Lear* and *Twelfth Night*

Eternal Child

Dark Shadow: Immature ("I won't grow up"); careless and irresponsible; unaccountable; don't fulfill commitments; desire to depend or rely on others; fearful of growing older

Light Shadow: Playful, fun-loving, and lighthearted without sacrificing quality or responsibilities; take care of self while you free yourself and complete commitments; follow your heart and take on only what you are responsible for

Examples: Peter Pan, Mary Poppins, Toad from *Wind in the Willows*

Gypsy

Dark Shadow: Move from place to place, person to person, or project to project when challenged for who you are or questioned about your abilities or way or life; never complete things; never put down roots; lack of commitment

Light Shadow: Accept unconventional ways of living; enjoy new places, cultures and people; carefree; free spirit; eccentric, upbeat, and creative; quirky; enjoy change; delight in the unexpected; individualistic

Examples: Hans Solo in *Star Wars*, Odysseus, Oden, Johnny Appleseed, Phoebe in *Friends*, Emma in *Emma*

Destroyer

Dark Shadow: Impulse to destroy or sabotage self; driven to destroy others' or your relationships, dreams, careers, or the environment; addicted to the power of destruction; believe a greater outside power can destroy or ruin aspects of your life and the world around you; overly confronting; lash out at others

Light Shadow: Destroy conventions for others' best interests; able to let go of what no long works or what binds; renewal; rise like phoenix from the ashes to rebuild and restore self and others; deal with loss gracefully and move on; complete and release possessions, relationships, and projects that no longer serve you; risk everything or give up life to create a better order for others

Examples: Shiva, Shakti (Parvati), *The Alien*, Hemmingway's *The Old Man and the Sea*, Thoreau's *Walden Pond*

Explorer

Dark Shadow: Aimless wandering; alienation; flit from place to place; ungrounded; restless; always yearning; never fit in; never put down roots; escapism; misfit

Light Shadow: Freedom to find self and a more authentic life; journey to explore new things; discover the world and all its unique variety; openness to try new options and experiences

Examples: Margaret Mead, Marco Polo, Captain Piccard of *Star Trek*, Sacagawea

Hermit

Dark Shadow: Reclusive; withdrawn from society; live a solitary existence; hide your wisdom from others; keep safe; always reflect or study; invisible; always need to learn or know more before you can be, live, or act in the world

Light Shadow: Store your physical, creative and spiritual energies; seek Truth and gain wisdom through self-reflection or meditation in order to grow and bring back to others; receive guidance from within

Example: Obi-Wan Kenobi in *Star Wars*

Judge

Dark Shadow: Critical; authoritarian; judgmental; you deem the worthiness of others or quality of everything better than others do; endlessly criticize self; hold self back for fear of being judged; enforce your rule or standards over other people; stick to the letter of the law at the expense of humanitarianism

Light Shadow: Fair and just; able to clearly and easily discern and discriminate what's appropriate, beneficial and in the best interests for self and for all concerned; balance justice with compassion; high standards and ideals; work with universal laws of harmony and justice; realistic and fair

Examples: Solomon, scales of justice, Lady Liberty

Knight

Dark Shadow: Blind devotion and loyalty; save others and sacrifice self; absence of honor or chivalry; loyalty to a questionable ruler, principle, or cause

Light Shadow: Give appropriate service, devotion, and loyalty toward honorable people and noble causes; balance service with work, rest, and play; chivalrous; protector; loyalty and self-sacrifice to a greater cause

Examples: Lancelot, Parsifal, Joan of Arc, Captain Kirk in *Star Trek*, Knights of the Round Table, *Man of La Mancha*

Lover

Dark Shadow: Misuse romantic or sexual attraction to gain a sense of importance or to feel superior; play favorites; feel empty being alone or without a love relationship; promiscuous;

codependent; puritanical; envious; infatuated; seductive; obsessive; jealous; sacrifice own power to be with another; can't be alone

Light Shadow: Unconditional love for self and others; accept and celebrate vulnerability; love, passion, intimacy, and connection with others; strong, vital relationship with self; passion for life; loving, passionate, friendly; help people to connect and relate despite challenges or obstacles

Examples: Don Juan, Aphrodite, Venus, Paris, Romeo and Juliette, Tristan and Isolde, *Sleepless in Seattle*

Magician

Dark Shadow: Create illusion of skill, ability, or success; easily fall prey to other's charisma and manipulation; set self up as a "guru"; mysterious and removed from others, which contributes to your power; know what's better for others and manipulate things to bring about the transformation you desire; manipulative

Light Shadow: Create change with grace and ease and open all doors to manifest your dreams and visions; heal or transform situations; have the charisma and power to shape and influence events for the benefit of all; open to allow miracles to come through from the Divine; magical experiences of transformation; knowledge of how the universe works; make dreams come true; transform the world

Examples: Hypatia, Merlin, Voldermort in the *Harry Potter* series, Darth Vader in *Star Wars*

Martyr

Dark Shadow: Long-suffering to the point of exhaustion; sacrifice self in order to feel superior, get attention, or acknowledgement; service and suffering to manipulate others or your environment

Light Shadow: Give what you truly have to help a cause; give to others and situations unconditionally with no strings attached; make great sacrifices in order to further a belief, principle, cause, or others; service and suffering to help others; courage to represent a cause; suffering so others may be redeemed

Examples: Martin Luther King Jr., Aslan in *The Chronicles of Narnia*, Malcolm X, *A Tale of Two Cities*

Orphan

Dark Shadow: Deserted, dependent, rejected, alone; lack support that should have been there; oppressed and abandoned; have to survive alone; never had what you needed; seek support from outside self; bend backward to get minimal care and even those efforts are in vain

Light Shadow: Can provide for self in all ways; self-sufficient and self-reliant; independent; can survive and are resilient no matter what life brings; able to face difficulties and disappointment

Examples: Little Orphan Annie, Oliver, *A Series of Unfortunate Events*, Little Match Girl

Perfectionist

Dark Shadow: Unhappy or displeased by what doesn't meet your standards as this proves you have great aspirations, good taste or accomplishments; fear of failure; strict, exacting, and demanding; self-critical; get bogged down in detail; want to be the best over others; if can't do it perfectly, won't do it at all; overwhelmed or anxious because can't meet own standards

Light Shadow: Set high but attainable standards to benefit others as well as self; overcome challenges, accomplish higher goals, and help others do so too; aim for the best from self and accept self as you are; masterful in your field; want to be the best you can be

Examples: Scrooge, dilettantes, prima donnas

Procrastinator

Dark Shadow: Postpone needlessly; never fulfill promises or obligations; there'll always be another day; shun responsibilities; lazy; inertia; lack of commitment

Light Shadow: Tune within to know the appropriate point to accomplish something and follow that guidance; fulfill promises and obligations in a timely manner; clear about what you can truly do or take on before making agreements, promises, obligations, or responsibilities; committed

Examples: Cinderella

Rebel

Dark Shadow: Outlaw: fear you'll get stuck in a box or pegged; resist or defy authority or generally accepted behavior; go to extremes to break from the norm, perhaps in order to gain status; break free from conventions; defiant; outsider; criminal behavior

Light Shadow: Set self free from convention; free self to pursue own passions; break out of the box to help others or self; think outside the box; radical freedom; true revolutionary

Examples: Jesse James, Robin Hood

Ruler

Dark Shadow: Sovereign; authority figure; entitled; make decisions based on gaining authority; rigid and controlling; leave no room for criticism; exert authority over others; make choices without considering how it'll affect others; arrogance and authority get the better of you; want others to do as you say; dictatorial

Light Shadow: Make choices in the best interests of all others involved; skilled and benevolent leadership; use authority to promote growth, beauty, regeneration, health, and wealth of others; accept stewardship for a family, group, or organization for the highest good of all concerned; claim own power and authority

Examples: King Arthur, Cleopatra, Queen Victoria, Gilgamesh, Napolean

Sage/Scholar/Teacher

Dark Shadow: More special than others from own knowledge and achievements; know more than others and are happy to demonstrate that; absentminded professor; truth and reality are more important than connection and emotions; dogmatic; opinionated; more studying and thinking rather than doing or experiencing; retreat into own head; snobbish; disassociate from reality; dogmatic; skeptical and doubtful of others; study forever and never act; guide others for financial gain and control

Light Shadow: Guide others through wisdom; role model for good behavior; possess insight and understanding beyond the ordinary; guardian of special knowledge; helper or advisor; serve others through own studies and wisdom; walk your talk and help others through doing so; uncover truth, wisdom, and freedom from learning what is real; openminded and curious; dispassionate analyst; objective and fair; master; expert; discoverer of truth

Examples: Gandolf from *Lord of the Rings*, Spock in *Star Trek*, Hypatia, Taliesen, Vivien (Lady of the Lake), Yoda in *Star Wars*, Dumbledore in *Harry Potter* series, Mr. Miagi from *The Karate Kid*, Robert Duvall in *The Apostle*, *Meetings with Remarkable Men*

Scapegoat

Dark Shadow: Outcast; blamed for everything whether responsible for it or not; the one always singled out for unmerited negative treatment; excluded or banned by others, groups, or events for some real or imagined cause, crime or curse; the object of irrational hostility; the fall guy or whipping boy; views the world as hostile; alone and unwanted

Light Shadow: Takes the brunt for others, willingly makes a noble sacrifice to help another or a situation, sacrifices for a greater need, bears the blame for others

Examples: Piggy in *Lord of the Flies*, Snowball in *Animal Farm*, Dorothy from *The Wizard of Oz*, Cinderella, Monster in *Frankenstein*, Heathcliff in *Wuthering Heights*

Seeker

Dark Shadow: Always look and rarely find; grass is always greener; always search outside self for what is within; aimless wandering; obsessive need to be independent; need to do it yourself; lost soul on an aimless journey; disconnected from goals; run away from journey or leave goal behind; always wandering; always trying new experiences but not growing or learning from them; lost in a quest

Light Shadow: Put self to the test; search for deeper meaning; independent, individualistic, self-sufficient, adventurous; explore capabilities; search for the highest truths to grow and help others; search within for all that is needed; search for deeper meaning in life; find a better way of life for self and others; gain truth, wisdom, and insight

Examples: Siddhartha, Luke Skywalker in *Star Wars*, Davy Crockett, Jason of *Jason and the Argonauts*, Parsifal

Trickster

Dark Shadow: Fool, messenger, transformer, and creator to make others look at things differently, usually in uncomfortable ways; play malicious jokes on people; wander through the world with humor and carelessness; fond of sly jokes and malicious pranks; manipulative through tricks or pranks

Light Shadow: Childlike with strength and wisdom; can maneuver out of situations; can make others look at things differently through light-hearted means

Examples: Coyote, Raven, Monkey, the wizard in *The Wizard of Oz*, Cheshire Cat in *Alice in Wonderland*, Puck, Joker and the Riddler in comic books, Faust

Warrior

Dark Shadow: Engage in frequent conflict; don't set boundaries; ruthless in beliefs and principles; frequently defend self or engage in senseless battles; attack others; victory at any cost

Light Shadow: Confront conflict in a loving way; choose battles wisely or for the highest good of all concerned; perseverance in the face of obstacles; set flexible boundaries; bold, dynamic, and give direction, and focus; appropriately defend self and others; stand up for self and ideals; strength and discipline to achieve goals; physical strength and ability to protect, defend, and fight for one's rights

Examples: Athena, Thor, Bodicca, Brunhilda, Bhima, Andarta, Durga, Amazon warrior women, John Wayne, Barbra Streisand in *The Way We Were*, *Seven Samurai*

Wounded Healer

Dark Shadow: Ignore, stuff, or circumvent your wounds; stuck in or obsessing about own wounds; complaining about own wounds and doing nothing about them; take advantage of those who help or need help; make false claims you can heal any illness

Light Shadow: Suffering and vulnerability contribute significantly to your ability to heal; hurts and wounds enhance your power to heal and be of service to others; empathy, compassion, and understanding of others' pain; ability to help others heal; experience wounding as the numinous event that it is and extract the gold; willingness to face your wounds and receive their blessings

Examples: Chiron, Asclepius, Apollo, the Fisher King, Black Elk in *Black Elk Speaks*, Garuda, Meditrina, Ellen Burstyn in *Resurrection*

Visionary

Dark Shadow: Hold own visions back out of fear; think your visions are more important than others'; live in visionary work and ignore reality; difficulty developing a vision for own future

Light Shadow: Share your visions to help others and the world; confident in own viewpoint and ideas; follow your visions for what might be accomplished; know how to implement your visions; can energize others by inspiring them through your visions; share your visions and allow others to help decide how that vision is realized; unite people under a common vision

Examples: Blake, Don Quixote in *Man of La Mancha*, Sybil, Cassandra

Fairy Tales and Folk Stories

Many people grew up learning fairy tales and folk stories. They are loaded with archetypes and universal truths that teach us how to live, understand, and reconstruct our lives. As well, they show you how to reconnect with your wild, instinctual self.

Fairy tales are generally made up whereas folk stories usually contain a kernel of truth in them and may even have historical basis. Many heroes are people who actually lived and their lives took on mythical proportions. Perhaps a particular fairy tale or folk story has stuck with you throughout your life, and you didn't know why. It may indicate a major pattern or your soul's journey.

Example Fairy Tales:
"Cinderella," "Jack and the Beanstalk," "Sleeping Beauty," "Puss N Boots," "Bluebeard," "The Little Match Girl," "Goldilocks and the Three Bears," "Little Red Riding Hood," "Three Little Pigs," "Hansel and Gretel," "The Frog Prince," "Rapunzel," "Snow White and the Seven Dwarfs," "Rumpelstiltskin," "The Pied Piper," "The Ugly Duckling," "The Emperor's New Clothes," "The Princess and the Pea," "Thumbelina," "Aladdin and His Lamp"

Example Folk Stories:
Paul Bunyan, Jesse James, *Blackbeard's Ghost*, Brer Rabbit, Ghost Train, Pecos Bill, Davey Crockett, Johnny Appleseed, Yankee Doodle Dandy, Sasquatch, "Three Billy Goats Gruff," "The Heron and the Hummingbird"

Imagery

Images speak volumes. Have you ever noticed that a good movie or vivid dream can produce the same effect on your body as if it were really happening? Even though you know the movie is staged and the dream isn't real, your body reacts as if it were. The same is true of your subconscious mind.

Images present a big picture that holds much information. They allow the right side of the brain to process information more globally. Before you do something, you usually envision yourself doing it. Our minds encode information as images, so one aspect of an experience can bring back the whole experience, much like a hologram.

To find an image as your universal story, choose one that feels right and that resonates with how you feel. The images that have the most impact are those imbued with emotion. You can find images in magazines, online, on billboard paintings, drawings, and so forth. You can also use one of the many card decks available, such as the tarot. You are not using these for a game or divination but just for the images. To use them, set your intention that you find the perfect card for your pattern or belief. Then either look through the cards and find one that represents how you feel or place the cards face down and pick one that you are drawn to.

In addition, you can make your own images, such as a collage or card of the images that impact you, have meaning, and direct your attention to what you want and how you want to feel. If you don't find an image that fits, use your heart or body wisdom as described in "States of Consciousness and Stories" at the beginning of section II. For example, imagine you feel frustrated, like you're mired in your life. Tune within, and find where you feel this energy.

You discover you feel it in your head. You allow an image to arise, and you "see" mud on a windshield. This is the image to process ceremonially.

Discover Your Soul's Journey

Your soul's journey is your dominant life story, the purpose you have come to accomplish. Each of us has a major overall design, or theme, to our lives. This life's journey encompasses what you are learning, what you are giving, and what you are here to do. It is determined from your overall major life metaphor, myth, or archetype.

Your soul's journey gives instructions to the universe as to how you want to be treated and to be held accountable. Because it includes all your beliefs and sets of behavior, your soul's journey affects your whole life. It manifests on the literal level by informing your mental, emotional, and physical selves.

To determine your soul's journey, look at the entire life you've been living and what's happened to you. Take into account your passions and interests as well as major patterns, core beliefs, subconscious agendas, and so on. From there, you then determine the overall metaphor, myth, archetype, fairy tale, folk story, or image that represents how the culmination of your life themes feel. It's important to search for your own soul's journey myth. Once you discover it, ceremonially process it.

Your soul's journey may be comprised of several big myths. If you feel you've completed your soul's journey, then you are living another part of it that may not yet be clear, or the completed part may need to be expanded to the world at large.

Tools to Ceremonially Process Your Stories

The tools in this section will help you neutralize the energy behind your limiting patterns and beliefs by helping you shift perspective and ceremonially process them. When the energy is neutralized, you can create what you desire instead, which is covered in section IV.

Shifting Perspective

To unhook from your stories means viewing them differently than before, that is, by shifting your perspective. Such a shift occurs on the soul level, the level of the universal story, such as metaphors, myths, archetypes, fairy tales, folk stories, and images. These speak directly to your subconscious to neutralize the energy of old patterns and beliefs so you can replace them with those you desire instead.

Intention is key here, for this is the difference between performing any old action and creating a meaningful experience. In fact, the key ingredient needed to perform any ritual or ceremony is intention.

Ceremony and ritual allow us to bypass the limbic system, the place of fear. Additionally, they help us access the soul and universal energies in life, which then inform the mental, emotional, and physical levels. Here you can more easily see the larger pattern. You can also learn the teachings, messages, and gifts. This is how you alchemically transform your stories and reclaim the gold.

How Do You Know When a Pattern is Released?

Your body wisdom will indicate when a pattern or belief has been released. Feelings like a sense of release, peace, stillness, calmness, relief, or sensing there's no energy in it anymore or you are neutral around the issues all indicate its energy has been defused. When you feel any of these, your story has been neutralized and you may go to "Step Three Metaphor-phosis" in section IV.

Ceremony and Ritual

Ceremony and ritual differ from daily routines with one important trait—intention. Drinking hot tea or reading the paper first thing every morning is a type of ritual, even a habit. But if you drink your herb tea intending all the while that it heal a particular health problem, you create meaning that invokes different energies, which influence your body, mind, and spirit. Because the key ingredient to any ceremony or ritual is intention, state what you intend at the beginning and stay focused on it throughout. Intention is what gives instructions to the universe for what you want to achieve.

Ceremony and ritual are symbols in motion, capable of imprinting upon your subconscious the truth you know in your heart. We all have ceremonies and rituals in our lives. Examples include lighting candles on a cake, throwing rice after a wedding, and memorials or wakes for those who died. There are cultural, religious, and personal ceremonies and rituals and more.

When you have determined your universal story, choose or create a ceremony or ritual to process it. It could be as simple as lighting a candle or creating an altar or as complex as undertaking a vision quest. With whatever ceremony or ritual you choose, pay attention to what memories arise, images you see, feelings that come, and thoughts you think. These are messages from your subconscious and threads to follow so you can reach the core truth and source of the universal story.

Even if they don't seem to make sense, trust the process and stay with it. Often what comes up leads to deeper, more hidden memories, so realizations and understandings flood forth and your perspective shifts. It's not usually a logical or linear process, so go with what presents itself and let it take you to the root of the matter.

For example, once when I was performing a process with someone, an image kept coming to me. It made no sense until finally I asked the person about it. The image triggered many memories for this person that got us to the core of her issue so she could make a major shift. If I hadn't trusted the image that popped up, this same result would not have happened.

Ceremony and ritual pull us out of everyday, mundane awareness and link us with greater energies. Through them, you connect with your Higher Self and Source energies. They also balance, heal and put us into right relationship with others, the natural world, and ourselves.

As the language of the soul, ceremony and ritual bypass the limbic system of fear, other limiting emotions, and the neocortex brain of mental loops and rationalizations. Instead, they connect you to your soul and, through that, shift your perspective and inform you anew. When we ceremonially process something, we honor it. This is a deep acknowledgment that means, "I see you. I hear you. I receive you."

How to Process Your Universal Story

There are many different rituals or ceremonies possible to process your universal story, and you may create your own as well. Take your time choosing what to do. Brainstorm with a friend or consider a group for support participation and witnessing. Choose whichever best fits your universal story. It will dictate what needs to be done.

Just because you realize or understand your universal story, it doesn't go away. Rather, you actually have to learn from it to diffuse its energy. It's there for a reason. Learn what that reason is. Do this by asking questions during your ceremony or ritual or by setting them as your intention before you start.

Whatever ceremony or ritual you do, open to the universal story and acknowledge its presence, energy, and message. Look for the teachings, messages, understanding, or gifts and how they have shaped your life. Come to a place of understanding. See if you can claim the medicine gift or teaching in the place of wounding or where the universal story is caught.

Questions to ask while ceremonially processing your universal story:

- Why are you here?
- What do you want to tell me?
- What do I need to know?
- What is your message?
- What is your teaching?

- What do you need from me in order to heal?
- What is your gift?

The Shift

Once you've discovered the teachings and gifts behind your universal story, you will feel a shift inside. It can be subtle or strong. It could be a sudden realization, change of perspective, altered perceptions, or sense of peace. When you can truly hear the teaching or sharing of your universal story, you receive its gift and the energy behind it dissipates.

Some issues need to be ceremonially processed over time before they release or else they'll come back. If your issue still shows up, go back to ceremonial processing.

There are many ways to ceremonially process and these follow. Choose what seems most appropriate and inspires you the most. When you feel the shift, the exercise is complete and you can go to "Step Three Metaphor-phosis."

Tools to Ceremonially Process Your Universal Story

Dialoguing

Dialoguing is a process of holding a "conversation" with something you want to talk with yet can't talk with. It is a great way to uncover the root of your patterns and beliefs, shift your perspective, reveal connections, and allow realizations to arise. This is what helps create those "ah-ha" moments, when a flash of insight alters how you feel about something.

You can dialogue with anything. It can be a dream image or character; an animal or rock in nature; your pet dog; a health issue, such as hypertension or back pain; a piece of music; the brother who treats you poorly or your dead mother. You can also dialogue with another person or situation through open chair gestalt (see below). Additionally, you can have different parts of yourself dialogue together. The possibilities are endless although the process is the same.

To dialogue, either write or speak aloud (and electronically record) your name and your question. Then write/speak the name of what you're "talking" to and write down/record its answer to your question. Allow a stream of consciousness to occur as you do this, avoiding any mental editing. Continue this even if the answers seem unrelated or are distant memories. There are reasons for this, and as the process unfolds, the understanding or revelations come. Keep this back-and-forth dialoguing going until complete.

As you begin this process, start anywhere. Don't get hung up on trying to do this "properly" or linearly. There is no right way. What matters is to just do it so your subconscious floodgates open and memories, ideas, insights, and realizations flood forth. Even better, combine some form of movement with dialoguing. Set your intention and then move in some way—drum, sing, hike, or stretch. I actually write best while I'm walking since more comes to me in this way.

The key to dialoguing is that it must be done in writing or spoken aloud and not mentally in your head. Mentally processing keeps you in a stuck loop and does not access your subconscious mind. Writing or speaking out loud accesses the subconscious so memories, connections, revelations, and insights rise to surface awareness. While some people have an encyclopedic memory of stories, most only remember when triggered by something. It's the same way with your subconscious. The process of engaging the body in writing or speaking makes all the difference in accessing your hidden information.

For example, we often internalize those aspects we don't like about others in how they treat us. I internalized my dad's critic and judge. It got so that I would judge everything I did as either productive or frivolous. If something was nonproductive, I would not allow myself to engage with it long even if it was pleasurable. Nonproductive for me might be a walk or to rest instead of doing something to support a productive project. Yet for me, walking and resting allows my mind to relax, and when it does, I can hear my intuition, which ultimately helps my productivity.

I dialogued with my internalized father critic and asked him why he was there. I learned that he gave me discrimination and good judgment. I told him I would turn to him when I needed him, but that I was in control from then on. Ever since, I've been able to follow my internal urges and flow without self-judgment.

Exercise One: Dialogue with Illness

You can dialogue with any illness or body area. This is a simple method of "talking" with it either out loud (record it) or through journal writing. Ask it questions and write, or speak aloud, the responses. After each question, sit silently a moment and listen. Then immediately record the response you receive. Don't try to make sense of it right then or edit it with doubts. Just let it flow as it comes. Then respond with another question or comment as needed. Continue this process until it feels complete.

Possible questions to ask:

- Why are you here?
- What are you trying to tell (teach) me?
- What do you need in order to heal?

- What am I doing to cause you?
- What changes should I make to feel well again?
- What is your gift?

Exercise Two: Dialogue with Consciousness

Have your universal story (superconsciousness) dialogue with your subconscious. Repeat with your conscious self. Then have your subconscious dialogue with your conscious self.

Open Chair Gestalt

Gestalt therapy[21] is a method of direct awareness. It emphasizes feeling and acting rather than interpretation and adjustment to a preconceived idea. In the open chair technique, you place a person or issue into a chair (or other object) and dialogue with it. When you've completed what needs to be said, you sit in the chair (or stand around the object) and speak from the other person or issue's perspective as if you were that person or issue.

Consider such questions as:

- Why did they do or say what they did?
- What was their motivation?
- What patterns or core beliefs were acted out?
- What is that other person's perspective?
- What do you learn about the other person?
- What new revelation or understandings arise from this shift of perspective?

Exercise: Open Chair Gestalt

This process is similar to dialoguing, except that you physically step into each aspect of your universal story and have it dialogue with you. This is how to do it:

- Ready your space, and set your intention.
- Choose an object to represent each major aspect of your universal story.
- Set each object in a different place around you as it feels appropriate.
- Choose one of these to work with first. Now "step" into that object by physically turning around and stepping around that object.

---

21   Gestalt therapy was developed by Fritz and Laura Perls in the 1940s.

- Next, speak as if you are that object representing that dream element. Become that thing/person/animal/place and so on and speak as if you are it. Write this down or speak it out loud and electronically record it.
- When complete, step out of the aspect, move to the next one, and repeat.
- After you are finished with all aspects of your universal story, you can have certain parts or all of them dialogue together. Do this by stepping into one at a time and have it speak to another aspect. Step out of it, and then step into the other object and have it reply back.
- When the entire process is complete, close your space.

Journeying

Journeying is the path of direct revelation. There are many styles of journeying found throughout the world and all time, but they all have several characteristics in common. One enters nonordinary reality at will to acquire knowledge, personal power, and healing.

In shamanic journeying, there are three worlds to which one journeys, the Lower World, the Middle World, and the Upper World. Each has an infinite number of levels along with spirits, teachers, animals, guides, and helpers with whom you can talk and from whom you can learn. It's important to know you have complete control of where you go and to whom you talk in any of these worlds.

There are many different styles and methods of journeying from around the world. Several good books give guidance and instruction, some even including a CD of rattling or drumming to induce an alpha state of alternative consciousness (see Bibliography). For our purposes, body journeying is extremely useful for working with patterns and beliefs (see below). Alternatively, you may do the following:

- Determine what you want help with, answers to, and healing about.
- Ready your space, and set your intention.
- Journey to a special place you love or imagine in nature.
- Find an opening, such as a cave, cavern, tree, stream, waterfall, or hole.
- Go inside, and travel down into the earth. Keep moving downward, deep, deep down, until you come out to another place.
- Find a cave or room filled with doors.
- Find which door calls to you and open it.
- Walk into another room. There you find helpers and healers who share their wisdom and guidance.

- When complete, give thanks, leave the room or cave, and travel back up the opening, going up and up, back to your nature spot.
- Return to your body.
- Record your experience in your journal.
- Close your space.
- Act on anything you were told.

Body Journey

An effective way to ceremonially process any issue is with a body journey. Body journeying is especially effective for health issues but may be used with any universal story. Besides journeying into the body, you may also use this process to see what other people's energies are there that shouldn't be and journey into chakras and subtle energy bodies.

Journeying into the body helps you discover the gift, truth, information, and wisdom around a particular health issue. The difference between journeying in the body and looking into the body is that when you look into your body you see it from a mental perspective, whereas when you journey into the body, everything looks huge, like you're actually there.

When you journey into your body, you may visit different organs, tissues, or other areas and from there be guided to more places. You may even sense guidance to travel into the earth, to the stars, or to a past or future life. In addition, different parts of the body may want to talk to each other, state their needs to each other, and make agreements. There are no

My Body Journey

I spontaneously discovered body journeying over thirty-two years ago when I had a terrible sore and swollen throat and couldn't go on a family Thanksgiving trip. My partner left in anger, which triggered my own anger. I immediately wrote down how I was feeling and vented all I wanted to say but had been holding back. In other words, I gave voice to my true feelings. Then I journeyed into my throat.

When I did so, I dialoged with it. A memory came of an experience early in life when my best friend and I were talking with an adult. The adult sided with my best friend, and I began to doubt myself. As a result, I learned to not speak my truth or say what I wanted to say to certain people. Not only did it not feel safe, I also didn't want to take flack or be put down.

I learned that wanting to express myself but holding back created the chronic sore throats. After this realization, my swollen throat immediately released, and I felt well again. It seemed a miracle had happened, and I received an incredible teaching about the power of the physical body.

"should's." Just stay open, and follow the journey where it guides you. Listen to what the body says and teaches, and act on its advice.

Exercise: Body Journey

- Ready your space, and set your intention.
- Scan your entire body. Where do you feel pulled? What wants your attention? What health symptom calls the loudest?
- Imagine you are very small and enter a magic glass elevator behind your eyes. It can go up, down, sideways, and diagonally as needed.
- Get out of the elevator and explore your body area through all your senses (look, touch, smell, listen, and taste.) Any colors? Movement? Textures? Images? Symbols?
- As the elevator descends, you pass your mammoth nose, giant lips, huge chin, large throat, and enormous glands, continuing in this manner to the body area.
- Get out of the elevator and explore your body area through all your senses (look, touch, smell, listen, and taste.) Any colors? Movement? Textures? Images? Symbols?
- If you don't know where to go, ask your heart. You can jump into your bloodstream there and let it carry you where needed. Or go anywhere you have sensations. You may feel pulled to the site of pain, discomfort, or trouble.
- You may see cords go to other places, such as organs, to past lives, to the lower or upper worlds, and so on. Follow these.
- Now dialogue with that body area or other place you were taken or shown. Let it speak to you while writing it down. Ask questions, such as:
  - What is causing you distress?
  - What do you need or want?
  - What is your message?
  - What do you want to tell or teach me?
  - What do I need to hear, learn?
  - Do you have any advice for me?
  - What are your gifts?
- Record the answers. Keep dialoguing until complete (you'll know because you'll receive an understanding, "ah-ha," or other information).
- Take the elevator back up to behind your eyes and step out.
- Close your space.

Soul Retrieval

When you experience a traumatic event, a part of you may separate from your overall energy field. That piece is supposed to come back, but if that's too difficult, it disassociates and creates soul loss. Traumas can include accidents, abuse, traumatic fights, verbal engagements, and other shocking events. Signs of soul loss include listlessness, apathy, severe depression, hypersensitivity, and hypervigilance. Soul loss has also occurred if you've never felt the same after a particular traumatic event or time period in your life.

Lost soul parts may be retrieved. Generally, this is done by someone practiced in soul retrieval. However, if you suspect you have soul loss, you may call that part back to yourself. Here are a few possible ways:

- While in meditation, in your sacred heart space, or at night while reversing, call any lost parts back to you.
- Ask your helpers and healers, such as angels, to help as well.
- Identify and clear any limiting patterns or beliefs that block its return.
- Determine a universal story for that lost piece and ceremonially process it.

Duplication

Western mysticism has long taught that to best invoke the power of something into manifestation, you fully act as if it is so. You can do this by duplicating your universal story in all its possible ways. Dress in the same manner, set up props, create its space, and act out its personality. Step into that metaphor, myth, archetype, fairy tale, or image and sense its energies. Rather than use words, tap into how your universal story *feels*. Allow it to move through you, and speak its truth. Revelations and realizations will come as a result, and your perspective will shift.

Prayer Arrow

A prayer arrow is a ritual for releasing your universal story. Here are the steps:
- Ready your space, and set your intention.
- Find a stick you like.
- Decorate it as desired. Say prayers or state your intentions the entire time.
- Find a place in nature to plant your stick.
- Blow your intention and prayers into the prayer arrow for what you want to release.
- Plant it in the earth.
- When your universal story is neutralized, ceremonially burn the prayer arrow.

- Close your space.

Altars

Altars may be created for many purposes. They may even be made for dead ancestors or pets as they help relieve grief. Create altars for something you want to release or something you want to bring in as well. Sometimes an old pattern or belief needs to be processed for a while before it will release. An altar is a great way to do this.

Place items on your altar as appropriate for your universal story. Some ideas include photographs, pictures or drawings, flowers, candles, seeds, food, incense, blessed water, or other items. This keeps the honoring process alive. In general, keep altars out of your bedroom so they don't affect your sleep. When your process is complete, dismantle the altar.

Feather Ritual

A feather ritual helps you make tough either/or decisions, such as, "Should I do this, or that?" It gives valuable insight to your true hidden feelings and desires, making your decision clearer and easier. To do a feather ritual:

- Get a feather.
- Take the feather with you to an open place in nature.
- Ready your space, and set your intention.
- Think about your two choices, and decide which you choose, even if you still feel uncertain about it.
- When ready, state the choice you are letting go out loud.
- Release the feather.
- If that decision reflects your true subconscious feelings, you'll be able to let the feather go and even sense liberation as it flies away.
- If you can't let it go, it doesn't reflect your deeper desires. You may even chase after to retrieve it.
- If you couldn't let the feather go, repeat this ritual with the opposite choice. That is, state aloud that you release the opposite choice, and let the feather go.
- You might still have resistance, but find it easier to release than the first choice. Now you know which choice to make.
- Close your space.

Sandpainting

Sandpaintings are used by many cultures and traditions throughout the world, notably Tibetan, Hindu, Navajo, Inca, and Buddhist. They are created in different ways and for different purposes. Sandpaintings are transient and as such are quite powerful. Some traditions use colored sand while others employ wood to burn or other objects. In most, specific patterns are created to achieve certain results.

A sandpainting is a way of connecting with your soul and Source energies to work on an issue and to ceremonially processes your universal story. This way Spirit works on your issue rather than it working on you. Whenever you are triggered, create a sand painting and leave the issue and its emotions for the universe to work. This helps you shift on all levels.

> ## The Power of Sandpaintings
>
> **I once participated in an East Indian yogic fire ceremony (*yugya*) in which a particular sandpainting was created to evoke rain during our seven-year drought in California in the nineties. Sure enough, the day after the ceremony, it rained. This was in August, when it never rains in our area, let alone during a drought! I learned then the power of sandpaintings.**

Exercise: Sandpainting

- Ready your space, and set your intention.
- Draw a circle on the earth (if indoors, use a small box of sand or sheet of paper).
- Using natural found objects, create a "picture" in the circle of how your issue or universal story *feels* in your body. Put your emotions in it but *not any people*. Allow it to "paint" itself. You'll know when it's done as it will feel right inside.
- Stand back and look at the whole picture. Understanding, realizations, or insights may come at this point, and your energy may shift. If not, leave the sandpainting "open."
- Later, return to your sandpainting, and look at it with fresh eyes. You may find that nature has changed it in some way. You may also modify it if needed so it feels right at that point. Know that when the sandpainting is altered, your life changes to reflect this.
- As long as your sandpainting is open, you're still in process with your issue or universal story; it's still working for you and on you.
- You'll know when the sandpainting's work is complete because your inner wisdom will feel it's done.

- When finished, close the sandpainting by taking out any remaining objects and smooth the circle over.
- Close your space.

Mind Mapping

A mind map is a diagram where words, ideas, tasks, and other items are linked to and intuitively arranged around a central key word or idea. It may be used to classify, visualize, structure, and generate ideas, solve problems, make decisions, and take notes. Mind maps can also help with memory recall, elicit realizations, see connections, and shift how you view an issue.

Exercise: Mind Mapping

- Ready your space, and set your intention.
- Draw a circle in the center of your paper.
- Draw an image of your universal story inside. Use at least three colors.
- Draw branches off the central circle, and write key associations on them. Include images when possible. Be sure to connect the lines with the circle.
- Draw branches off the branches as needed to group related items together.
- Use different colors and line thicknesses to code the groupings.
- Show associations by linking them with a line.
- Use your inner wisdom as guide, and be creative!
- When finished, look at the whole picture metaphorically. Look for the following:
  - *Colors:* Where is the most color? Least? What is the predominant color? The least used or not used color?
  - *Light and dark:* Where is the most light? Dark? Overall, is the picture dark (heavy, difficult, deep, buried, mysterious) or faint (are you invisible in your life)?
  - *Form:* Gaps? Chaos? Crowded? Lively? Linear? Cyclical? Geometric?
  - *Shapes:* Remind you of _____? Empty spaces?
  - *Activity:* Bland? Some activity? Active? Too active?
- What realizations arise or connections occur from these answers?
- When you feel complete, close your space.

Collage

Make a collage of your universal story as a ceremonial process (see "Tools To Discover Your Stories" at the end of section II). Choose images and objects that represent how it feels. You may also use it to determine your soul's journey by choosing images that represent your passions, stories, and life journey, or that just call to you for some reason. Arrange them according to what feels right. While this process alone ceremonially processes your universal story, you can use it with other rituals or ceremonies, such as dialoguing, dancing, drumming, and journeying.

Fire Ceremony

Fire is an archetype for transformation, purification, and rebirth. It is one of the core ceremonies in many ancient traditions. A fire ceremony is done to release something and to bring in the light to symbolically ignite the new. Fire provides the vehicle to let go of old stories and drama and to transform, renew, and be reborn.

Through fire ceremony, you ceremonially process your universal story or issue by placing it in the fire and turning it over to Source. When you release it to the fire, you heal at the level of the soul without having to experience it literally or physically. Any time you seem "blocked" or are focusing on a manifestation, fire is an incredible tool to help you shift.

Exercise: Fire Ceremony

Before coming to the fire circle, create an offering out of burnable materials, such as a small stick or piece of paper, on which you have written the issue, pattern, core belief, or universal story that you desire to release.

- Ready your space, and set your intention.
- Prepare the fire, candle, fireplace, fire pit, or bonfire.
- Light the fire, candle, fireplace, fire pit, or bonfire.
- Connect with the universal story you are releasing. Acknowledge the lessons, teachings, and gifts you have received. Using your breath, blow this intention or prayer into the offering three times.
- Make your offering to the fire. Repeat with all offerings until done.
- Stay with the fire until everything burns to ashes.
- If appropriate, use your hands to pull the firelight into and over you to kindle and feed your new universal story/intentions.
- Close your space.

The Inca say there is a two-week period following their fire ceremonies during which "instances of opportunity" appear to translate your intentions into reality. This means it creates an opening for healing, opportunities, or whatever else you need to appear. Look for these and seize them while allowing the universe to care for the details.

Vision Quest, Walkabout, and Earth Power Walk

Traditional people went on vision quests or walkabouts to find their way, mark progress, seek vision for their people, and discover answers. You can choose to do a formal or informal vision quest or walkabout as you are drawn. If you choose to do a formal vision quest or walkabout, I suggest you seek a teacher to watch over and guide you in this process.

A walkabout is a traditional male Australian Aborigine rite of passage during which he journeys through the wilderness along ancestral "songlines" for periods up to six months. While you may choose to follow your ancestral paths on a journey, you may also do a shorter walkabout, even for just one day. I call this an Earth Power Walk.

An Earth Power Walk is a dawn-to-dusk walk during which you can fast or not as appropriate. It is a focus on self-communion, listening to nature, and looking for signs from the universe. It is a powerful way to process your universal story and discover deeper aspects of yourself.

Exercise: Earth Power Walk

Before your walk:

- Choose a place in nature that calls to you and is safe.
- Tell a friend or family member where you are going and when you intend to return. Leave a note stating this information as well.
- Decide if you are going to fast or not.
- Take a daypack, water, emergency kit, appropriate layered clothing, journal, pen, ritual items, food (if desired), cell phone (keep off and use for emergencies only), hat, sunglasses, sunscreen, mosquito repellant, and comfortable walking shoes.
- Be at your starting point at dawn and stay until dusk. A full walk is necessary and important for your process.
- Call the park rangers before hand (if this applies) and tell them approximately where you'll be and when you plan to return. Ask them for specific information you need regarding parking lot openings, wild animals, ticks, trail conditions, and other important details.
- Be informed regarding appropriate behavior of the wildlife in the area in which you're walking (including cougars, red ants, bears, and others in your area).

To begin your walk:

Create a threshold of some sort to formally delineate the beginning of your Earth Power Walk. This can be as simple as drawing a line on the earth, which you then cross upon your return. Or you may choose to mark the outer doorway to your dwelling in some way so that when you pass through it you begin or end.

While you are on your Earth Power Walk:

- Open to the influences of the natural world. Be aware of:
    - Who and what you think about
    - What you explore
    - What you see
    - What animals, plants, rocks, and other natural objects draw your attention
    - How you feel in your body
    - Anything else that draws your focus and attention
- Perform any planned or spontaneous rituals as appropriate.
- Write in your journal, and reflect on what you learn.
- Dialogue with nature as she presents herself.
- Reflect on your universal story. Ask for answers, help, and guidance from nature to both clarify and shift it.

To end your walk:

Cross a threshold again to mark the end of your walk. Erase or in some other way remove the threshold you created.

When you return from your walk:

- Notify the park rangers you are back.
- Inform your friend or family member you have returned.
- If you fasted, break your fast slowly by eating lightly that evening.
- Wait to share your in-depth, personal experience with others until you've processed your experience and are ready. Just tell people you're back and are okay. You can discuss general parts, such as the weather and that you walked, sat, and looked at scenery or other simple details.

About fasting:

- Fasting is an excellent way to focus solely on your walk and process.

- If your body requires some food for health reasons, be sure to take easily accessible and edible food and eat as needed. Pack out your trash.
- Whether or not you fast, take some emergency food with you in case it is needed.

How to Process Your Earth Power Walk:

- Several days later, review the journal entries you made during the walk.
- Look for overall themes. Note the highs, lows, and what stood out, such as a certain place, animal, or event.
- Dialogue with each piece you noted. Ask it questions, such as:
  - Why did you happen or come to me?
  - What is your teaching?
  - What do you want me to know?
  - What is your gift?
- Act on what you received during the walk or during your dialogue after the walk.

Healing and Divine Triangulations

The pathological triangle of victim, hero, and perpetrator keeps you stuck in limiting stories whereas the healing and Divine triangulations reframe your issue so your perspective shifts. You may also use this with any people or situations with whom you are on the pathological triangle.

Exercise One: Healing Triangulation

The outcome of a healing triangulation can be quite amazing. I've seen a complete reversal of behavior and experience through this process. Where once there was no communication, communication occurs; disrespect, respect; and lack of touch, touch. This transformation occurs without having to do anything externally. Instead, it arises from the shift inside because you now hold the person, people, group, or situation differently. This then allows for a healing to occur.

- Draw a triangle.
- Put your name in the bottom left corner and your universal story (or person or issue) in the bottom right corner.
- At the top of the triangle, put the state or quality you desire to experience with your universal story (or person or issue), such as compassion, ease, love, touch, patience, communication, equality, wisdom, respect, openness, understanding, or peace.

- Continue focusing on the desired quality between you and the other until the desired result is achieved.

Exercise Two: Divine Triangulation

Do the same process as a healing triangulation, only put Source (or your name for the Divine) at the top of the triangle and let the Universe determine what's needed for healing.

Reframing

Reframing is a process of shifting your words and phrases to a positive context. When you reframe situations, it quickly shifts how you feel about them. For instance, instead of saying you are in "crisis" or are experiencing a "disaster" in your life, reframe it to you are at a "turning point" or in "transformation."

Reframing is not sticking your head in the sand about what is happening. Rather, it helps you approach the issue from a different perspective, one that is more open to other possibilities. It also improves how you feel rather than staying closed, stuck, or depressed about the situation. Reframing your language around your universal story helps you process it and receive realizations and new understanding.

Repattern

Repatterning is used to review a difficult past event and recreate the desired outcome. This diffuses energy from the past, including limiting patterns and beliefs. This does not change the event itself but shifts how you feel about it.

For example, David remembered a time when his beloved grandfather died and he couldn't attend the funeral. To repattern this, he readied his space, set his intention, and calmed his breath. Then he relived the event, not by how it had happened, but by how he wanted it to have happened

He saw himself getting excused from school and being driven by a friend's parent to the funeral. Then he imagined sitting with everyone else, listening to the ceremony, standing up and saying what he wanted to share, and celebrating his grandfather's life with everyone else. He visualized the procession, the burial site, and watched the burial. He said, "Thank you, I love you, and I forgive you" to his grandfather in his heart. David completed every detail of the event until he felt complete and had the experience he wanted.

You can do this with any past event to energetically shift what happened. This creates an internal change that affects how you feel about it. You neutralize its impact on your nervous system too.

Exercise One: Repattern 1

- Ready your space, and set your intention.
- Choose a past event you would like to have experienced differently.
- Go back to right before the event occurred, maybe thirty–sixty seconds.
- Relive the event but with what you would like to have happened instead. Arm yourself with any needed protection or tools. See the image to completion.
- Track it out to the future to make sure it works. Tweak as needed, and edit the newly inserted image. When it works in the future, you are done. If it doesn't work in the future, go back and repattern some more until you are complete.
- Close your space.

Exercise Two: Repattern 2

- Ready your space, and set your intention.
- Choose a past event you would like to have experienced differently.
- Go back to right before the event occurred, maybe thirty-sixty seconds.
- Take the original event out and tear it up, throw it away, see it dissolve, or some other method that destroys that memory.
- Go back to a prior joyful time and implant that memory instead.
- If there isn't one, create a joyful event and implant that memory.
- Track it out to the future to make sure it works. Tweak as needed, and edit the newly inserted image. When it works in the future, you are done. If it doesn't work in the future, go back and repattern some more until you are complete.
- Close your space.

Healing Core Beliefs and Values

Here's a useful way to shift beliefs and values. Hold your journal or paper and a pen and do the following steps:

Exercise: Healing Core Beliefs and Values

Hold your journal or paper and a pen and do the following steps:

- Ready you space, and set your intention.
- Close your eyes, and breathe deeply several times.
- Journey to a special place you love or imagine in nature.
- Ask yourself the following question, and record the answer:
  - What are my core beliefs and values?

- ♦ Take the first core belief or value and ask:
    - Is this really my own idea, or did I adopt it?
    - Why do I have this belief or value?
    - Does this belief empower and serve me?
    - What would I have to give up to change this belief or value?
- Record the answers in your journal, and continue until all your questions have been answered.
- Return to your body.
- If appropriate, release that core belief or value in ceremony.
- Close your space.

Releasing Emotions

When you've determined the major emotions you tend to experience, here are several ways to release them.

Exercise: Cultivate Virtues

Often our emotions, attitudes, and self-perceptions are physiologically based rather than emotionally. In Traditional Chinese Medicine (TCM), when organs are imbalanced, their corresponding emotions either become exaggerated or repressed. When the organs heal, their corresponding emotions diminishes. These emotions may be used for healing in two ways: by cultivating virtues and by providing the organs with their essential needs.

In ancient times of TCM, physicians worked with patients to shift their vices (adverse emotions) to virtues, called "culturing the virtue." You can do this as well by focusing on the corresponding virtues (beneficial emotions) to your excessively expressed or repressed emotions (the vices). Further, each organ benefits from certain activities and qualities of being, which, when supplied, lessen their corresponding vices. The following chart lists the organs with their essential needs, vices, and virtues.

Ancestral Patterns

Once you've discovered your ancestral patterns in "Tools to Discover Your Stories," there are several excellent techniques to clear them.

Exercise One: Dialoguing

Dialogue with the ancestor either through writing or speaking out loud.

HEALING WITH THE EMOTIONS			
ORGAN	**ESSENTIAL NEED**	**VICE/INJURING QUALITIES**	**VIRTUE/HEALING QUALITIES**
HEART	Love, joy, beauty	Overexcitement; overachieving; excess joy, fright (shock), sadness, or unhappiness; excessive laughter, talking, partying, or reading; excessive worrying/ thinking; fear, anxiety, shock	Compassion; caring for yourself; following your heart's desires and spiritual path; love; working with your emotions; psychotherapy; joy, beauty, enthusiasm, joy of life, openheartedness, and laughter
LUNGS	Confidence, time and space	Exposure to cold; grief, sadness; criticism (from others or self); shallow breathing (you don't give yourself enough breath or breathing room); unworthiness (don't feel worthy of living/breathing); reclining excessively; not living in the present but holding onto past sadness & hurts (pain in the present = hurt; pain in the past = anger; anger directed at self = guilt)—get the old-hurt stuff out!	Protect yourself from cold (especially at back of neck); conscientiousness; feeling good about one's self; creating room for yourself—enough time & space; confidence (its more important to act confident than to be confident); gratitude (it gets you breathing and allows what you desire to come to you); being in the present moment

ORGAN	ESSENTIAL NEED	VICE/INJURING QUALITIES	VIRTUE/HEALING QUALITIES
LIVER	Relaxation, peace, herbs	Anger, frustration, resentment, irritability, impatience, depression, annoyance, timidity, or cowardice; repressing or stuffing your emotions; excessive and prolonged anger; any long-term repressed or stuffed emotions	Kindness, forgiveness, respect, esteem, and benevolence; service; decisiveness; a healthy drive; creative expression; physical movement; appropriate emotional expression and release; naturally induced altered states; bravery; assertiveness; courageousness; herbs and medicines
SPLEEN	Nurturance, nutrition, giving to others	Obsession, worry, pensiveness, or brooding; confusion; always caring for others without getting the care you need; dwelling on the past; eating on the run, while doing business, or standing up; poor diet (especially excessive intake of cold, damp foods and drinks); excessive sitting	Empathy, centeredness; right action; instinct and intuition; nurturance (being nurtured on all levels); good nutrition and giving yourself what you need (don't expect others to give it to you); quit giving it away (i.e., nurture yourself!)
KIDNEYS	Rest, quiet, sleep, meditation, drinking water	Fear, paranoia, worry, fright, apprehension, mistrustfulness, stubbornness, or procrastination; excessive weight lifting; sitting on damp ground	Courage; wisdom; meditation; resting; sleep; drinking water; cultivating wisdom (knowledge plus experience); holding to a purpose in life—being resolute, determined, firm, and enduring

Exercise Two: Open Chair Gestalt

Imagine your ancestor sitting in a chair opposite you. Say what you need to say to the ancestor. Listen to what the ancestor says back, or sit in the ancestor's chair and respond to what you said from the ancestor's perspective.

Exercise Three: External Techniques

There are two excellent techniques developed by other people to clear ancestral patterns. Both are well-developed systems and available in book form or online (see the Bibliography).

Releasing Roles

Roles are released through some form of ritual or ceremony.

Exercise: Releasing Roles

One of the best and simplest rituals I know for this is to "burn" your roles. You will need a small stick or a slip of paper for each of your roles and a fire, such as a candle with a fireproof bowl or other container, a fireplace, or an outdoor fire pit. Once you have everything assembled and are ready to go, follow these steps:

- Ready your space, and set your intention.
- Choose a role and blow it into a small stick or write the role on a slip of paper. Now "talk" with the role, thank it for what it's given to you, what it's allowed to happen in your life, what you've learned from it and anything else you need to say.
- When complete, burn the stick or paper in the fire.
- Repeat this process with all the roles.
- When finished, be sure that all the sticks/papers burn to ash.
- Put the fire out.
- Close your space.

This role-burning process is very freeing and revealing. You'll know which roles you can release and which you can't. With the roles you can release, you'll experience new freedom and a life change. The ones you can't let go indicate where more personal work is needed or where more hidden patterns lie. Burning your roles may go against your strongest instincts. This is also an indication of a pattern or belief.

If you can't burn a role, ask why you need it and what would happen if you no longer had it. Whether or not you know the answer yet doesn't matter. First become aware of it, and then decide if you still want it. If you don't, burn the role, and the universe will help you transform.

Dream Work

Once you remember and record your dreams, here are several ways to ceremonially process them and shift their energy. Working with your dreams can be an incredible experience that brings insight and even healing. Although there are many books written on interpreting dreams, the most accurate and powerful interpretation is your own.

Exercise One: Dream Dialoguing

This technique works for any dream but especially helps with confusing ones. View your dream as a mythic story by putting it in third person form (he or she rather than I). You may also do this process with Open Chair Gestalt. Review the dream for:

- Its various actions
- Any adversaries
- Helping or healing forces
- What or who is being hurt or harmed
- Who or what is being healed
- What actions the dream suggests
- What the dream wants from you
- Circle any symbols, what stands out or has special meaning, is frightening, intriguing, curious, what you can't figure out, or want you want to know more about. Include inanimate objects or places. Include the adversaries, helping, or healing forces, and what or who is being hurt or healed.
- Ready your space, and set your intention.
- Now dialogue with each of the circled items, asking:
    - Why are you here?
    - What are you trying to tell or teach me?
    - What do you need in order to heal?
    - What am I doing to cause you?
    - What changes should I make to feel well again?
    - What is your message?
    - What is your gift?
- After each question, sit silently and listen. Record the response you receive. Don't try to make sense of it or edit it with doubtful thoughts. Just let the words or message flow as it comes.
- Respond to the answer with another question or comment. Listen and record the response you receive.

- Continue this process until it feels complete, which will be obvious to you.
- Close your space.

Exercise Two: Dream Divination

If you have a puzzling dream you can't figure out even after dialoguing with its parts, do a journey using a divination posture. This will not necessarily yield a specific interpretation but will give a general sense of its meaning. The posture used for this is "Nupe Mallam."[22] An "ecstatic" posture means it changes consciousness by altering the body through posture. In this case, the body is the ritual while the posture establishes the intent. Here is how to do it:

- Ready your space.
- Set your intention to ask what your dream means or what you should learn.
- Sit on the floor.
- Bend both legs at the knees with both feet pointing to the right and positioned so that your left foot is resting just to the left of your right knee.
- Lean toward your left, and support yourself with your left arm.
- Hold your left arm rigid with your hand at a right angle to your body and pointing away from it.
- Place your left hand at a spot three to five inches to the left of your body and just behind a straight line drawn along the back of your buttocks.
- Place your right hand on your left leg where the muscle indents about halfway down your calf.
- Move your head slightly to the left so you are looking over your left knee.
- Close your eyes.
- If this side causes discomfort, you may do the posture facing the opposite direction in a mirror image of the position described above.
- Do your journey, ideally listening to a CD of rattling or drumming (see Bibliography). As you journey, ask, "What is my dream about? What should I learn from this dream?"
- When the journey is complete, record it in your journal.
- Close your space.

Exercise Three: Dream Journeying

Journeying with your dreams is particularly useful for scary dreams.

---

22   This posture is from *Ecstatic Body Postures: An Alternate Reality Workbook* by Belinda Gore. Bear & Company. Rochester, New York, 1995, p. 106. Reprinted with permission from Belinda Gore..

- Ready your space, and set your intention.
- Journey to a special place you love or imagine in nature.
- Arm yourself with all the tools and protections you need and want.
- Relive your dream armed with your tools and protections.
- As you work with each scary part, use your tools and protections. Know that new tools or protections will appear as needed.
- Ask questions, such as:
    - Why are you trying to get my attention so strongly?
    - What is your message?
    - What is your gift?
- Use whatever tools necessary to neutralize the scary parts. For example, use a lance or arrows or enter the cave with your torchlight.
- When complete, return to your body.
- Record your experience in your journal.
- Close your space.

Exercise Four: Dream Archetypes

See the major elements in your dream as archetypes. For example, recognize the sword in your dream as the Sword of Truth, or the dark night as the Black Knight guarding, protecting, and guiding you through the instinctual world. Then work with the archetype that you discovered or its universal story and take that to ceremony or ritual.

Death Work

In "Tools to Discover Your Stories" at the end of section II, much was said about death and death work. Here are two death preparation ceremonies that help release patterns, beliefs, and universal stories. Take both seriously, for we don't know when we will die. It could be any day or any minute. This is it. When you truly sense you're dying, you shift to true priorities, unfulfilled desires, and regrets.

Exercise One: Death Walk

Take one day to prepare for death in this way:

- Ready your space, and set your intention.
- Spend one day as if it were your last. See the sun, tree, and flower as if you'll never see it again. Notice everything.
- Be fully in love on your last day, and note what comes up and what really matters.

- Say, "I love you," "I apologize," "I forgive you," and "I thank you" as needed.
- Ask questions, such as:
  - ♦ If I were to die tomorrow, what do I wish I had accomplished? Felt? Shared? Told someone? Heard from someone?
  - ♦ What is not working for me now?
  - ♦ What is it I want instead?
  - ♦ What is the burning desire in my heart?
- Close your space.
- Act on your answers.
- Repeat the Death Walk one day a week or month until complete.

Exercise Two: Death Circle

A death circle is the opportunity to finish what needs completing before you die. It's a chance to forgive and say your needed, "I love you," "I forgive you," and "I thank you" before you die. You can also complete with anyone with whom you still resent, have old wounds or anger, or have things left unsaid. Releasing in this way neutralizes old patterns and creates a change of heart.

In a death circle, you face the core people still affecting you and say exactly what needs to be said, listen to that person, get emotions out, understand the situation from both sides, and acknowledge that person and yourself. This is not done in person but alone. That means you can do this with people who have already died. It is a very powerful process and so takes full intention to do. Trust the process!

How to do a death circle:

Before starting, ask these questions, and make a list of the answers:
- What resentments, old wounds, anger, or regrets do I carry in my heart and with whom (living or dead)?
- Who in my life have I been unwilling to forgive (living or dead, including my self)?

To do the process:

- Find a place in nature where you can be alone and won't be disturbed. Take everything you'll need for a couple of hours—water, journal, pen, layered clothing, sunscreen, your notes from the above questions, and a blanket to sit on.

- Build a circle of stones large enough to hold you and all of your stuff (this is a wheel of protection and intention).
- Ready your space, and set your intention.
- Remove a stone in the south and enter, bringing everything you need in with you. Close the stone circle behind you. Get seated and comfortable.
- Imagine you are about to die and need closure with your people. Look at your list of everyone with whom you haven't yet completed.
- Invite in one person at a time and out loud talk with that person. Tell them:
    - Exactly how you feel—what's made you mad, sad, or upset.
    - What you've always wanted to say to them but couldn't for whatever reason.
    - What you've always wanted to hear from that person but never did.
    - What gifts you received from that person.
    - Say, "I forgive you," "I love you," "I apologize," and "I thank you" as appropriate.
    - Say whatever needs to be said with that person until you've released all the pain, hurt, grievances, and judgments that you've been holding.
    - Next, hold a dialogue with that person. Invite them to speak back to you, again out loud. Just speak their words as if you are that person. If you need to physically change positions to do this, do so. After, you can respond to that person. Continue until done. Trust the process!
- When you've finished with one person and experience clarity and completion, see them leave your circle.
- Invite in the next person, and repeat all the above steps.
- When you have spoken with everyone *or when two hours are up*, leave the circle through the south. Dismantle the stones and smooth the earth, leaving the place as you found it.
- Close your space.
- Two hours of emotional work can be draining, so if you are not complete, stop, rest, and repeat the entire process another day.

Exercise Three: Death of Emotions and Memories

You can also do a death circle with each memory, thought, emotion, or experience that has brought you sorrow. Here's how:

- Follow the steps for a Death Circle.

- Instead of inviting in a person, call in what brought you sorrow.
- Feel its pain with all its emotions.
- Dialogue with it. Ask such questions as:
  - Why are you here?
  - What are you trying to tell or teach me?
  - What do you need in order to heal?
  - What am I doing to cause you?
  - What changes should I make to feel well again?
  - What is your message?
  - What is your gift?
- When complete, say, "I love you, I accept you. Come into my heart now. It's over."
- Release it, and see it leave.
- Repeat with the next sorrow and the next.
- Repeat until you are complete with everything, *or when two hours are up.*
- Next, imagine you're sitting by a river and memories float by. Look at them in whatever order they come (usually it's not chronological). As they arrive, complete any unfinished business with each one.
- Again say, "I love you," I forgive you," "I apologize," and "I thank you" as needed.
- Repeat until you are complete.
- When complete, follow the finishing steps for a Death Circle.

Self-Generated Ceremonies and Rituals

If none of the ceremonies and rituals given here fit, generate your own. Ceremonies and rituals are fun to create and can be simple or quite elaborate. They can be done alone or involve other people. They may include music, singing, dancing, drumming, gestures, prayer, statements of belief, offerings, and movement.

You can also employ the natural elements in various ways, such as fire (fire ceremony), earth (sleeping on or in the earth or burying something), air (using flowers or feathers or throwing something into the air), and water (ritual bathing, anointing, submerging in water).

Additionally, you can exchange gifts, tie hands together, make offerings, destroy the old, change clothing, or paint something new. In group rituals, each person could grind a seed into a paste and use it to anoint, or tie a knot in a string with their blessings. Other possibilities include singing, dancing, drumming, painting, writing a poem, composing a song, or building a structure with your universal story; dance with your fear; drum with your anger; or write a poem about your grief.

You can combine various elements to create your own ritual or ceremony. For example, you could dance with your universal story, allowing it to move through you and express itself. Then stop and draw it on paper with colored pens, crayons, chalk, or watercolors. Then dance again and draw again, repeating until you are complete. Or you could do this same process but with drumming or using voice or another musical instrument and then dancing or even writing a poem and repeating the back-and-forth process until complete.

Whatever ritual you create, I suggest you begin with smudging to ready your space and then set your intention (instructions for smudging are given in "Essential Tools for Change" at the end of section I). Several ritual elements to try are listed in the following table. Combine as appropriate for your needs and desires.

RITUAL COMPONENTS

ENDINGS	TRANSITION	BEGINNINGS	OTHER
Cutting hair	Symbolic clothing	Hair style change	Smudging
Smashing	Solitude	Clothing style change	Journal writing
Burning	Vigils	Feasting	Gestures
Cutting	Making vows	Tying/knotting	"Power" or Night Walks
Tearing	Wearing masks	Mending	Incense/ Smoke
Burying	Period of silence	Symbol of new status	Singing/ Chanting
Washing	Immersion in water	Weaving	Collages
Veiling	Fasting	Unveiling	Lighting candles
Cleaning out stuff	Celibacy	Gifting	Music
Crossing a threshold	Stay in sacred space	Recrossing threshold	Prayer
Stripping away	Name change	Joining together	Offerings
Purification	Nakedness	Donning symbolic clothing	Dancing/ Movement
Forgiving	Touching sacred objects	Fusing/joining objects	Invocation

IV

Ceremonially processing your universal stories can have different results. Sometimes a realization brings enough understanding that the old is swiftly released and neutralized. Other times, a pattern needs more than one session or approach to clear it. Deep, long-lasting issues may need processing over time to peel more layers before it is cleared. All of these were true for me.

All the ceremonial work I did through my vision quests, rituals, journeying, dialoguing, gestalt, dream work, and other techniques created huge shifts inside of me that manifested in my outer life too. Some issues would clear as soon as I reached a realization or understanding. Others took processing over time. I worked on the really big patterns for years.

I would approach an issue from one perspective as much as possible, and then if it reappeared months or years later, I'd work on it again. However, every time it would be less severe, last a shorter time, and clear more swiftly. I'd also reaffirm the new universal stories I chose over and over. Sometimes if I reworked an issue months or years later, I'd choose another universal story as it morphed.

As for the issues I had been working on, those of feeling alone, lack of nourishment on all levels, an inability to let love in, and not finding my place in life, after I cleared them, I chose new universal stories that encompassed what I wanted instead. Here are several examples.

My first vision quest helped me gain clarity about my life and healing work. After it, I got married, birthed and raised my son, and started my career. My second vision quest helped me to further claim my place. I wrote my first book and quickly found a publisher. A second book I thought my husband should write, he turned down. When I realized it was my vision instead, I wrote the book myself.

I planted a new flower garden as a metaphor for the shift I was making. I dismantled the old box structures and designed a new garden that was open and free-flowing. This garden symbolized the transformation I felt within. In its center, I put mosaic stepping-stones I had created of various archetypes that guided me. Again I had daily visual reminders that helped to reinforce these new guides in my life.

I processed different health issues through several techniques. For instance, I focused on my recurring sore throats by journeying my throat. There I realized that whenever I didn't speak my truth but held it inside, my throat would swell or get sore. I needed to give voice to what I felt but in ways that could be heard and received by others. In a journey a tigress appeared to give me courage to verbally express my truth. This new universal story still continues to help.

After my birthday ritual, I truly began to know I deserved love, abundance, and nourishment. One of the gifts I had received helped this transition occur. It was a tale that spoke volumes to me. Since I had spent most of my life trying to fit in, that also meant I had not always been living my authentic self. This realization came clear in this simple but powerful story.

The essence of the tale is that wherever your arrow falls is your target. That way you continually hit a bull's eye. To me, this said that I had been trying to hit other people's targets all my life. Instead, I must now shoot in the direction of my passions and inner guidance, for then I will always hit the center of my destiny.

The entire birthday ritual helped me understand the essence of my issues, and that I needed to listen to my emotions, speak my truth, and respect myself. I drew all three of these on a paper heart and tacked it up so I could regularly see it as a reminder. I began to socialize more and experienced increased creative energy. My sleep improved greatly, although I still had periodic bad bouts that would drain me.

I was able to reach out to my dad first through touch and then words. One day, I spontaneously massaged his back, and another time, he came and massaged my shoulders. We were touching! I also began to tell him that I loved him. It took a few years, but eventually he began to say he loved me back. The power of working on myself helped my dad too and freed us both from this ancestral pattern.

A few years later, a friend invited me to co-lead vision quests, and this brought into manifestation one of the last pieces I had received during my second vision quest. I knew this offer arose because of the extensive inner work I had done so that my self-worth and confidence increased. The world indeed reflected back to me my inner conversion.

After shifting my old story of feeling unloved to the new one of "My community loves and respects me," I began teaching at many new events and seminars. Indeed, a colleague in one of these communities passed my name on, and I was invited to fulfill a dream of mine: to teach on a cruise.

I often made collage cards of some new universal stories I chose. Just the procedure of creating them was a tremendous support to my process and helped my new universal stories come even more alive. I taped them on a wall together, and every morning, I'd wake to those images as a daily reminder of the new life I was creating. As well, I spontaneously grouped the collages together, which elicited new meanings and understandings that years later continue to unfold.

From the old story of the Hanged Man and Wounded Healer going round and round the Wheel of Fortune, I chose the new universal story of the tarot card the Magician. She stands strong and solid in her garden and uses the many tools there to enact her destiny. From this, I incorporated the many techniques I had learned over thirty years and created several different class series, which I continue to update and offer today. People's lives changed from this; some found the relationships of their dreams or joy in their jobs, while others recovered from miscarriages and then celebrated new pregnancies.

In terms of the Gates Work, I had ceremonially processed my descent at each stage. This helped me shift my issues and integrate them to inform my life anew. I remembered someone once teaching the essential action of each chakra and reviewing that amazed me. The first chakra is "be" (water gate); the second, "grow" (earth gate); the third, "do" (fire gate); the fourth, "love" (air gate), the fifth, "speak" (ether gate), the sixth, "see," and the seventh, "have." The essence of each chakra not only matched the energy of each gate, but it also manifested that way in my outer life as well! Truly a greater force was orchestrating my life than I could ever have imagined.

As I processed the issue around finding my place through all my various dreams and the Gates Work, my outer life shifted to reflect this. Within three years after my second vision quest, I had created my own retreat space at home and was taking one half day a week as retreat time. Additionally, I had moved into a new clinic space. My practice until then had been meager, but after the move, it expanded and thrived. I brought more and more of the many tools I had learned over thirty years into my practice and, along with the new shamanic techniques, integrated them together.

To work with my issue of lack, I used my body wisdom to determine its source. When I tuned within, I realized that the problem wasn't nourishment, as I was surrounded by it, but rather somehow I couldn't take it in. So I drew a circle on the earth and imagined everything that nourished me around its circumference. Then I stepped inside the circle and, with my hands, symbolically pulled the different items toward me as I claimed aloud, "I step into my nourishment and feed myself."

Something deep inside shifted as I did this, and I truly felt open to receiving my nourishment. To this, I added the new belief, "I respect and honor myself." I mind-mapped this on paper, drawing a heart at the center and all the nourishment I wanted stemming from this. This then morphed to, "I am open to all possibilities."

After this, I again created a new class series and began to offer this different work to my clients and community. Of course I had a night dream to reflect these shifts. In it, I experienced what I loved and realized I deserved and could have it all. At the same time, I understood the life-long themes that created my sense of lack. I identified the people involved and did *Ho'Oponopono* with them and myself. I also clarified the gifts I had received and gave thanks. I created an altar to my ancestors and honored their gifts in my life. I knew then that everything I need comes to me.

Finally, on a journey a few years later, Laughing Buddha appeared and told me, "Be the joy that you want in your life!" I embraced this wisdom deep within and took it to heart. Anytime I didn't feel joy, I identified why and chose to experience joy instead. This was a powerful practice that changed my life.

While I claimed my place more and more in my outer life, I felt layers of emotions release and shed. My nightly dreams now carried the message that I was finally in my room and with my people. Other dreams reflected inner adjustments, such as rebirthing myself (pregnancy dreams) or growing my inner female and male selves (having little girls or boys).

After twelve years, my butterfly self formed, and I began to emerge from the chrysalis. I knew my destiny, started my new Radiance Energy Medicine work and my Radiance Quest class series, and had two of my books published in other countries. It was then that I learned about the sacred heart space, the final key that put it all together.

As I dove within to explore my sacred heart space, I received much guidance and wisdom. Only then did all the pieces finally fall together. Rooms, Inner Man, Hanged Man, the Key, and spirit dreams, and the gates work along with the descent journeys, all merged into this one place, my sacred heart space. I learned here that this spiritual place is my room, my place, and my destiny. My old universal story of Inanna's descent to the underworld now transformed into a heart with a shining star inside. Interestingly, I discovered that on a whim I had already created a collage card with this exact image five years prior. The outer and inner worlds were merging!

Only as I write this have I exited the Inanna descent and, sixteen years after the ether gate, have entered yet another, one that promises new life. Only after being fully purified could I ascend again to clothe myself with the new powers of joy, clarity, abundance, nourishment, intuition, body wisdom, and heart wisdom. My soul's journey has been an alchemical transformation to reclaim my wholeness.

I used to always search, seek answers, or feel unsettled, unhappy, discontented, things weren't right, something was off, this person bugs me, that person is a problem, and other discontent. Now I am at peace. Yes, I've matured and have more space in my life, but I've also transformed so many of my stories of pain into power.

After all of this work, I've regained some of what was stripped away during my descent years. I've enlarged my community, embraced more friends, broadened my diet, traveled more, and, in general, felt more freedom. I've created my own healing work and expanded my creative expression too.

I've changed so much with this work. The major shift I experienced and now express in the outer world, however, is that I feel much more joy and contentment. Many issues have completely resolved, and others I've even forgotten. I'm not nearly as hooked by old patterns, and if I am, I can quickly release them. I'm much more open to seeing my stuff and letting it go.

To me, contentment means you are okay with the way things are. It doesn't mean you won't alter anything or that you don't want something to be different. It also doesn't mean you have perfect health, all of your dreams have come true, that you've finally reached a certain place or achieved your goals, or are even happy. Rather, contentment means that you accept whatever is right now. This means you don't get hooked. It means you accept your self, and that your world and life stem from this inner peace and are not swayed by your outer environment. For me, this alone has been worth the work.

My own journey has been about developing self-trust and listening to my intuition. Doing so has brought me many gifts and taken me places I never would have imagined. I've learned to follow my gut instinct to know when to go there, do that, make that call, or talk to that person. As well, I've learned to trust my gut about when not do something, don't call now, or don't go there. In the past, I would have overridden my gut reaction with logic only to later learn that my intuition was right. It's the thinking part that derails us. Gut instinct comes from our subconscious and superconscious, both of which know more than our conscious mind alone.

I've worked on many other core beliefs and patterns throughout my life, including lack of self-worth, the belief that I have to do it all and be self-sufficient, and that I work really hard but receive little recognition or remuneration. Currently, I am reclaiming my masculine self that I cut off when my brother turned five, so I'm getting stronger at setting boundaries, standing up for myself, and becoming visible. I've more to reclaim, but through it all, my main focus is to manifest my authentic self along with helping others transform their lives.

I still periodically have insomnia, but it doesn't affect me nearly as much as it did before. Gone is the deep despair and pain. I have months on end of good sleep now. Clearing many of my emotional conflicts by unhooking from my stories was a huge reason my sleep improved.

I've used all the tools included in this book in order to uncover and ceremonially process these patterns and themes. And I've used them with many other people to help them change their lives too. It is for this reason that I now offer them to you. May they help you transform your stories of pain into ones of power. May your life metaphor-phosize into the garden of your dreams.

Determine Your Desired Stories

You've learned to identify your stories, uncovered your patterns, discovered your universal story, and processed it ceremonially. You've shifted your perspective and are ready to move on. Now what do you do? How do you write a new story and live a changed life? How do you rewire your brain and reprogram your subconscious with what you desire instead? And how do you activate this new journey?

These are all important questions to explore as you take the next step to create the life that you desire. The old has been neutralized, but it needs to be replaced; the vacuum created by clearing needs to be filled, so you have a new story to live. You do this work by choosing your new universal story and facing forward with it. This is where you come into alignment with your authentic self so you can cocreate your destiny.

Determine Your Life's Purpose

Usually people know very well what they don't want, but when asked about their visions or life's purpose, they are unsure. For some, this is because they don't think what they envision is possible. Others may have general ideas but aren't clear about the specifics. Still more are caught in the daily grind, just trying to keep one foot in front of the other let alone think about what they desire instead. There are several clues to help you define your life's purpose. Many are covered here and in "Tools to Create Your New Life" at the end of this section under "Tools to Manifest the Life You Desire."

Destiny Versus Fate

Fate and destiny are two very different concepts. According to the dictionary, *destiny* comes from the French word, *destinée*, meaning "purpose and intent," and from the Latin word, *desinare*, meaning "to make firm or establish." Fate comes from the Latin word *fata*, meaning "prophetic declaration, oracle, or prediction."

Like stories of the Greek Fates or Norse Norns, fate is the cloth that has already been spun. It is predetermined, so you have no choice. Fate traps you as a victim on the pathological triangle, seeming like you're doomed to the same experience forever. To move into a life of your dreams and visions, it's necessary to step off this triangle and out of fate.

Fate is deeply imbedded in our language. Many of us say things like, "It's doesn't matter what I do," "It's my fate," "It's my karma," or "I did X, so Y happened to me." In one sense, our future is predetermined but only because our past actions create our probable future. Most of us live according to fate, but with our old patterns and beliefs neutralized, we can choose our new life from a place of destiny instead.

Destiny claims that you can influence the design of your life's fabric. According to the Inca, you are born with both a gold and a silver book of life. One book is filled with your current life while the other is blank, ready for a new story to be written. The filled book is your fate while the blank book is your destiny. In other words, fate is probability while destiny is possibility.

Destiny is stepping out of karma and into dharma, your individual unique path in life. In Taoism, it is the "way," or the natural flow of nature in life. If you go with your own natural flow, that is, with your passions, talents, and gifts, doors will automatically open and your desires come.

But What *Is* My Life Purpose?

I'll never forget in high school when it was finally my turn to look at the book of careers. I was very excited when my school counselor presented it because I knew that somewhere inside I would find what I'd do for the rest of my life. I quickly paged through the book and searched the possible professions for my special career. Yet list after list didn't reveal a thing. Nothing fit or felt right. Although I had known from age thirteen that I'd help people, I didn't know how or through what means. Unfortunately, that book didn't tell me either, and when I closed it, I felt more confused than before.

Here I'll tell you what I wished someone had told me all those years ago. Destiny is not something you discover and then set about to pursue. Rather, **destiny manifests as you develop and actualize your unique talents, gifts, passions, inclinations, and highest creative potential.**

In other words, destiny is what you long to express in partnership with creation. It is doing what you love, what brings you joy and energy, and what expresses your true self and deepest yearnings. Destiny helps you flourish in such a way that it serves a higher purpose and the world at large.

It's important to determine your life's purpose according to what you *desire* rather than on what you *want*. Desire is different from want. Want implies need; it is from lacking something. Derived from the French phrase, *de sidere,* meaning, "from the stars," desire is an aspiration for something. This is where to aim your dreams and set your intentions. For example, instead of,

"I want a job," try something like, "I desire right livelihood that fulfills and inspires me and uses my gifts and talents to help the world."

How to Determine Your Life Purpose

Every one of us is responsible for discovering our own life purpose. Our soul's journey encompasses our life purpose, but it's not written out; we're not given a user's manual when we are born. It's something we feel and attune to. You'll discover yours when you allow your innate, inborn potentials to express and when you align with your true authentic self. Then you become a conduit for divine energies to flow through you to gift others and the world.

My teacher, Evelyn Eaton, always said to smudge ourselves before we smudge others, for then we would be centered and able to extend more outwardly (instructions for smudging are given in "Essential Tools for Change" at the end of section I). This means you need to attend to your own process first. When you don't align with your passions, skills, and inclinations, pain, misery, and illness can occur, which not only affect you but others as well.

A wonderful example of this is Joseph Campbell, well known for his saying, "Follow your bliss." Instead of getting a formal job after college, he spent five years doing only what he wanted—studying mythology and playing jazz. It was following these passions that ultimately led him to become one of the world's foremost authorities on mythology. Through this, he influenced thousands of people and changed many lives.

To help you follow your bliss, ask: What's my passion? What are my natural talents and gifts? What do I deeply desire to express, experience, and create in my life? What do I truly desire to contribute to the world? What engages and nourishes me? What brings color to my face? What puts a spring in my step or a song in my heart? When does my face light up, my eyes open wide, and my energy zoom? These are the true indicators of passion and bliss, the qualities of your destiny. Follow such energies and interests, and tune into how your body feels and reacts as a result. They are the true signs that you are in destiny rather than fate.

Remember, the universe always mirrors your internal world back to you. So what do you desire to see in that mirror? With what do you desire to fill your garden? Weeds or roses? Mud or healthy soil? Mealy bugs or butterflies?

We all have a burning bush inside of us, a passion to fulfill. So what's your passion? What's your dream? What do you feel called to do and be? What is the intense fire inside your heart? What does your quiet inner voice prompt for you?

Your deepest desires propel you into action. These come from your heart; it's heart-based desires that orchestrate your Self in the world. When you consciously follow your heart's desires, it only benefits you and others because it comes from your soul's connection with the Source of all life.

> ## Clues You Are Living or Are Not Following Your Life's Purpose
>
> *You are living your life purpose if you feel* at home; it's the right place; like you can grow there, be nurtured, and supported.
>
> You will know your destiny when it feels right. Your heart will be at peace, and doors will automatically open. People generally know when they are "in the zone" or on track with their lives, for there's something inside each of us that knows when we are on or off the beam. To realize your destiny, tune into how your body and heart feel, for they are your true guides.
>
> *You are not living your life purpose if you feel* it's not right in some way, uncomfortable, out of alignment, or out of integrity.
>
> Clues that you are not following your life's purpose include the outer and inner voices that ask: Is it productive? Can it support me? Will it please others? It also includes the outer and inner voices that say, "I have to," "Thou shalt," or "You should." We all know the doubts, the buts, the even-thoughs, and the what-ifs. They surround us and can infuse us. Such limiting beliefs are very effective at stopping us in our tracks and keeping us in fate. Colluding with such cultural beliefs glues the pages of our blank book together so we can't write in it.
>
> When I face any self-doubt or uncertainty about my own path or even about what to do, I track where my energy and attention desire to go, what gives me energy, and what makes me excited. Then I go with the answers. I learned this years ago when my husband suggested there should be an herb book for children. I loved craft books as a child, so I quickly warmed to his idea, had a strong vision of the book, and encouraged him to write it.
>
> Several years passed, and still he had not written it. I'd periodically ask him about it but never received a proactive response. Finally, one day he told me that not only would he not write the book, he had never intended to do so. I was stunned until I realized that I was the one who had envisioned the completed book. My own ideas had created it in my mind. Once I realized the book was actually *my* passion, I wrote and published it in 2000. Today it is still available as *A Kid's Herb Book*, selling not only in the United States but in other countries too.

You Don't Have to Know the Details

This might surprise you, but you don't need to know the details of what you desire to manifest. In fact, it might be better not to because then you can allow for something even better to occur than what you might imagine. Rather than search for specific details about what to do or be, keep focused on your deepest passions, talents, and skills. Follow your bliss, and watch your destiny unfold.

The soul speaks in metaphors, myths, archetypes, and images. It doesn't necessarily say, "Go live there," "Get that job," "Meet these people," "Marry that person," or "Be a teacher or a musician." Instead of setting specific goals, choose a new universal story from the level of the soul. Anything specific you desire, such as a new home, partner, career, or health, will occur as a reflection of this universal story.

When you feel worthy, you attract different people and opportunities than when you feel unworthy. When you feel accepted, trusted, or helped, through resonance and coherence, you experience situations and people who accept, trust, and help you. You set the big picture first, and the rest follows.

The key here is the state of being that evokes these feelings in you, not outside specifics, objects, or achievements. Once you attain your desired feeling state, all the rest follows in alignment with that.

A Guide to Determine Your New Universal Story

A general guide for choosing your new universal story can be the Goddess Maat myth. The ancient Egyptian archetype of truth, honesty, balance, order, law, morality, and justice, the Goddess Maat regulated the stars, seasons, deities, and mortals to set the universe to order after the chaos of creation. Her feather symbolized these qualities and was an important representation of her.

Typically, Maat holds a set of scales, upon which a heart is weighed on one side against her feather of truth on the other. The Egyptians believed we are asked two questions when we die: Did you feel joy in your life? Did others feel joy from you? In other words, if your heart is light as a feather, Maat's scales balance, and you can successfully reach the paradise of the afterlife. Your answers to those two questions can help guide you in choosing your desired life.

Do You Need Talent or Skill to Follow Your Dreams?

Yes and no.

In my twenties, I wanted to be a dancer. I loved to dance and took lots of dance classes. I even dreamed of starting a new career as a dancer. Then one summer, I attended a two-month intensive with a modern dance company. As I auditioned for one of four levels, beginning-to-advanced, I thought surely I'd be placed in one of the upper levels. Instead, I was put in the beginning group. I was shocked to learn I had no talent. Despite this, I stayed and ultimately enjoyed the summer program. But I learned a major lesson: to create your desired life, it's important to match your passions with your talents and skills.

At the same time, if you really have a desire but no talent, you can create a new path. I may not be a dancer, but I turn on music and dance to my heart's content as this nourishes, inspires, and heals me. I also encourage my patients and students to do so because movement circulates stuck energy, which heals many physical and emotional ailments. So rather than a career in dance, I use dance in other ways.

If you don't have or can't gain the talent or skill needed to manifest your dream life, you can still incorporate that dream in other ways or use it as a springboard to fashion something new. Look at the artists who changed tradition and gifted the world with their visions, such as Hildegard of Bingen, Mirabai, Beethoven, Picasso, and James Joyce. Each followed his or her own natural inclinations and created his own art form. So don't get stuck in the acceptable or productive mode of thought, or fitting the pigeonhole of what is the "true" artist, healer, musician, writer, or athlete. Such cultural beliefs are limiting. Instead, create your own path; gather your own unique bouquet of flowers from your garden and extend that to the world.

Step Three Metaphor-phosis: Create the Stories You Desire

Transcendence occurs when you change your mind about who you are and what you believe about yourself. You know you are not worthless, unaccepted, distrusting, or helpless anymore. So what is the new story you desire to create? And how do you create a life you can love?

There are three parts to complete Step Three Metaphor-phosis:

- Ready your space
- Set a new universal story
- Go manifest it

As you follow this process, be sure to refer to "Tools to Manifest the Life You Desire" in "Tools to Live Your New Life" at the end of this section for further help, ideas, and techniques.

Ready Your Space

Step One

If your space is already open from "Step Two Metaphor-phosis," proceed to step two. Otherwise, ready your space. Call in your helpers and healers (create sacred space), close your eyes, relax your muscles, calm your mind, and breathe deeply.

Step Two

Sense a magnetic field surround and infuse you. As you do so, you may experience various physical sensations, such as tingling, trembling, or a sense of great peace. In this altered state, ask if your old story is ready to be transformed into a new one. If the answer is no, return to "Step Two Metaphor-phosis" and do more processing through ceremony or ritual with your old universal story.

You may balk at this idea, but the new will not hold unless the old is completely neutralized. That means there's no sense going on until you've fully unhooked from your old pattern. There is more to learn, more gifts to gain, and this can only occur by returning to the old through ceremony and ritual. However, if the answer is yes, you are ready to set your intention.

Set Your Intention

Set your intention to create a new universal story.

Go to a New Universal Story

Now that you have neutralized your old story, you can create a new universal story. Universal energies inform and encompass all other parts, so the new universal story will inform the mental, emotional, and physical parts of you.

To determine your new universal story, choose the metaphor, myth, archetype, fairy tale, folk story, or image that encompasses how you desire your new life to *feel*. Pick what feels right deep in your gut, blood, and bones. It's about a search for your soul's expression and your authentic self, so use your body wisdom as your guide. Try one of the following to set your new universal story.

1) Use Self-Inquiry

If needed, go to "Tools to Determine Your Desired Stories" in "Tools to Create Your New Life" in this section to find information, tools, and techniques to help you determine the life you desire to live. Consider your destiny, your skills and talents, and your passions and inclinations together to help determine the new metaphor, myth, archetype, fairy tale, folk story, or image that encompasses how that new life will feel. Take your time with this step.

2) Use Your Heart Wisdom

Follow the steps to enter your sacred heart space given in "States of Consciousness and Stories" in section II under "Your Inner Wisdom." As you do so, set your intention to enter your sacred heart space and to discover your new universal story.

- Go to alpha
- Dive down and "travel" into your heart
- Observe your unique heart language (such as imagery, sensations, or an inner knowing)
- Receive understanding

3) Use Your Body Wisdom

As you consider the new life you desire, ask the following questions:

- What do you desire instead?
- How does this feel now?
- What emotion does this desire evoke?
- Where do you feel this in your body?
- Use all of your senses to describe the feeling in your body.
- Allow a new metaphor, myth, archetype, or image to arise that encompasses how your new desire feels in your body.

Act on Your New Universal Story

Now that you've set your new universal story, there is a last but vital step to Metamorphosis: act on your new universal story. As you do, it will inform the physical, emotional, and mental parts of you and also gives instructions to the universe and others for how you want to be perceived and treated.

There are four parts to manifesting your story: ready your space, set your intention, go face forward, and act by extending your new story to the world.

1) Ready Your Space

Tune into the Field of All Life, imagining you are immersed in and surrounded by a formless substance that is everywhere, limitless, timeless, spaceless, and contains all possibilities and abundance. Or sense you are surrounded by a magnetic field that attracts all of your desires.

See either field surround you and attract what is needed to manifest your new universal story. Let it infuse every cell of your being.

2) Set Your Intention

Choose your intention according to the inner experience/feeling you desire. It's how the intention makes you *feel* that matters. This is crucial because the feeling drives the manifestation. Remember that the subconscious does not know the difference between a real and an imagined event, so stay focused on the images and feelings of the new mythical life that you desire to manifest.

3) Go Face Forward

Imbue your new universal story with all the powerful feelings it creates. Let your new self-confidence saturate every cell of your being. See it as so with your imagination, and speak it as truth with your words. When your images, beliefs, thoughts, words, and actions match your desire, it becomes a reality. Your brain then rewires around this, and your subconscious replaces the old program with the new.

Now immediately create a power statement and trigger (see below) of how your new universal story feels. These serve as instant reminders to quickly invoke and reinstate how you feel right now. Both will inform all parts of you as to how to live your life from your new story.

Create a power statement

A power statement is created from how your new universal story feels. Examples are: I am appreciated, I am supported, I am surrounded by love, I am respected, I trust my process, I see the world as safe, and people help me. If possible, frame it as an "I am" statement, which invokes the words of creation. As you create a power statement, be aware that you might not yet feel it's fully true. However, it will help you reprogram your subconscious and generate new ways to manifest your intention.

Expand your power statement to include your people or the world. For example, to the statement "I am financially abundant," add "and my work blesses everyone with whom I do business." Or along with "I am wildly creative," extend this to "and my creations benefit ___," and fill in the blank to encompass your people.

Create a trigger

Now create a trigger for your intention and power statement. Triggers are extremely useful to help you remember the feeling that your new universal story evokes. A trigger is a stimulus, such as a picture, sound, touch, movement, or fragrance that is neurologically linked to a particular state. Create triggers for images and states that you want to manifest, and then you can invoke that state anytime you want by activating that trigger. For example, a trigger for stillness could be taking three deep breaths. Then anytime you desire stillness, just take three deep breaths, and it will immediately invoke this state.

When you shift your body posture or facial expressions, it alters how you feel. A trigger does the same thing. In this case, it quickly brings back the whole gestalt of your universal story. A trigger can be a body movement or posture, sound, smell, taste, or other sensory experience.

I strongly urge you to create a body posture or movement as your trigger or in addition to any other trigger you choose because it directly accesses your body wisdom and thus bypasses the mental and emotional levels. To do this, get into a posture or do a physical movement that evokes how your new story feels. Repeat it several times. Do it again, only smaller. Repeat it even smaller this time. Next, make it very tiny. Now do it only in your mind's eye.

Once you have it in your body, you can do your trigger mentally while in line at the store, talking with others, or during some other task, and it'll still bloom with all the feelings of your new universal story in those moments. To anchor this, physically do your trigger several times daily for three weeks. This strongly helps reprogram your subconscious to create your new desired story.

Give thanks

Just as you readied your space, it's important to close it too. This is your opportunity to give thanks to any helpers, healers, angels, or others whom you may have called in for helping with your process. Also ask for help in bringing your manifestation about with grace and ease.

You might say something like, "Thank you _____ (list the names of the spirit helpers, healers, power animals, guides, guardians, and/or directions that you called in when you opened your space) for coming, protecting, and guiding me. I ask that you help bring about _____ (name your new universal story) with grace and ease."

Face forward

Focus only on your new universal story. This is like driving while looking through the front windshield. It brings your desire forward and collapses all the undesired probability waves of other possible futures. Resonance and coherence will then bring your new vision to life so you can receive opportunities that didn't seem to exist before.

To face forward, focus on your new universal story, and imbue it with your intention and all you desire to *feel*. Western mysticism has long taught that if you desire to evoke particular energies, you need to create the entire "field" for this. This may mean rearranging your space, dressing in certain clothing, or obtaining the implements that evoke these feelings. Make choices and perform actions that are based on your new life vision, cultivate relationships that support your new self, and surround yourself with people who back your vision.

All of this is done literally. However, you can also do so somatically. In fact, just mentally holding the images, feelings, sounds, and tastes of what you desire to manifest can be just as effective as doing so literally. Further, the longer and more often you hold this focus, the sooner it will come to you. The strongest and fastest effects occur when you both focus internally and take the outer literal steps in alignment with this.

Like planting a seed, your new universal story needs attention, feeding, care, and nurturance. Feel your new universal story with every fiber of your being, and imagine it as so. Act from a place of joy, excitement, and anticipation. Set a daily routine that includes activities to reinforce your new story. Hold absolute certainty and gratitude that your universal story is so. Create hypothetical relationships for it. In other words, "fake it till you make it" or act as if it is so, no question about it, it is yours to experience.

> ### Write Your Future Play
> We are all actors in our own life plays. Once I had a spontaneous clear vision of how we create our own realities. As well, I saw how our Higher Selves make decisions to help us act out our stories. It seemed to me we both direct and star in our own plays. Through this experience, I not only saw how I had created my current play but also how I was creating my future play. As a result, I focused on the new images of what I wanted to see happen, knowing eventually they'd take form.

Derive your current sense of self from your future self. Align with who you desire to be in the fullness of your potential. From that, work backward to the steps needed to expand into that future self. Focus on how that future self feels and go from there. Create your future backward, and step into what you need to grow and develop in order to walk this destiny path. Then everything you need will be magnetized through coherence and resonance.

Keep your language in line with your intent. Rather than tell others about how things are or have been, make statements that encompass your new vision and improve how you feel. This will keep energy flowing in the direction of your new self and desires. You have to desire it, visualize it, work toward it, and know it is so. Then it will manifest for you.

4) *Act by Extending Your New Story to the World*

Ceremonially process your new universal story

It can be most helpful to take your new universal story to ritual or ceremony. This helps you learn more about it, including its teachings, gifts, and any steps needed for its full manifestation. Simple processes work well here, such as dialogue, journey, fire ceremony, or sandpainting.

Set a concrete step

Develop a concrete step, and follow that through to completion. Determine the specific skills needed to develop in order to attain your future vision and develop them. Make your first step small and doable so you start a pattern of success. Start with a part of your project you can easily accomplish. As you finish it, this creates the energy of completion that builds momentum. After it's completed, set another concrete step, and repeat.

It's extremely important to follow any information or guidance you may have received while creating your new universal story. This honors it and so anchors its energy.

Extend your new story to the world

As you focus on your new universal story, extend it to the world as well. Notice how this new self might help others. Feel it fully, and then release it into the world. Hold no agenda, apology, or need; just affirm your new story and your place in the world with it. Spread this power, presence, and radiance outward like a lighthouse beam to bless others. The more you shift, the more joy and contentment you will bring not only to yourself but to those around you.

In addition, dream a bigger dream. State something like, "This or something greater comes to me for the highest good of all concerned." This is a major lesson I learned while co-leading women on vision quests. In the past, questers sought vision and answers not just for themselves, but for their people too. They brought news back to their villages so hunters knew where to find game, leaders knew when to move the tribe, and people knew when to plant and harvest food. The tribe made decisions based on the visionary among them, and that visionary worked with universal energies for the good of his or her people.

I suggest you extend your gifts to the world, not as one more thing to add to your "to-do" list but as an attitude to hold with your new universal story. As you do so, doors will open and opportunities will appear for you to automatically gift others with your dreams and visions. This is channeling your "bliss" into action so you serve your people along with helping yourself. Doing so engages more universal energies to not only assist you but also to help evolve the world.

I learned the power of this when I saw Sai Baba.[23] A number of us who had attended the first International Healing Congress in 1989 in India went to his ashram after hearing him speak. We waited for days to gain a personal audience but were just a few in the endless lines of thousands. Finally, my husband and I left to tour India only to realize we weren't complete and should return. When we did, one of the people we knew suggested we form a group together and try to see Sai Baba that way. It worked. I learned then that there is power in numbers, that truly when "two or more are together" something greater can happen than when on one's own.

Ultimately, destiny is not just about actualizing your full potential, but also taking your place in the world as you are meant to do. Extend your new self to others and bless them without any expectations. This is living your ultimate destiny.

Our Examples

Pattie:

In "Step Two Metaphor-phosis," Pattie had just "talked" with her pressure cooker image and learned that allowing her husband and others to take advantage of her was actually perpetuating her mother's abuse and father's lack of protection. The tension in her gut dispersed, and the pressure cooker image disappeared. Instead, she felt calmness and peace enter her body. Her true self became visible, and a new image emerged of a star shining so brightly that its light infused the earth below.

Pattie talked with the star and learned that her true self was whole and perfect. She felt this truth resonate inside and knew that never again could she surrender her own needs to others' demands. She painted a picture of a huge jaguar as the image of this new belief. When I saw it, I could feel its power jump off the page. It was simply amazing. Pattie had shifted her perspective from an invisible person of whom others took advantage to a woman of truth and power.

When I asked Pattie later if she felt any guilt about standing up for herself, she received another shock. She said that although it used to rule her entire life, she no longer felt any energy around it whatsoever. In fact, she hadn't even thought about the guilt and had no idea why. She now realized how huge this "subtle" shift had been in her life. With this newfound confidence and power, she set about making the changes she had so long desired but hadn't been able to make before.

Tom:

Tom's original feelings of being disrespected and ignored by his boss and treated poorly by his workmates had expanded into the pattern that men weren't there for him but attacked

---

23   Sai Baba was an Indian saint revered by millions around the world.

him instead. In "Step Two Metaphor-phosis," he created a drawing that revealed the gifts he had received from this pattern, self-protection and strength. Tom's new belief became "I am respected." As he spoke, an image arose of a giant tree surrounded by dozens of different animals that admired and thanked the tree for its gifts.

He carried that image and new core belief into his life. That very day, he saw his boss at a store and was amazed at his friendliness. His boss was even solicitous of his wife and voluntarily told him about some work-related decisions and plans. Tom realized that these decisions had nothing do to with making his life miserable after all. Ever since, he never again felt his boss was "out to get him" or wasn't acting on his behalf.

After Metaphor-phosis, Tom's workmates also treated him differently. Problems with others at work just seemed to smooth out "all by themselves." Tom said exactly what he needed to say and finally felt heard. He was amazed because he had never told his office mates how he felt nor did he do anything different. Instead, he realized it was the inner shift that had altered his world. Other job offers and opportunities came in from his searches, but Tom decided to not move or leave his job because he now felt content where he was.

How to Live Your New Life Story

Now that you've created your new universal story, how do you live your life differently? After all, stuff still happens—a dear friend dies, the economy tanks, a family member leaves, business wanes, the aging process continues, health problems arise, and more. Plus, what do you do if your old story tries to rear its head again? As you begin to live your new universal story, the following tips can help you gauge your progress, get unstuck, and handle roadblocks along the way.

How to Gauge Your Progress

To reinforce your shift, it's important to periodically check in and gauge your development. I suggest you do so once every two to four weeks. This work is usually subtle and gradual, so you need some distance before assessing any changes in your life. The following clues can help determine your progress.

Look for Subtle Shifts

It's important to know where and how to look for your desired changes to manifest. You may experience immediate and life-changing results or small, subtle shifts over time. A rose bud doesn't open to a full blossom overnight; rather it unfolds in stages, bit by bit. Similarly, when you look back at yourself weeks from now, you will see the bud of your new universal story opening. And in six months or so, you may find it has blossomed, the shift has occurred, you feel very different, and your life has altered.

Anything is possible, but to be more specific, you might feel more respected, supported, loved, and seen for who you are. You might also feel less anxiety or depression or a health issue may resolve. You don't get as angry as before and are less triggered, and so you can deal more easily with issues at hand, have heightened intuition when needed, or experience a greater ability to receive the positive elements of life that inspire and fulfill you. This work can act indirectly by bringing to you whatever is needed in order to heal or change as well. These are just a few of the possible shifts to expect.

Change is interesting. It doesn't necessarily appear where you think it will or happen as you believe it should. We think life is going one way or is going nowhere, and then suddenly it shifts and opens up. Quite often it's already present but in a different way and form than you expected. For instance, what you seek may not be a new partner like you thought but a better partnership with your self. And when that's occurred, you'll attract an even better outer partner than you would have if you were still operating from the old story. In the meantime, stay focused on how you desire to *feel,* for that is the true indicator of transformation.

Clues of Change

Here are several clues to help identify your shift. As your inner world alters, your outer world will generate evidence of this in different ways.

Self-Inquiry

To help identify your change, ask questions such as:

- Am I free of the drama from the past?
- Am I calmer and more content?
- Am I freer inside?
- Am I handling things a little differently than I did before?
- Am I not as pulled in by them, not quite as reactive?
- Do I more quickly see a way out or alter how I respond faster?

These are the indicators of change upon which to confirm your growth.

You'll Feel Different Inside

When the shift occurs you'll feel different inside, although you may not be able to name what is happening. It could be a relaxation of tension or pressure, an adjustment of your body and how you feel in it, a shift of how you hold yourself, a greater sense of peace, or an alteration in how you look at the world. You could seem less burdened, like a weight has fallen off your shoulders. You might experience fewer emotional ups and downs or are happier with whatever you are doing. You could also hear from others how much you've changed.

Your Emotions Will Respond Differently

If your old story arises again, you will deal with it differently because you'll respond differently. You might let it wash over you, feel nothing at all, or act anew. This is true freedom.

It is the freedom to choose how you wish to respond and the freedom to experience joy and contentment no matter what happens.

Your Body Will React Differently

Another way to gauge improvement is to assess your physical reactions because the body is a true barometer of change. In general, if your physical reaction decreases around a person or situation, you are progressing. The following is a sample range of reactions and how they might shift as you do:

IN OLD STORY	violent reaction	gut wrenching	feels like someone sitting on your chest	sharp pang	feels hollow	just a twinge	no reaction	it's for-got-ten	**IN NEW STORY**

Ultimately, the more joy, contentment, ease, and gratitude you feel inside, the more you have transformed. And when you are in such a joyful state, your endorphin receptors fill, which, through resonance and coherence, will draw even more joyful experiences to you, so the positive feelings will continue to grow and grow.

Changed Behavior

As you live your new story, you will eventually notice how you act differently with others and that people respond to you in new ways too. You may extend yourself in fresh ways or experience reconnection with your work associates. Your creativity may zoom, new energies may unleash for your life and work, more opportunities may appear, or blocks you experienced, disappear. All of these are clues that your new universal story is manifesting.

Enhanced Intuition

Intuition guides us through quiet promptings and a still, inner voice. It can appear at any time and in various ways. For example, without knowing why, you might sense an urge to develop bookkeeping or marketing skills, or you might be "told" to go see your mother that day, know you must pick up certain groceries, or sign up for a class you've never taken before. Then later, understanding dawns when you're prepared for a new opportunity, you meet someone important, or you prevent a problem, all of which might not have happened otherwise.

An inner urge might direct you to discover new help that heals your chronic knee pain, understand the feelings behind your reluctance to complete a certain project, or guide you to do something you normally wouldn't have and that's when you receive a break. We all have a quiet inner voice that directs us. As your new self emerges, you will hear it more clearly.

Messages from the Universe

Just as the macrocosm reflects the microcosm, so the universe reflects what is going on inside of you. This reflection can be experienced in many ways. For example, ants in your kitchen may reveal that something is bugging you; a dream about being unable to go into your normal parking space indicates its time to correct an old habit; a book passage, scene in a movie, or something on TV answers a burning question inside; or the yield sign you see while driving suddenly jumps out at you so you now know how to handle an overwhelming situation.

When you receive such messages, they strike a cord and give you guidance. They actually occur all the time when you live life connected with your authentic self. You can even purposefully put out a thought or question and look for the answer to come in such ways. Additionally, new doors may open or things automatically happen that bring help, information, and direction in alignment with your desires, questions, and new universal story.

Grace and Ease

Amazingly, when you align with your new universal story, life will flow to achieve your dreams. Just by focusing on your desired feeling state, it will be drawn to you through resonance and coherence. The idea of "doing" is a core belief that one has to work hard to get what one desires. However, when you manifest your new story, things will move naturally to and for you.

Strive to be in such alignment with your new universal story that everything flows so you don't have to push, work hard, or try more. Instead, allow the universe to put you where you need to be for what's needed to happen. Keep facing toward your new universal story, and you will live your new self with grace and ease.

You'll also discover that you don't have to literally work on an issue, such as resolving your all-consuming shame. When you ceremonially process the old universal story, it will alter itself so that it disappears even though it ruled your life before. Not only is there now no energy to it, it's a nonissue entirely. This is the real freedom and true shift that occurs through Metaphor-phosis.

Of course, you still need to hold to your intent and new universal story and do what's needed to manifest that. It may well be necessary for you to take steps to help your new life unfold. If any of these or other tasks call to you, it's important to follow them, such as develop skills and capacities needed to take the next step, generate your own new experiences, reconnect with what is true for you no matter what happens along the way, or stay open for something even greater to happen than what you can imagine.

Synchronicity

Synchronicity is the experience of two or more events that "coincidentally" happen together in a meaningful manner that is not explainable by conventional cause and effect. As your new universal story unfolds, you'll notice that more synchronicity occurs in your life.

For instance, you might think about someone and that person immediately calls; you might need to find someone to help you, and without even looking for or talking about it, that needed person comes; or you might desire something to happen, and it occurs without effort. Synchronicity arises when you are in alignment with your authentic self. The universe then conspires on your behalf to make things work smoothly for you.

Life Automatically Reorganizes

You'll also find that you won't necessarily have to act differently, but that your outer world reorganizes around your new self. Without saying anything, you may find that people respond to you in new ways, or you feel loved, accepted, seen, or appreciated when you didn't before. Even partners or workmates might act so changed that you wonder what happened to them!

Because you've transformed your inner world, people in your outer world will respond differently to you. This can seem like a miracle. You didn't talk to anyone about your issue nor did you outwardly alter anything. It was the internal change that occurred, and because of this shift, your outer world reorganized to reflect it. This is resonance and coherence at work.

If You Get Stuck

Sometimes as the old dissolves and the new is forming, we hit roadblocks, plateaus, or seem stuck along the way. We might feel shaky or unsure; things are not as they were, but we don't know how to move into the new. Often this occurs because we can't see the whole picture yet, we may need to clear more patterns or beliefs, or we may need to look in a different place for help. There are several possible ways to handle these situations.

Identify Your Butterfly Stage

You might seem in limbo while you are shifting. Your life is not what it was, and you can feel it's different, but it's definitely not how you desire it to be either. Being in limbo means you are still in process. The shift is occurring, but it is not yet complete.

In this situation, it can help to compare where you are with the metamorphosis of a butterfly. Genetically, the butterfly is imprinted in the caterpillar, yet it undergoes an amazing transformative process. This begins when the caterpillar latches onto a tree or leaf and weaves its chrysalis. Inside, the caterpillar begins to digest itself from the inside out. As it does, the digestive juices turn the old body into food, which is then used to build the new butterfly. When the butterfly is formed, it breaks out of its chrysalis as a completely different creature.

This is a beautiful metaphor for the alchemical transformation you undergo with Metaphor-phosis. As you shift perspective and ceremonially process your old universal story, you digest your old self, release the dross, and use the resultant "food" to build a new life. It's as if you "feed" off the gifts of your old patterns and core beliefs while you neutralize them. When you choose a new universal story and manifest it, you complete your own Metaphor-phosis and break through your chrysalis as a new person. This is true inner alchemy.

As you undergo this transformational process, you may stay in different stages of the process longer than others. For instance, if you linger in the chrysalis stage, you may actually feel like your life is breaking down rather than getting better, like you're dissolving into goop. You're not the caterpillar you used to be, but you're definitely not the butterfly yet. This can be a confusing and uncomfortable place where things might seem strange or worse than before. However, instead of falling apart, know that you are actually coming together but in a new way; you just don't know it yet. The point is, confusion means something else is going on underneath. Stick to the process, and trust it.

If you are stuck, uncertain, or in meltdown, remember that your new self is already inside of you. It's just a matter of continuing to neutralize the old patterns and face toward your new universal stories until they emerge. To help you know where you are in this process, gauge your progress according to the following metamorphosis stages:

The Onion or the Artichoke?

Sometimes after we change, the universe presents us with opportunities to handle old situations in the new way. To us, it looks like the old has returned, but instead, the universe is asking, "Are you sure you want to change? Have you really changed? Show me you've changed!"

Growth is not linear and, in fact, can be quite circuitous. It's an ongoing process with continual practice. No matter how much you have changed, you might briefly get caught in the old again. If you continue to face toward the new, the old can't hook you when it reappears. Or perhaps you just briefly dip into it, recognize what is happening, and quickly get back out. You might even get caught in the old pattern or belief a short while until you recognize what is happening and face toward the new again.

HOW YOU FEEL	CHRYSALIS STAGE
You want to change your life.	The caterpillar is weaving its chrysalis.
You're in the process of changing your life, but don't feel anything shift yet.	The caterpillar is in its chrysalis, preparing to undergo its metamorphosis.
You feel like you're breaking down or falling apart; nothing looks the same; you don't have an experience or picture of your new self yet, but you're definitely not your old self either.	The pupa is digesting its old body and is undergoing its major transformation. The caterpillar is no longer a caterpillar, but neither is it yet a butterfly.
You begin to experience some changes in your life for the better.	The pupa is using its digested old body as food to form its new body.
You have a stronger sense that you've shifted; the old stories still come up, but they don't affect you as strongly.	The butterfly is now formed but is still within the chrysalis.
The stories come up but barely affect you at all, although you are still defining your new self.	The butterfly is breaking free of its chrysalis.
You discover that you're living your life completely different from before, and the stories and emotions of the past not only don't hook you, but you hardly remember them, if at all.	The butterfly now flies free, drinking nectar and living a completely different life from the original caterpillar.

When we first change, we feel great, and then another layer may surface to be cleared or a new facet of the pattern needs tending. I call this clear-repeat-clear-repeat cycle "the onion or the artichoke." Both are comprised of layers that must be peeled in order to reach their core, or heart. As each layer is peeled, it's not quite as severe or otherwise seems different from before. It might have less energy, be less intense or of shorter duration, or is altered in some other way. Because you already peeled off a layer, your issue is different even though it may not be entirely gone.

Take Baby Steps

Only work one small issue through the Metaphor-phosis process, and let the change anchor in for one to three weeks before working on a new issue. It's important to allow each new universal story to take root, for otherwise it can split your focus and attention. Instead, give yourself a chance to align with your new story before beggining another. Starting with a small issue sets up a better chance of success and can lower the emotional and mental risk levels.

Your Soul's Journey

When issues continuously repeat in different forms, it's generally part of your soul's journey. Learn from such repeating matters as they are key lessons for your life and have gifts for you. Your soul's journey is comprised of the really deep issues that might last much of your life, so you may continue to work on them in one way or another for a long while. Frankly, if you're still here in this body, there's usually more to work on!

Stuff happens, but when you work with that stuff from the level of a universal story, answers come, synchronicities occur, realizations flash, and choices appear that you'll know how to implement. You no longer seem boxed in by your life but rather feel freer, more contented, or joyful. So don't be discouraged; just recognize another layer of the onion or leaf of the artichoke to peel. Eventually, you'll get to the core of that problem to receive its key gift, and then it will dissolve from your life.

Facing Challenges

When you are challenged, the following steps can help you break free from your old patterns or beliefs.

Honor the Old Universal Story More

Sometimes as you watch for your new universal story to manifest, you may actually find you're still dwelling on the old story. If you find this happening, don't blame yourself. It is actually a message that you may not be fully ready to let the old pattern or belief go. That is okay! Acknowledge this, and turn back to your old story. It simply needs more ceremonial processing and so is calling to you.

Refocus

Rather than berate yourself, simply turn your attention back to your new universal story. This is where the trigger you created in Step Three Metaphor-phosis especially helps, as it quickly brings back the feeling you first experienced when creating your new universal story. To refocus, stop what you are doing, look at how you are reacting, choose how you desire to respond instead, do your trigger, and focus on your new universal story.

Face Forward Again

Regardless of what challenges arise, face toward your new universal story. Your new self needs food and nurturance to grow, just like a baby or a new plant. Remember how your desired life feels in your body, do your trigger, and continue facing forward.

Mirror the Situation

Rather than view a challenging situation literally, look at what is externally happening as a mirror of different parts of your internal universe instead. That is, examine the situation metaphorically and see what fits. Remember that when you alter internally, the external changes around this. That means, to alter the outer world, you need to first shift the inner world.

For example, if Tim is ignoring you and all the work you've done or contributions you've made, look for what part of you is not acknowledging another part of you. In other words, what part of you is trampling, suppressing, or confining another part of you? How does a part of you beat up, berate, judge, criticize, abandon, ignore, or not see another part of you? Now identify that other part of yourself, listen to it, learn what it needs, and then do what it asks.

Use the Metaphor-phosis Process

If you face challenges, there may be another layer or aspect to your issue that needs clearing, so the new self doesn't fully manifest yet. If so, take the current issue through the entire Metaphor-phosis process, and continue to peel your onion or artichoke.

Find a Growth Partner

We all love sympathy from our friends, and this is important to help lessen our pain. However, it's very useful to have one partner who will call you on your stuff, help get you back on track, stand for you and the changes you are making, and be there for you every step of the way.

A growth partner is someone whom you trust not only to share your deepest truths and process, but who will tell you when you are off base, speaking or acting from an old story, or not fully aligning with your new self. They do not give advice, do therapy, or try to correct you, but they will name what they see and give emotional support. They help you reach authentic and honest places within so you can transform with support.

Your growth partner will probably not be your life partner but a good friend living near or far. Tell them what you are striving for and your visions and desires. Ask them to gently help hold you accountable for your process. Regularly check in, and perhaps even make agreements together about how you discuss and handle what comes up.

Live in Your Heart

Learn to live in your heart rather than your brain, and approach life from a heart-centered place. Most businesses are mentally based and lack heart, acting through the world of duality with its "us versus them" attitude. Living from the heart means existing in both the inner and outer worlds at the same time. This is operating from your true Self and receiving wisdom from the divine Source within and acting on that in the outer world. It serves everyone and the planet, not just ourselves.

The more you live your authentic self, the more quickly you will be aware of your stories, double blinds, roles, assumptions, habits, and triggers. This means you can clear these sooner and more easily. It also means

> ### The Limitations of Thinking
> Thinking and the brain are important and essential for life. However, as Ralph Waldo Emerson purportedly said, "The mind is a great servant, but a terrible master." In discovering and unhooking from your stories and then creating the life you want instead, shifting from the brain to the heart will yield much better results.

you can quickly rectify something that's off, have deeper connections, and be very aware of what's working in your life and what isn't. This brings even more experiences to keep you congruent with your authentic self.

Living from your heart is waking up to wonder again. It is a life based on joy, playfulness, relaxation, laughter, gratitude, compassion, unconditional love, and delight. It means you don't dwell in emotions of anger, sadness, or grief because you are no longer hooked by your stories. Then if someone treats you poorly, you can respond with compassion or even understanding instead.

A wonderful tale that demonstrates this is about the Dalai Lama and a journalist. The journalist was extremely nervous when approaching the Dalai Lama to do his interview. As the Dalai Lama turned his attention to the journalist, he seemed to understand what was happening because he next did the unthinkable: he tickled the journalist. That broke the tension so the journalist could easily proceed with his work. All it took was one person living from the heart to playfully interrupt the mental and emotional tension of another, and everything changed. This is something we can learn to do as well when we live a heart-based life.

Keep on Keeping On

One of my teachers, Evelyn Eaton, or Grandmother Eve as we called her, was a college English professor and an author. She transformed this life and became a pipe carrier for the Paiute in Eastern

California, helping many people with their "big and little ills." In the latter part of her life, she was in and out of the hospital seven times with colon cancer and almost died those seven times. Yet even then people would seek her prayers and blessings. She learned that it didn't matter if she was sick; she could still help others. This taught her to keep going regardless of what happened. From this, she coined the wonderful phrase, "Keep on keeping on."

And so I say that to you as well: Keep on keeping on! Keep on discovering your stories, keep on transforming your patterns, and keep cocreating the life of your dreams. As you do so, stick to this key: Stay focused on your new universal story, and keep any stuff that comes up on the metaphorical level. Don't engage with the literal, but let the universe work on it. Remember that although stuff happens, it's not about what happens to you, but rather if you suffer from it or transform it that matters. It's about the choices you make. It's about saying yes to your journey and facing forward every step of the way.

Keep on keeping on with your process, and watch your life metaphor-phosize into the glorious garden of your dreams!

Exercise

Gauge Your Progress

Make a list of all that has changed in your life from doing the Metaphor-phosis process. Include such areas as finance, relationships, career, creativity, friendships, family, behavior, and emotional evenness. Put the old story, belief, emotion, or reaction on the left-hand side of the page and your new story, belief, emotion, or experience on the right-hand side of the page. Compare them, and see how you've transformed!

Tools to Live Your New Life

The tools in this section will help you determine your life's purpose, manifest the life you desire, and live your new life.

Tools to Determine Your Life's Purpose

Your life's purpose is greater than a specific career or job; it encompasses all areas of your life. To determine your life's purpose and destiny, focus on your new universal story. This creates possibilities for something even better to occur than what you imagine. Go for a dream much bigger than you think you are!

When you align with your new universal story, you won't have to grunt and push but will experience where you need to be for what's needed to happen with ease. To align with your new universal story:

- Know that anything is possible
- Choose the final result you want to feel
- Choose from a deep sense of purpose
- Realize your intuition is your guide
- Choose the inner feeling and emotions you want to experience from your new universal story (this is the major motivating power to manifest your new life)

Exercises

Although you can do each of the following exercises individually, they are most powerful if done together and in this order:

Exercise One: Determine Your Life's Purpose

Write the answers to the following, look at them together, and determine the patterns. These point to your destiny.

- My inborn gifts and abilities are:
- My natural inclinations, passions, and talents are:
- This is easy for me to do in life:
- My natural self-expression is:
- The meanings I have created in my life are:
- I am most at home when I:
- I feel most alive, directed, fulfilled, and purposeful when I:
- I feel most myself when I:
- I love to:
- I feel I'm destined to:
- I feel I can grow and express my highest potential when I:
- My deepest passions and reasons for living are:
- What's inside of me that must be expressed is:
- The messages, truths, and yearnings that want to come through me are:
- What I have to give to the world is:
- What I have to say that the world needs to hear is:

Exercise Two: Guided Journey to Visit Your Dream Self

The following journey gets you in touch with your dream self.

- Ready your space.
- Set your intention to meet your dream self.
- Imagine you are sitting in a bubble of formless substance that is everywhere, limitless, timeless, spaceless, and contains all possibilities and abundance. Here nothing happens until you have a thought.
- Journey to a special place you love or imagine in nature.
- Find a cave and go inside.
- Search the cave until you find a door.
- Open the door and walk through.
- Walk into a room where you find two chairs facing each other.
- Sit down on one of the chairs.
- The door opens and your dream self enters and sits on the opposite chair.
- Talk with your dream self. Ask any questions and record the answers. Write even if just one word or it doesn't make sense.
- When you feel complete, your dream self says good-bye and leaves.

- Now you leave the room and go back into the cave.
- Leave the cave and walk back into your nature spot.
- Return to your body and open your eyes.
- Write down your experience.
- Now refine your dream self and life with what you just learned.

Exercise Three: Reversing

Not only can you reverse your life at the end of a day or year by year, but you could also reverse your life to the time before you were born. While most people can't remember their birth, let alone before they were born, in a journey this information can come to you.[24] To do this:

- Ready your space, and set your intention.
- Journey to a special place you love or imagine in nature.
- See your current life as if on a screen or 3-D before you.
- Reverse your life year by year or decade by decade.
- Go back to your birth.
- Go back to being in the womb.
- Go back to before you were born.
- Remember what you came here to do and what you set as your life's purpose.
- When done, return back to your body.
- Record your experience.
- Close your space.

Exercise Four: Your Dream Self and Life

Make a description of how your dream self and life feels. Imagine that anything is possible. Use your answers to the statements in Exercise One. Detail this for all areas of your life, particularly health, work/career, where you live, relationships, spirituality, finances, and creative expression. Keep it in the present tense and in the positive outcome form. For example: I am with a partner with whom I feel (fill in all your desired qualities in a partner and partnership).

Exercise Five: Draw Your Dream Self and Life

Create an image for each of the areas in Exercise Two. Draw all your images together on a sheet of paper or make a collage or vision board with them (see below).

---

24   There is a technique called Life Between Life, which brings forth such experiences and information (see the Bibliography).

Tools to Manifest the Life You Desire

Manifestation

Life doesn't happen to you; rather, life responds to you. How you feel and the images you hold determine your life experiences. ***You are already dreaming your world into being.*** To shift your experiences, change your dreaming; to change your dreaming, focus on the emotions you desire to experience. Emotion is the power that attracts; it is energy in motion, or e-motion, the motivating power that activates its manifestation. Use the emotions you want to experience to draw what you desire to you.

You could also use imagery to help you manifest; envision yourself doing, having, and being exactly what you want. Imbue that with all the emotions you want to experience, and use all of your senses.

Exercises

As you do the following exercises, focus on whatever you want to manifest—your new universal story, life's purpose, or dream self and life—in the following ways:

- Step into your desire using all your senses.
- Imagine the desire in all its details.
- Feel all of its emotions, joy, and expansion throughout your being and in all areas of your life.
- Experience, expect, and set your desire *as if it is so.*
- Declare this and feel it as happening in the moment.

Exercise One: Golden Pyramid

The golden pyramid temple of transcendence is a space that enhances the manifesting process. Here's how to use it:

- Ready your space.
- Set your intention to manifest your new universal story, life's purpose, or dream self and life.
- Imagine a golden pyramid temple of transcendence come down around your body.
- Focus on your desired manifestation.

- Expand your energy to 360 degrees around and three feet outward, visualizing this like doors or flowers opening.
- When you are complete, release the golden pyramid temple and close your space.

Exercise Two: Lighthouse

Here you blast your manifestation out like a lighthouse beam to energize its expression.

- Ready your space.
- Set your intention to manifest your new universal story, life's purpose, or dream self and life.
- Focus on your desired manifestation.
- Holographically view your desire. See its every part contained in the whole.
- Beam this outward like a lighthouse to the entire world. See it bringing back to you exactly what is needed to manifest your desire.
- When you are complete, close your space.

Exercise Three: Track Into the Future

It can be even more powerful to track your desired manifestation into the future to clear the way for its success. This step may be added to any of the other manifestation processes.

- Ready your space.
- Set your intention to manifest your new universal story, life's purpose, or dream self and life.
- Focus on your desired manifestation.
- Follow your desired manifestation far into the potential future. Make sure it is clear, and manifest.
- If the future is clear with your desired manifestation, close your space.
- If there are any blips, focus in to what they are and adjust them. If this doesn't work, clear the energy behind that limiting belief or pattern through the Metaphor-phosis steps. Then return to this manifestation process.

Exercise Four: Write a Letter

Write a letter to the universe describing your new universal story, life's purpose, or desired dream life. In the present tense, write it according to how you will feel emotionally, using all your senses. Describe it in every aspect and area of your life. Put your letter on your altar or another special place. Leave it for the universe to work on.

Tools to Live the Life You Desire

To live your new universal story, it's important to act as if it has already become the magical story of your life. See it already manifested on all levels—physical, emotional, mental, spiritual—and at all times and ways, such as while sleeping, driving, running errands, working, playing, and exercising. In time, your new universal story becomes your ordinary life. It's not about technique. It's about residing in a different place with a different perspective and holding your life differently.

Bring Source Energy Into Daily Life

After sitting with your new universal story, or even with your soul while in your sacred heart space or meditation, it can be difficult to hold that space when entering the world of duality again. Deep within, you know eternal truths, such as "I am whole," "I love everyone," "I am prosperous," and more. But back in daily affairs, however, the "yes-buts" arise in your mind. For example, when connected to Source energy, you know you have abundance, but in the outer world, you also have lack. Or, you know you're connected to everyone but wonder why your daughter doesn't talk to you. So how do you keep the feelings of truth, such as unconditional love, connection, and abundance, alive while living in the world? Here's a technique that can help you.

While you are in your new universal story (or the sacred space of your heart or meditation), write five to ten statements of the truth you know. When dualistic thoughts arise later, immediately pull out your truth statements and read them. Try to come back into the same feeling space you had as when you wrote them, and hold to that energy. For example, if you want to focus on relationship, you could write truth statements, such as:

- When I feel connected, I feel open and trusting.
- When I have clear communication, I can clear up any misunderstandings with grace and ease.

It's important to find ways to distract yourself from duality "reality" and align with your greater truth instead. Duality is either/or, and as long as you focus on what isn't working, you reinforce it. How's that working for you? Choose to focus on your authentic self, and live a life of either/and instead.

Symbolic Gestures

A symbolic gesture is an insignificant action that you create as a symbol for success. Invent a symbolic gesture for your new universal story and complete it. Here are a few examples:

- *To get things done:* Create a "to do" list, such as brushing your teeth or combing your hair, and check these off your list as you do them.
- *To enjoy the finer stuff in life:* Buy an expensive bar of soap.
- *To create a new self-image:* Buy some new clothes.
- *To manifest financial abundance:* Put $100 in your wallet.
- *To experience more time:* Take five-minute vacations to smell flowers, read a book for pleasure, swing in a hammock, or do nothing.
- *To manifest a new home:* Convert a room or space into exactly how you want your new home to be.
- *To climb a mountain:* Hike a small hill.
- *To walk through the "fires" in your life:* Do a fire-walk.

Make a Choice

This process helps you realign with your new universal story. It can be done anytime and anyplace, regardless of what is happening in the moment.

- Place your left hand forward and say, "I surrender to everything that is."
- Place your right hand forward and say, "And I choose _____," filling in your new universal story.

Refocus

If you get off track with your new universal story, refocus in the moment to help bring its energy back. Refocusing is used to stop reacting and instead be proactive about your choices. Use this technique every time you become aware that you are focusing on what you don't want instead of your new universal story. Here is how to refocus:

- Stop what you are thinking about and dwelling on. Step back and become fully aware of the conflict and your feelings about it.
- Look at what is going on and what you are doing. Become fully aware.
- Choose what you want instead. Say: "I choose _____," and fill in the blank. Be sure to choose the emotions you want to experience and feel it as if it's already happening.

- Let go. Allow your new universal story to manifest.
- In the future, when the issue comes up, repeat this process until all you need say is, "I choose _____," and the feeling of what you want to experience immediately arises.

Collage

Make a collage of your new universal story (see "Tools to Discover Your Stories" at the end of section II). Choose images from photographs, magazines, or other sources that evoke how your new universal story feels. Arrange them together on a card or other background as you are inwardly guided. When it is complete, place it in a visible spot where it will remind you of how to hold your new universal story.

For example, I made collage cards of my new universal stories and tacked them to a wall together as their arrangement felt right. When I looked at them together, I saw new meanings and relationships. As well, I made a crown collage of a new universal story and wore this during a group ritual.

Vision Board

A vision board is a collage of something specific you desire to manifest in your life. You choose images that encompass everything you desire to experience around that goal. You may also include objects, such as coins, written messages, celebratory ribbons, or streamers. All are glued together on a large board and placed in a visible spot where you will regularly see it. This helps you feel as if your desire is already manifested and reinforces it into your subconscious. Examples include a particular car, job, home, trip, or relationship.

Map Your New Life

Like mapping the life you've already lived, create a metaphorical map of the life you desire to live. Using crayons, colored pencils, or paints, create a metaphorical image for each area of your life that represents how you want to feel. Map these images together on one large sheet of paper or board. Arrange them according to their relationships or follow your intuition and inner guidance. When complete, look at your overall picture to glean new meanings, messages, and guidance for living your new life.

Create Future Memories

Create future memories of how you want to feel. Then figure out a way to feel that way *now*. Imagine who you will be even ten thousand years from now and inform yourself from this. Create an image of how this feels through a collage, vision board, or map.

Pay It Forward

One of the best and surest ways to create what you want to experience is to **give what you want to receive back.** Whatever you want to experience on all levels, give it to others, such as love, respect, support, or appreciation. In time, you will realize these qualities yourself.

Fake It Till You Make It

Pretend, play-act, and fake it until your new universal story fully manifests. Through play-acting, you bring out of the soup of possibilities what you want manifested into existence. Do this for the love of the thing itself and not to get anything back. This is key, for doing something to get something in return holds you in a place of want, need, or something being off. When you act from a place of appreciation for the thing itself, you are acting as if it has already manifested.

For example, as Emerson supposedly said, "Poverty consists in feeling poor." To fake abundance until you make it, pay your bills with love and gratitude; appreciate people who have money and even get excited for them; say yes to money; give some money away, even if it's pennies or a dollar, and do so for the love of sharing and what money can do; feel good about money in general.

Evolutionary Partners

An evolutionary partner is someone who helps you learn and grow so you both evolve beyond your current state. This not only helps your manifestation, but it also helps the other person's and the world at large. Further, you become who you spend time with, so find people who align with your new universal story and desired life. Cultivate such relationships. Ask such people to help you stay on track with your manifestation process and stand for theirs as well.

Nourish Your New Universal Story

Do what supports and nourishes your new universal story, life's purpose, dream self, and life. Here are a few possibilities. While some may seem strange or unrelated, they actually help alter old routines or create movement in your life, which enables your new story to manifest.

- *Listen to or read inspirational writings:* Inspirational writings do just that—inspire you, which shift your emotional state.
- *Walk two or more miles a day:* Walking quickly shifts energy and emotions. If you can't walk, choose some other form of movement.
- *Choose something you've always wanted to do and do it now:* Even if it's just once a week for only a half hour, do something you truly want to do. For example, I know of

one woman who when she is down, walks through a nursery since the plants give her energy.

- *Change your routines:* Do one thing differently today or modify its order, such as drive a different route, delegate, or offer to help.
- *Clean your closets:* Rather than clearing out what you don't want, try taking everything out and only putting back what you really desire and supports your new universal story.
- *Look at a photo of yourself when you felt "on top of the world":* Focus on how you felt, and bring those feelings alive now. Keep focusing on them, especially right after you wake up in the morning and right before you go to bed at night.
- *Develop practices:* Choose ones that help you feel compassion, beauty, fearlessness, and other experiences you desire.
- *Start your morning off to support your new life:* Here are some possibilities:
    - Imagine you are the multidimensional editor of the quantum field. How do you want to write the script of your life production? How do you want it filmed and edited?
    - Out of the limitless possibilities that exist, what do you want to experience today? Out of the soup of the universal energy say, "I choose ____," and fill in the blank. Focus on it, intend it as so, and pretend and act as if it is already so for the rest of the day.
    - Imagine your day and feel love for it going well. Place the force of love ahead of you.
    - Feel gratitude for everything as you move throughout your day. Send love to everyone around you. Ask yourself throughout the day how you are doing and how you could feel better. Ask what you need, listen to it, and act on the answer. For example, while driving ask, What is the best road to take? While at the store ask, What else do I need?
    - Visualize what you desire for the joy of it, and stay focused on that joy throughout the day regardless of what is.
    - Read your gratitude journal first thing every morning. Focus on each positive thought for ten seconds and then move to the next one.

Helping Others

It can be difficult to see others suffer, but we can't change them or do their inner work. However, if you know someone who is having difficulty, you can help by offering some of the techniques in this book. The following are particularly useful to share with others:

- Gratitude
- *Ho'Oponopono*
- Movement
- Creative Expression
- Healing Triangulation
- Divine Triangulation
- Sandpainting

Tools for Feeling Stuck

Besides the tools and techniques given in the three prior "Tools" chapters ("Essential Tools for Change" at the end of section I, "Tools to Discover Your Stories" at the end of section II, and "Tools to Unhook from Your Stories" at the end of section III), here are a few more to help you get unstuck.

Exercise One: Stuck?

Do something different, *anything* different. It could be driving a different route than normal; walking outside your door and turning a new way; calling someone you haven't talked to in a while; connecting with the earth, sun, or moon; or gazing at the stars at night. Do something simple that is radically different and notice how it shifts your feelings on all levels.

Exercise Two: Still Stuck?

If you have an issue that persists regardless of what you do, try these techniques. They may be used with an emotional state, such as anxiety or depression, a cyclical pattern or limiting belief, or your universal story.

Befriend it: Give your issue a name. Ask it how it's doing. Listen to it like a long-lost friend. Ask what it needs and give it. If that's not fully possible, make an agreement to do what you can.

Treat it Like a Beloved Teacher: Ask your issue for its lessons and teachings. Really listen as if you are being taught by a beloved teacher.

Exercise Three: Health issues

Rewrite the script of your health issues. See it as a play or movie in which you are the main actor. How would you like to script to be? Include how you want to feel physically, emotionally, mentally, and spiritually. If any limiting patterns or beliefs arise, take them through the Metaphor-phosis process. If any information comes to you through intuition or inner knowing, *act on it*.

Exercise Four: Handling Distractions

When a distraction tries to pull you off track, here is a simple question to ask: "Do I have time for this?" Your honest answer can quickly guide you back or reveal more limiting patterns or beliefs to clear.

Exercise Five: Handling Challenging Situations

When you are challenged:

- Place your left hand out and say, "This is challenging ..."
- Then place your right hand out and say, "But/and I still move forward."

Epilogue

After I wrote my story, something very profound shifted inside of me. I felt empowered and liberated, as if I had come into the light. It also allowed me to incubate and recreate my inner journey. I realized that by telling my story, I had honored it, and in doing so, I could let it go. This meant I could now truly face forward with my new universal story in my sacred heart space.

I have cleared many of my patterns, but I know some still remain. However, even though some old stories may still pop up, I'm able to quickly release them and create what I desire instead. Here's an example.

This last holiday, I found myself moving into an old story as I performed the multiple preparations for Thanksgiving. As the day approached, old thoughts arose: Why do I have to do it all, and why is no one helping me? I felt alone and overworked from all the necessary preparations for the family gathering. I watched others do what they wanted as I put my own projects on hold, yet again.

Not only was I shopping, getting the house ready, and preparing the meal, but I also had houseguests, some business deadlines, and my mother in the hospital, for which I was the main advocate that week. I felt surly, crabby, and soured on the entire holiday. My husband and I once more decided to never again host it.

Then I went for a run and thought about how I was feeling. It wasn't typical for me to experience this anymore. These were old feelings I thought I had transformed. Then I realized it was just an old pattern rearing its ugly head again. I used to have trouble asking for help because I hated being turned down or told no. Now just realizing it was an old pattern was enough to help me disengage. Once I acknowledged the pattern, I could let it go. This understanding made all the difference.

Afterward, I decided what help I needed and asked for it. Next, I thought about what I looked forward to about the holiday. I had a new recipe I wanted to try and felt excited to do so. I was also curious about who would ultimately come, as there were frequently last-minute cancellations and new arrivals.

Once I let go of the pattern and looked forward to the day, everything shifted inside of me. I didn't even think of it again but moved forward with my plans. I felt a mixture of anticipation and curiosity for how the day would turn out. Indeed, everything fell into place without my doing anything extra. I asked for help and immediately received more than I asked for. The new recipe turned out great, and I enjoyed preparing the meal and serving everyone.

After the day ended, I had two people tell me it was their favorite Thanksgiving ever. I agreed, for it was one of my best too. It felt easy and flowed naturally. When I compared the day with what I had experienced in the past, this time felt quite amazing. It wasn't until I reflected on this that I realized the transformation had started when I recognized the old pattern, let it go, and faced forward with what I wanted instead. All the rest switched from this.

To me, the Metaphor-phosis process is a search for true freedom. Most think freedom is not being under the control of some outside person or power. But to be truly free is to be out from under the control of your inner limiting patterns and beliefs. These are the true chains that bind, for they curb your power so you fall short of your potential. What stops us is inside of us and not outside. Clearing old patterns and beliefs not only brings joy and contentment but also true freedom.

Recently, I visited Mariah again and told her about writing this book. I began to mention one of my old patterns, but before I could name it, she jumped in and said, "Oh, the one about not being able to feel or take in love."

I stopped talking and stared at her. I had no idea what she was talking about. "No, that wasn't it," I said.

"Yes, it was," she countered.

"I never had that issue," I continued.

"Oh, yes, you did," she insisted.

I stared at her some more. Then a faint image surfaced of sitting at a table across from her and telling her that very thing, that I had a difficult time feeling love from others and taking it in. Soon other memories flooded forth as I recalled events and experiences where I used to feel that way. But no longer. That issue had been completely erased. Not only am I no longer triggered by that old pattern and belief and it is now a nonissue, but I had forgotten it entirely!

It is truly possible to change. It is possible to briefly dip into the old and quickly get back out. It is possible to create a new experience instead, one that realizes your dreams and desires. This is the power of Metaphor-phosis. You can transform your life and open to the infinite possibilities before you. Not only have I done it; many others have as well.

Ultimately, it's not about creating more stories for our selves but about *being*. By "being" I mean living in a state of super-awareness—awareness of the light being self; awareness of unconditional love and compassion for all life; and awareness that I'm you and you are me. One's focus shifts from one's self to a broader field of interconnection with all of life.

You also experience inner peace, that place where all lasting positive change and emotional and spiritual growth occurs. Not only are the old stories forgotten, but the need to create new ones grows less and less, and you live in a state of contentment and joy. I'm sure there's more beyond this that I can only imagine, and so my quest into radiance continues as a growing state of being.

So keep on keeping on. Keep saying yes to yourself. Keep discovering and clearing your patterns. Keep creating the stories of your dreams instead.

A traditional Buddhist prayer comes to heart here that is really a blessing to me. May it bless you, your life, and all those around you.

May all beings be well.

May all beings be happy.

Peace, peace, peace.

Here's to your metaphor-phosis!

Summary: Metaphor-phosis Steps

Step One Metaphor-phosis: Discover Your Conscious and Unconscious Stories

- Ready Your Space
- Set Your Intention
- Go to Self-Inquiry
- Go to Your Heart Wisdom:
    - Go to alpha
    - Dive down
    - Observe your unique heart language
    - Receive understanding
- Go to Your Body Wisdom:
    - What emotion do you feel?
    - Where do you feel that emotion in your body (any discomfort, stress, tension, or where something is "off")?
    - Go to that area. What sensations do you feel? (Use all of your senses.)
    - What memories come forth?
    - What images arise? Are they in black-and-white or color? Any smells, sounds, tastes, textures? Is it still, or is there movement like a movie?
    - When did you feel/experience this at an earlier time in your life? Keep going back and identify all the times you felt this way in your body.
    - What people and places are involved?
    - When did you experience the issue and feel this way at an even earlier time?
    - What is your earliest memory when this theme occurred?

- Pay attention to how your body feels while you do this, as it will tell you when you have found the originating memory where your source story lies.
- What roles did you play?
- What roles did others play?
- Do you still have this issue today?
- What did you lose that you are trying to get back?
- How have you been behaving because of that loss?
- What is the limiting pattern or core belief you discover?
- Act On Your Stories
  - Determine the pattern
  - Act on what you learned
  - Close your space or immediately go to Step Two Metaphor-phosis

Step Two Metaphor-phosis: Unhook from Your Stories

- Ready Your Space (if not already done)
- Set Your Intention
- Go to a Universal Story
  - Allow a metaphor, myth, archetype, fairy tale, folk story, or image to arise that represents how your limiting pattern or belief feels in your body.
  - If you don't find a universal story that fits, find your own image:
    - Use Your Heart Wisdom:
      - Go to alpha
      - Dive down
      - Observe your unique heart language
      - Receive understanding
    - Use Your Body Wisdom:
      - What is the pattern, belief or issue?
      - What emotions arise?
      - Where do you feel this in your body?
      - Go to that area. How does that area feel? Describe it with all of your senses.
      - Now allow an image to arise that encompasses how the area feels. Go with the first one that comes.
- Act on Your Universal Story through Ceremony

- Process your universal story through ceremony or ritual
- Learn from your universal story as appropriate. Possible questions include:
  - Why are you in my life?
  - What do I need?
  - What do I need or do you want me to know?
  - What do you want to share with me?
  - Do you need anything?
  - What are your lessons?
  - What do you want to teach me?
  - What are your gifts?
- Keep processing your universal story through ceremony as needed or go immediately to Step Three Metaphor-phosis.
- Act on what you received.
- Go directly to Step Three Metaphor-phosis or if not possible, close your space.

Step Three Metaphor-phosis: Create the Stories You Desire

- Ready Your Space (if not already done). Sense a magnetic field surround and infuse you.
- Set Your Intention
- Go to a New Universal Story
  - Use Self-inquiry
  - Use Your Heart Wisdom:
    - Go to alpha
    - Dive down
    - Observe your unique heart language
    - Receive understanding
  - Use Your Body Wisdom:
    - What do you desire instead?
    - How does this feel now?
    - What emotion does this desire evoke?
    - Where do you feel this in your body?
    - Use all of your senses to describe the feeling in your body.

- - Allow a new metaphor, myth, archetype, fairy tale, folk story, or image to arise that encompasses how your new desire feels in your body.
- Act by Manifesting It
  - Ready Your Space (if not already done)
  - Set Your Intention
  - Go Face Forward
    - Create a power statement to evoke the feeling of your new story
    - Create a trigger
    - Give thanks and close your space
    - Face forward
  - Act by Extending Your New Story to the World
    - If desired, ceremonially process your new universal story to learn its lessons and receive its gifts
    - Set concrete steps
    - Extend your new story to the world

Bibliography

General

Chandler, Steve. *The Story of You*. Career Press, Franklin Lakes, NJ, 2006.

Ferrucci, Piero. *What We May Be: Techniques for Psychological and Spiritual Growth*. Jeremy P. Tarcher/Perigee Books, New York, NY, 1982.

Ford, Debbie. *The Dark Side of the Light Chasers: Reclaiming Your Power, Creativity, Brilliance, and Dreams*. Riverhead Books, New York, NY, 1998.

The Four Winds Society. Their Light Body School teaches how to discover and clear limiting stories and beliefs along with shamanic tools for transformation: http://www.thefourwinds.com. The Four Winds Society by Alberto Villoldo. Accessed July 16, 2012.

Hicks, Esther and Jerry. *The Astonishing Power of Emotions*. Hay House, Carlsbad, CA, 2007.

Hotchkiss, Burt. *Your Owner's Manual*. Fernwood Management Company, Sweet Home, OR, 1992.

Shainber, Catherine PhD. *Kabbalah and the Power of Dreaming: Awakening the Visionary Life*. Inner Traditions, Rochester, Vermont, 2005.

Villoldo, Alberto PhD. *The Four Insights: Wisdom, Power, and Grace of the Earthkeepers*. Hay House, Carlsbad, CA, 2006.

———. *Shaman, Healer, Sage*. Crown Archetype, New York, NY, 2000.

Biology of Your Stories

Dispenza, Joe DC. *Evolve Your Brain: The Science of Changing Your Mind*. Health Communications, Inc., Deerfield Beach, FL, 2007.

Doidge, Norman MD. *The Brain That Changes Itself: Stories of Personal Triumph from the Frontiers of Brain Science*. Penguin Books, New York, NY, 2007.

Kenyon, Tom. *Brain States*. World Tree Press, Lithia Springs, GA, 1994.

Lipton, Bruce PhD. *The Biology of Belief*. Hay House, Carlsbad, CA, revised edition, 2008.

Lipton, Bruce PhD, and Steve Bhaerman. *Spontaneous Evolution*. Hay House, Carlsbad, CA, 2009.

McTaggart, Lynne. *The Field*. Harper Perennial, New York, NY, 2002.

Pert, Candace PhD. *Molecules of Emotion: The Science Behind Mind-Body Medicine*. Simon and Schuster, New York, NY, 1999.

———. *Your Body is Your Subconscious Mind*. Sounds True, Boulder, CO, 2004, compact disc, written and performed by Candace Pert. 3 CD's (2 hours, 30 minutes), 1 study guide (20 pages). ISBN-10: 1-59179-223-1; ISBN-13: 978-1-59179-223-9; Product Codes: 0451d, w451d, aw00451d

Talbert, Michael. *The Holographic Universe: The Revolutionary Theory of Reality*. Harper Perennial, New York, NY, 1992.

What the Bleep DO We Know? DVD, 20th Century Fox. Betsy Chasse, Mark Vicente, William Arntz, Matthew Hoffman writers. Released March 15, 2005. 109 minutes.

Heart Wisdom

Melchizedek, Drunvalo. *Living in the Heart: How to Enter Into the Sacred Space Within the Heart*. Light Technology Publications, Flagstaff, AZ, 2003.

Body Wisdom

Allison, Sue PhD. *Empowered Healer*. Balboa Press, Bloomington, IN, 2011.

Universal Stories

Baron, Renee, and Elizabeth Wagele. *The Enneagram Made Easy: Discover the 9 Types of People*. HarperCollins, New York, NY, 1994.

Baron-Reid, Colette. *The Map: Finding the Magic and Meaning in the Story of Your Life*. Hay House, Carlsbad, CA, 2011.

Bolen, Jean Shinoda. *Goddesses in Every Woman*. Harper and Row, New York, NY, 1984.

———. *Gods in Every Man*. Harper and Row, New York, NY, 1989.

Briggs Meyers, Isabel, *Gifts Differing*. Nicholas Brealey Publishing, Boston, MA, 1995.

Briggs Myers, Isabel, and Mary H. McCaulley. *Manual: A Guide to the Development and Use of the Myers Briggs Type Indicator*. Consulting Psychologists Press, Mountain View, CA, 1985.

Campbell, Joseph. *The Hero With a Thousand Faces*. New World Library, Novato, CA, 2008.

———. *Introduction: The Complete Grimm's Fairy Tales*. Random House, Inc., New York, NY, 1972.

———. *The Power of Myth*. Anchor, Garden City, NY, 1991.

Campbell, Joseph, and Johnson E. Fairchild. *Myths to Live By*. Viking Penguin, New York, NY, 1993.

Eisen, Armand, ed. *A Treasury of Children's Literature*. Ariel Books, Houghton Mifflin Company, New York, NY, 1992.

Hay, Louise. *You Can Heal Your Life*. Hay House, Carlsbad, CA, 2007.

Palmer, Helen. *The Enneagram*. Harper and Row, New York, NY, 1983.

Pearson, Carol S. PhD. *Awakening the Heros Within: Twelve Archetypes to Help Us Find Ourselves and Transform Our World*. HarperOne, 1991.

———. *The Hero Within*. HarperOne, New York, NY, 1986.

Pearson, Carol S., and Hugh K. Marr. *What Story Are You Living: A Workbook and Guide to Interpreting Results form the Pearson-Marr Archetype Indicator*. Center for Applications of Psychological Type, Inc., Gainesville, FL, 2007.

Pinkola Estes, Clarissa PhD. *Women Who Run With the Wolves*. Ballantine Books, New York, NY, 1996.

Ponsot, Marie, trans. *The Golden Book of Fairy Tales*. Golden Books Publishing Company, Inc., New York, NY, 1999.

Riso, Don Richard, and Russ Hudson. *The Wisdom of the Enneagram: The Complete Guide to Psychological and Spiritual Growth of the Nine Personality Types*. Bantam Book, New York, NY, 1999.

Ceremonial Processing

Farmer, Steven D. PhD. *Sacred Ceremony*. Hay House, Carlsbad, CA, 2002.

Villoldo, Alberto PhD. *Mending the Past and Healing the Future With Soul Retrieval*. Hay House, Carlsbad, CA, 2006.

Ancestral Patterns

Pacheco, Christa Rae. http://www.christaraepacheco.com. *Opus Lux DNAScan* by Christa Rae Pacheco. Accessed July 16, 2012.

Ruby, Margaret. *DNA of Healing: A Five-Step Process for Total Wellness and Abundance*. Hampton Roads Publishing, Newburyport, MA, 2006.

Shamanic Journeying

Baron-Reid, Colette. *The Map*: *Finding the Magic and Meaning in the Story of Your Life*. Hay House, Carlsbad, CA, 2011.

Goodman, Felicitas D. *Where the Spirits Ride the Wind*. Indiana University Press, Bloomington, IN, 1990.

Gore, Belinda. *Ecstatic Body Postures*: *An Alternate Reality Workbook*. Inner Traditions, Rochester, VT, 1995.

———. *The Ecstatic Experience*: *Healing Postures for Spirit Journeys*. Bear & Company, Rochester, VT, 2009 (includes CD of trance rhythms).

Ingerman, Sandra. *Shamanic Journeying: A Beginner's Guide*. Sounds True, Boulder, CO, 2004 (includes CD of trance rhythms).

Ingerman, Sandra, and Hank Wesselman. *Awakening to the Spirit World: The Shamanic Path of Direct Revelation*. Sounds True, Boulder, CO, 2010.

Wesselman, Hank. *The Journey to The Sacred Garden: A Guide to Traveling in The Spiritual Realms*. Hay House, Carlsbad, CA, 2003.

Death and Dying

Fitch, Linda. http://Dying Consciously. dyingconsciously.org./The-Greatest-Journey-CD. htm. Accessed July 16, 2012.

Hendricks, Gay. *Five Wishes*. New World Library, Novato, CA, 2007.

Create the Stories You Want

Newton, Michael. *Life Between Lives: Hypnotherapy for Spiritual Regression*. Llewellyn Publications, Woodbury, MN, 2004.

Villoldo, Alberto PhD. *Courageous Dreaming: How the Shamans Dream the World Into Being*. Hay House, Carlsbad, CA, 2009.

Rejuvenation Retreat

Rainbow Hearth Bed and Breakfast: Rejuvenation, hiking, and bodywork on Lake Buchanan, Texas: 512-756-7878; Mariah@rainbowhearth.com www.rainbowhearth.com

Biography

Lesley Tierra, LAc., Dipl.Ac. (NCCAOM), Dipl.C.H. (NCCAOM), RH (AHG), is the author of *Healing With the Herbs of Life* (Crossing Press/Random House, 2003), *A Kid's Herb Book* (Robert D. Reed Publishers, 2000; also published in Japan, 2010 and to be published in Estonia in 2012), *Healing with Chinese Herbs* (Crossing Press, 1997), *The Herbs of Life* (Crossing Press, 1992; also published in India in the late 1990s) and coauthor of *Chinese Traditional Herbal Medicine Volumes I and II* with Michael Tierra (Lotus Press, 1998). She collaborated with Michael Tierra to cowrite and produce the East West Herb Course and is dean of its school, The East West School of Planetary Herbalism. She's authored various articles in magazines throughout the country, such as *New Age Journal* and *American Herbalists Guild Journal*.

Lesley is a nationally and California state licensed acupuncturist and herbalist with a clinic in Santa Cruz she shares with her husband, Michael Tierra. In her practice, she combines acupuncture, herbal and food therapies, and shamanic practices along with lifestyle and inner growth counseling. She has taught natural health, herbal, and Chinese medicine classes throughout the United States and England since 1983. For five years, she co-led women on vision quests in the desert and has taught various series of personal growth classes, of which her latest is Radiance Quest, the classes teaching the Metaphor-phosis technique.

Lesley has studied ancient mystical, spiritual, medicinal, and shamanic methods along with modern psychotherapeutic techniques for over forty years, including herbalism, Chinese and Ayurvedic medicines, massage, psychotherapy, various journeying techniques, shamanism, yoga, Eastern and Western mysticism, dream work, tarot, and Hakomi.

To learn more about Lesley's offerings and classes, or to receive a consultation, go to:

www.metaphor-phosis.com
www.planetherbs.com   www.radianceenergymedicine.com
www.planetherbs.com/consultation/consultations.html
Call: 831-429-8066; ***Email***: eastwestclinic@hotmail.com

Index

H

Habits ix, 34, 37, 62, 81, 110, 222
Handling challenging situations 236
Handling distractions 236
Healing core beliefs and values 177
Healing triangulation 94, 175, 176, 235
Healing with the emotions 179
Health and your stories 39
Heart language 85, 139, 206
Heart, live in your 222
Heart, sacred space of the 67
Heart transplant 37
Heart wisdom 67, 68, 69, 84, 85, 139, 196, 206, 241, 242, 243, 246
Heart wisdom, how to use your 85
Helping others 148, 197, 235
Hidden agendas 81
Higher consciousness 35, 62, 63, 65, 131
    Shifting to 131
Higher Self 19, 35, 47, 67, 72, 80, 133, 161, 209
Ho'Oponopono 45, 46, 94, 114, 195, 235
How to achieve alpha alternative consciousness 66
How to appropriately express emotions 94
How to determine your life purpose 200
How to process your universal story 161
How to use your body wisdom 85
How to use your heart wisdom 85

I

Identify contracts 112
Identify your butterfly stage 217
Identify your mirrors 111
Illness ix, xiii, 33, 39, 40, 47, 63, 92, 97, 145, 146, 157, 163, 200
Image, find your own 139, 242
Imagery 36, 52, 64, 67, 69, 72, 84, 85, 119, 135, 139, 158, 206, 228
Imagery and your stories 36
Inherited 19, 20, 101, 120
Inner wisdom 67, 85, 89, 110, 127, 139, 145, 170, 171, 206
Institute of HeartMath 41, 67
Intention, set your 50, 51, 68, 71, 72, 76, 77, 84, 85, 103, 113, 137, 138, 158, 163, 164, 165, 167, 168, 169, 170, 171, 172, 177, 181, 182, 183,

184, 186, 188, 205, 206, 207, 226, 227, 228, 229, 241, 242, 243, 244
Intuition 64, 134, 135, 163, 180, 196, 197, 213, 215, 225, 232, 236

J

Journal writing 47, 55, 75, 163, 189
Journeying 16, 35, 64, 103, 119, 165, 166, 172, 183, 193, 247, 249
Journeying, body 166
Journey to visit your dream self 226
Journey to your shadows 103
Jung, Carl 62

K

Karma xiii, 112, 199
Kidneys 180

L

Life metaphors 146
Life purpose 19, 199, 200, 201
Life purpose, determine your 200
Life themes 18, 19, 20, 79, 159
Life timeline 99, 111
Limbic system 34, 142, 160, 161
Lipton, Bruce 39, 245
Live in your heart 222

M

Mammalian part of your brain 34
Manifestation 122, 168, 172, 194, 207, 208, 210, 228, 229, 233
Map your life 98, 100
Map your new life 232
Memories, create future 232
Messages from the universe 48, 55, 110, 111, 119, 216
Metaphorical map 98, 100, 232
Metaphors xi, 40, 119, 132, 134, 138, 139, 144, 145, 146, 147, 159, 202
Metaphors for illness 145, 146
Mind mapping 171
Mirrors 29, 105, 111, 200
Mirror the situation 221
Multiple personalities 33, 40